GABBA GABBA HEY!

Archie ®
CROSSOVER COLLECTION

The Ramones resemble cartoon characters just like the Archies, they are fascinating and fun. Johnny was always a lover of pop music like The Ohio Express, 1910 Fruit Gum Company and The Archies. So it was really fun and exciting to work with the Archie team. It felt like a perfect fit. It was exciting to collaborate with the artists, and to have Johnny Ramone come to life in the comics. Johnny was always into having his hair perfect, he made sure he always looked amazing and wore his leather jacket with ripped jeans. So going back and forth to make sure he looked cool from head to toe, adding special touches, giving him the punk legend persona he conveyed in real life was a cool experience. Johnny always said "I wrote the book on punk", and Johnny was always right, always.

Listening to "Sugar, Sugar" by the Archies and "Rockaway Beach" from the Ramones you can definitely see how this is a perfect collaboration

for Ramones fans and Archies fans alike. Johnny was an avid collector of movie posters, baseball memorabilia, monster magazines, etc. He thought collecting was good for your mental health and hobbies were good for your sanity.

Johnny would be thrilled to be meeting the Archies in a classic collectible comic. I hope everyone goes out there and enjoys the Ramones meeting the Archies!

Gabba Gabba Hey!
Linda Ramone

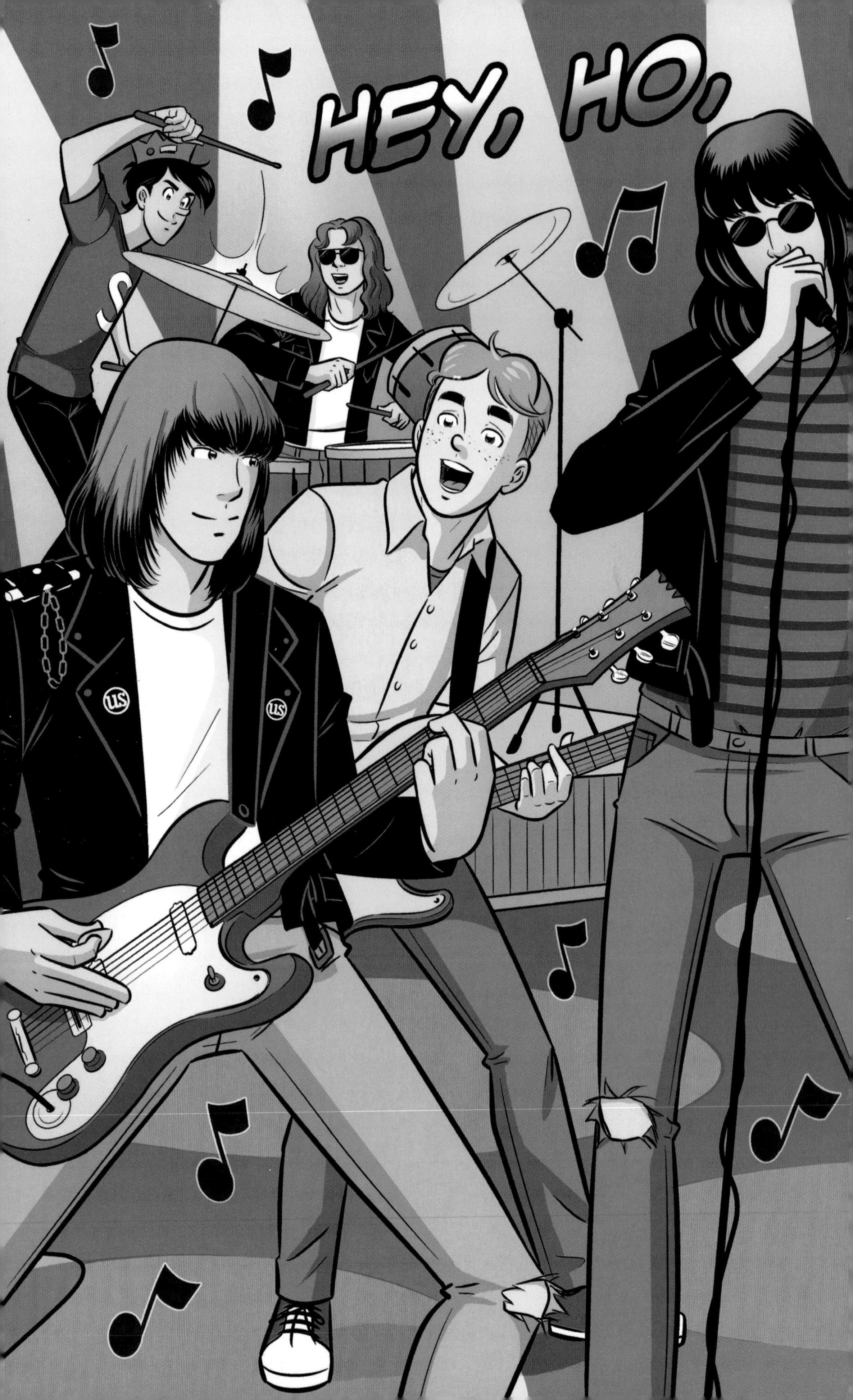
HEY, HO,

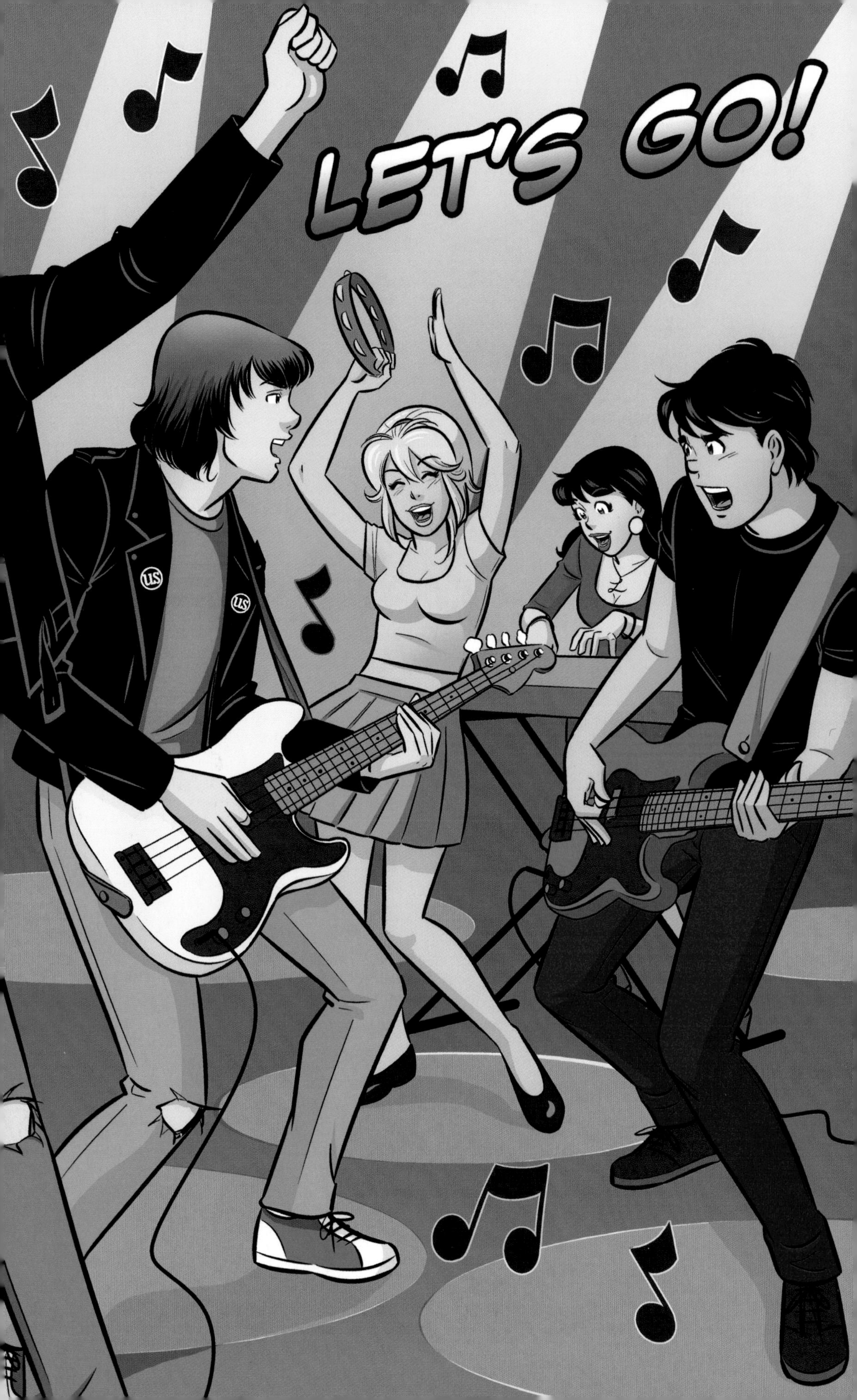
LET'S GO!

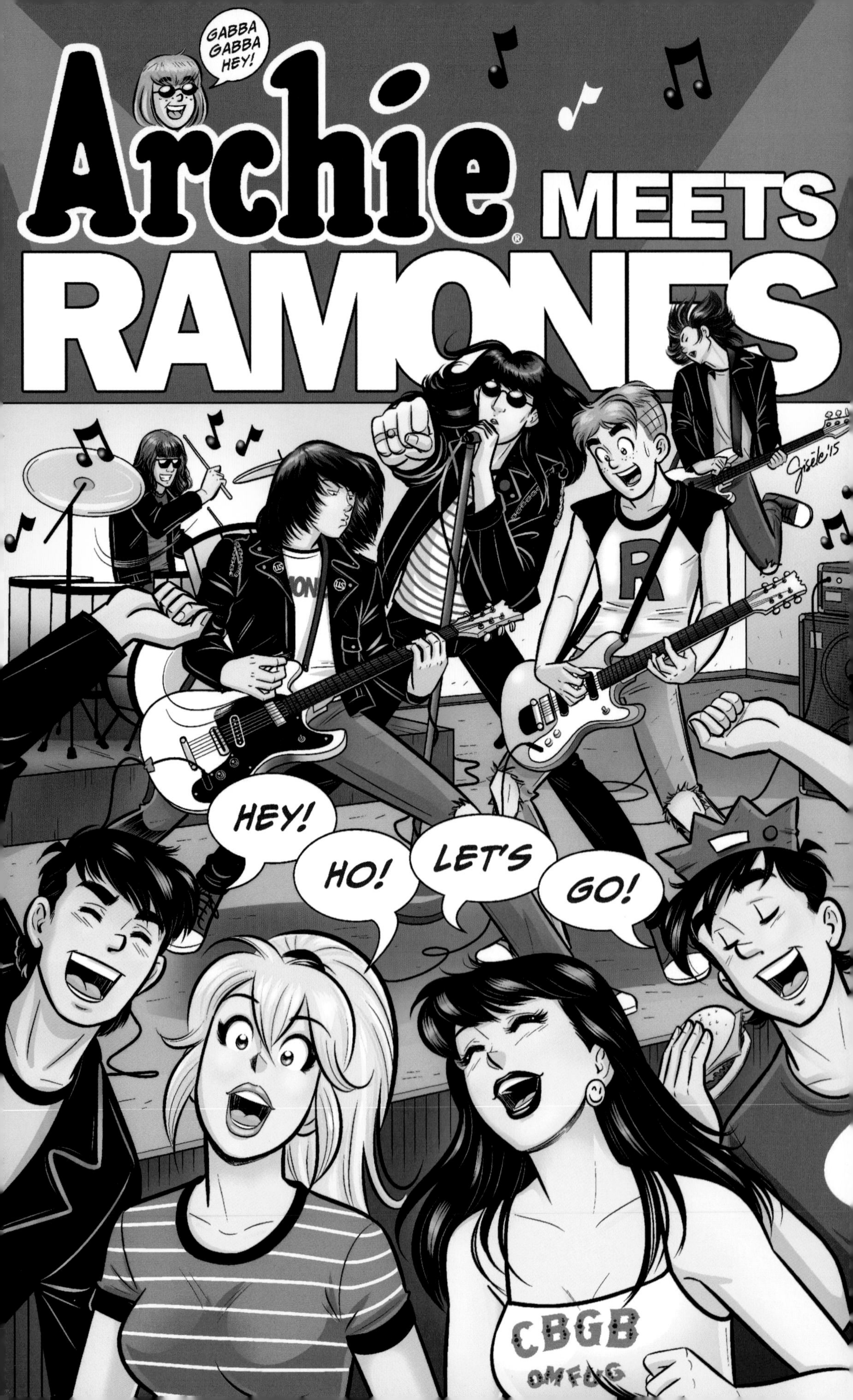
GABBA GABBA HEY!
Archie® MEETS RAMONES
Gisèle '15
HEY!
HO!
LET'S
GO!
CBGB
OMFUG

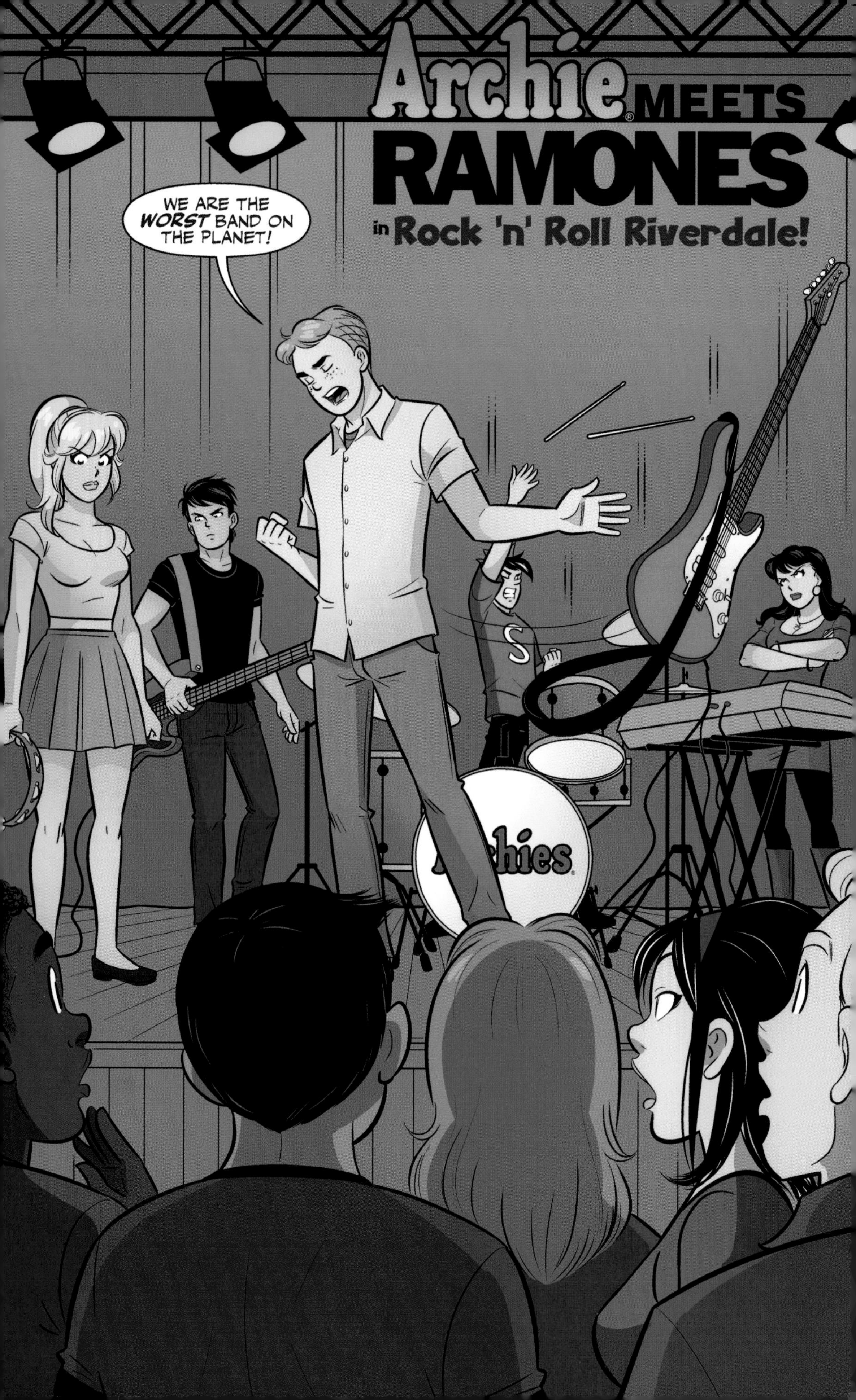
Archie MEETS
RAMONES
in Rock 'n' Roll Riverdale!
WE ARE THE WORST BAND ON THE PLANET!
Archies

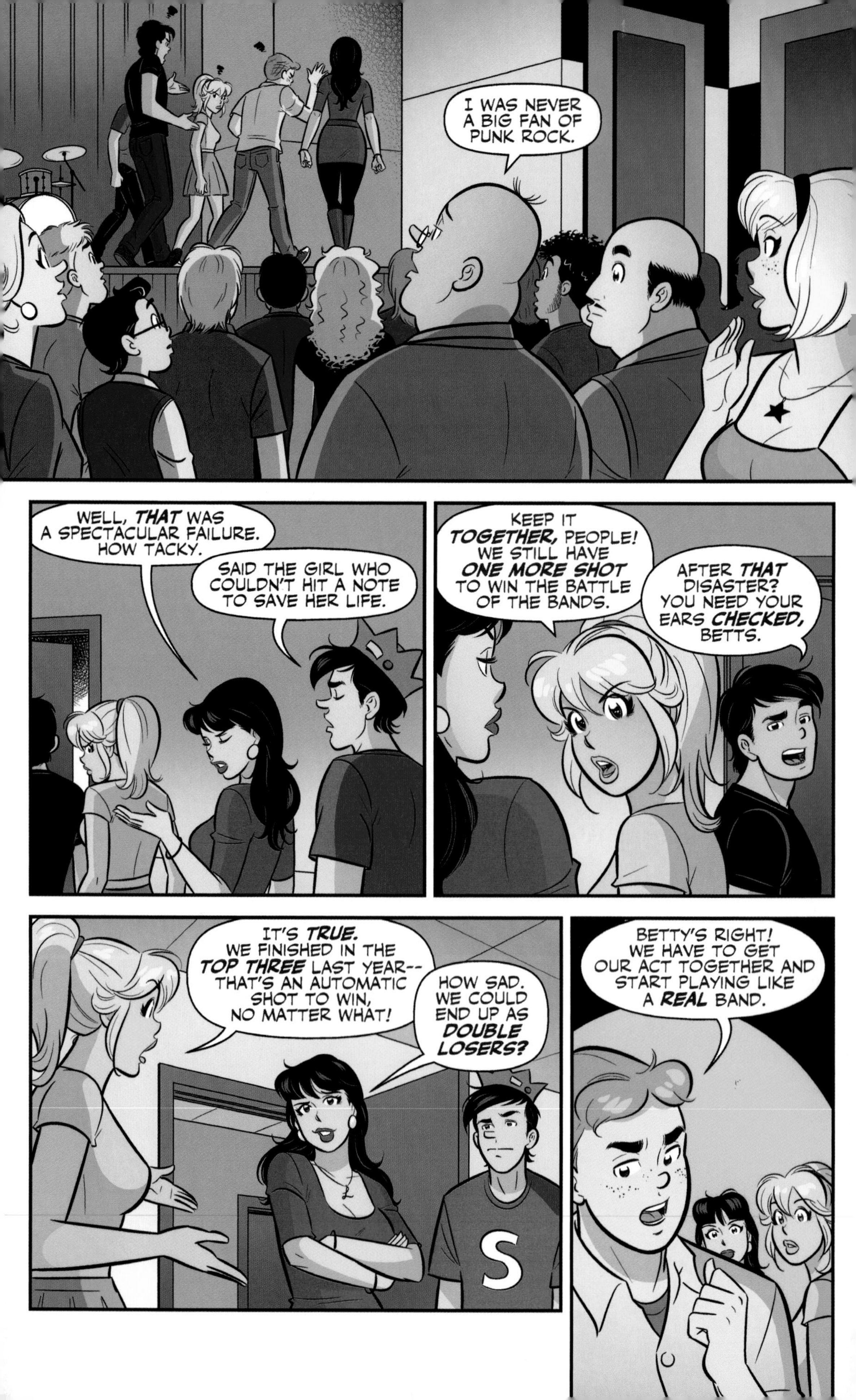
I WAS NEVER A BIG FAN OF PUNK ROCK.
WELL, THAT WAS A SPECTACULAR FAILURE. HOW TACKY.
SAID THE GIRL WHO COULDN'T HIT A NOTE TO SAVE HER LIFE.
KEEP IT TOGETHER, PEOPLE! WE STILL HAVE ONE MORE SHOT TO WIN THE BATTLE OF THE BANDS.
AFTER THAT DISASTER? YOU NEED YOUR EARS CHECKED, BETTS.
IT'S TRUE. WE FINISHED IN THE TOP THREE LAST YEAR-- THAT'S AN AUTOMATIC SHOT TO WIN, NO MATTER WHAT!
HOW SAD. WE COULD END UP AS DOUBLE LOSERS?
BETTY'S RIGHT! WE HAVE TO GET OUR ACT TOGETHER AND START PLAYING LIKE A REAL BAND.
S

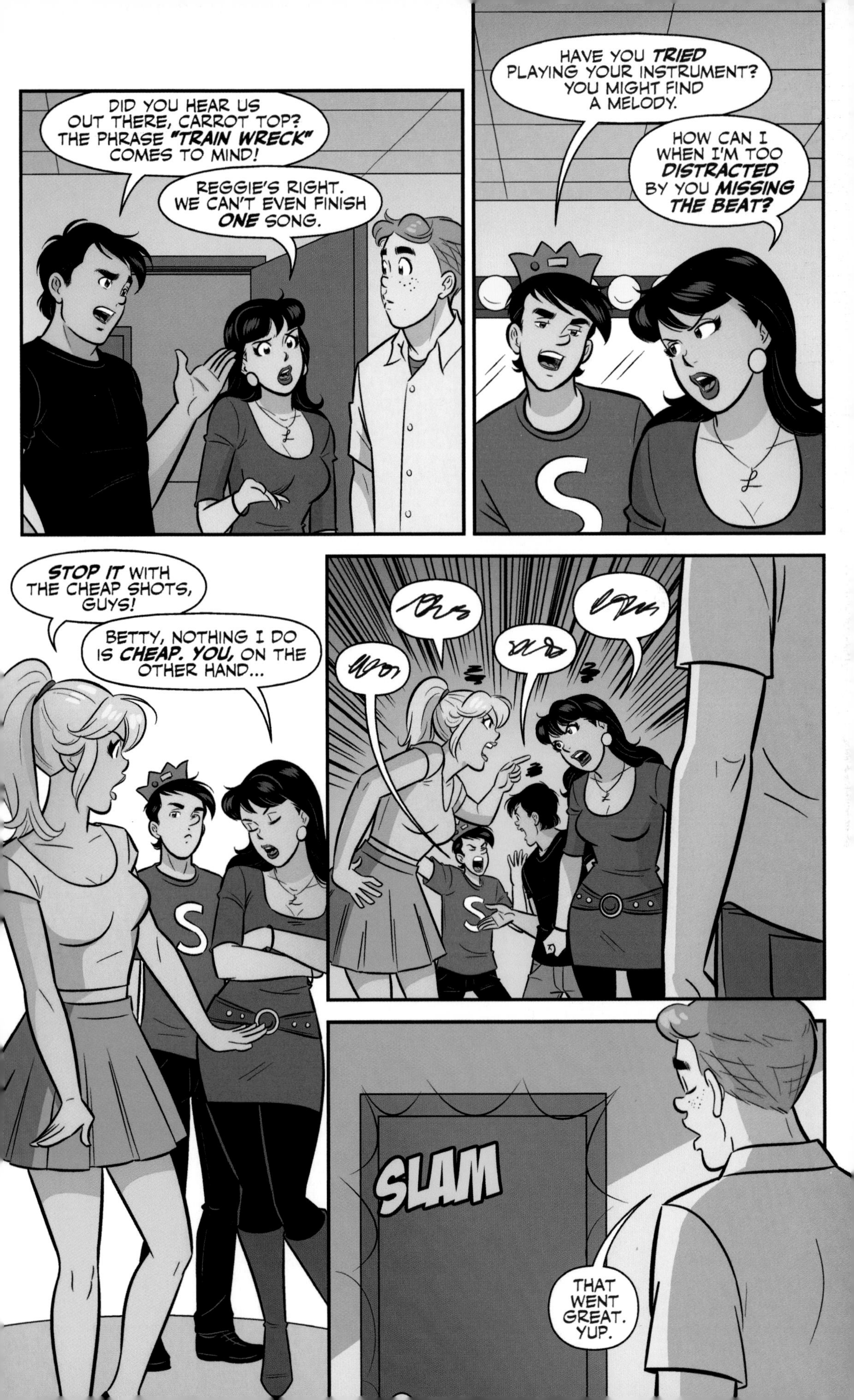
DID YOU HEAR US OUT THERE, CARROT TOP? THE PHRASE "TRAIN WRECK" COMES TO MIND!
REGGIE'S RIGHT. WE CAN'T EVEN FINISH ONE SONG.
HAVE YOU TRIED PLAYING YOUR INSTRUMENT? YOU MIGHT FIND A MELODY.
HOW CAN I WHEN I'M TOO DISTRACTED BY YOU MISSING THE BEAT?
STOP IT WITH THE CHEAP SHOTS, GUYS!
BETTY, NOTHING I DO IS CHEAP. YOU, ON THE OTHER HAND...
SLAM
THAT WENT GREAT. YUP.

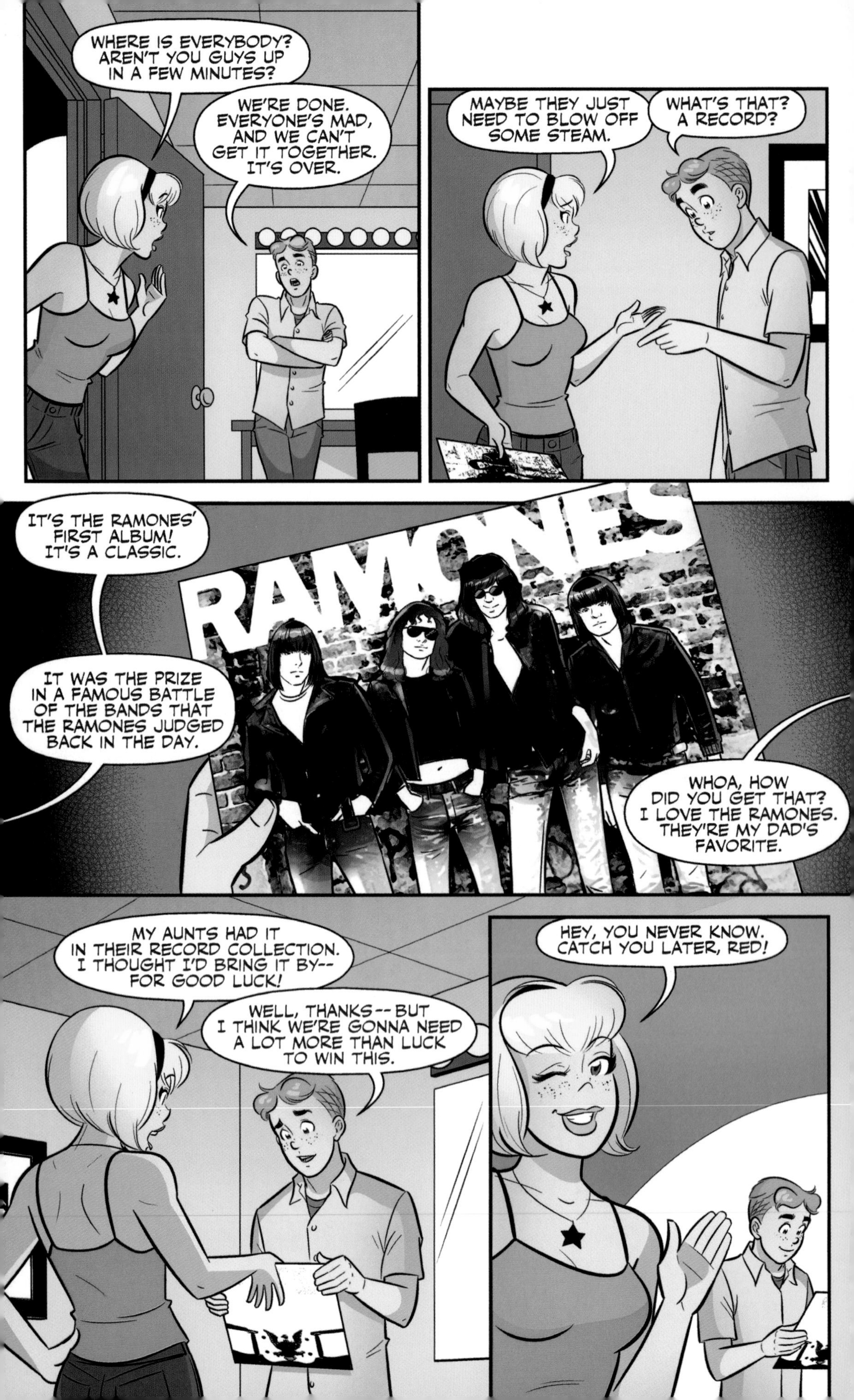
WHERE IS EVERYBODY? AREN'T YOU GUYS UP IN A FEW MINUTES?
WE'RE DONE. EVERYONE'S MAD, AND WE CAN'T GET IT TOGETHER. IT'S OVER.
MAYBE THEY JUST NEED TO BLOW OFF SOME STEAM.
WHAT'S THAT? A RECORD?
IT'S THE RAMONES' FIRST ALBUM! IT'S A CLASSIC.
RAMONES
IT WAS THE PRIZE IN A FAMOUS BATTLE OF THE BANDS THAT THE RAMONES JUDGED BACK IN THE DAY.
WHOA, HOW DID YOU GET THAT? I LOVE THE RAMONES. THEY'RE MY DAD'S FAVORITE.
MY AUNTS HAD IT IN THEIR RECORD COLLECTION. I THOUGHT I'D BRING IT BY-- FOR GOOD LUCK!
WELL, THANKS-- BUT I THINK WE'RE GONNA NEED A LOT MORE THAN LUCK TO WIN THIS.
HEY, YOU NEVER KNOW. CATCH YOU LATER, RED!

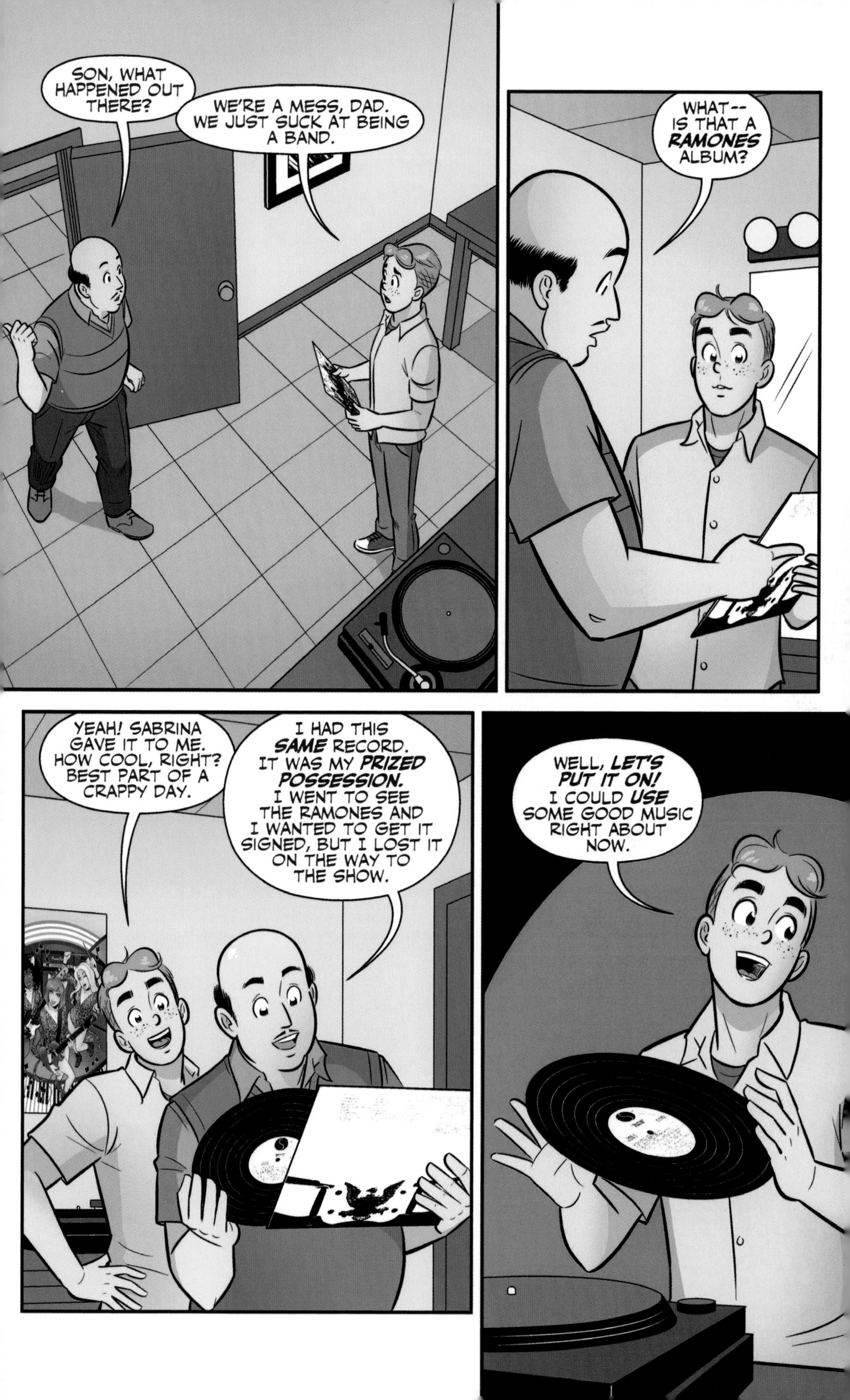
SON, WHAT HAPPENED OUT THERE?
WE'RE A MESS, DAD. WE JUST SUCK AT BEING A BAND.
WHAT-- IS THAT A *RAMONES* ALBUM?
YEAH! SABRINA GAVE IT TO ME. HOW COOL, RIGHT? BEST PART OF A CRAPPY DAY.
I HAD THIS *SAME* RECORD. IT WAS MY *PRIZED POSSESSION.* I WENT TO SEE THE RAMONES AND I WANTED TO GET IT SIGNED, BUT I LOST IT ON THE WAY TO THE SHOW.
WELL, *LET'S PUT IT ON!* I COULD *USE* SOME GOOD MUSIC RIGHT ABOUT NOW.

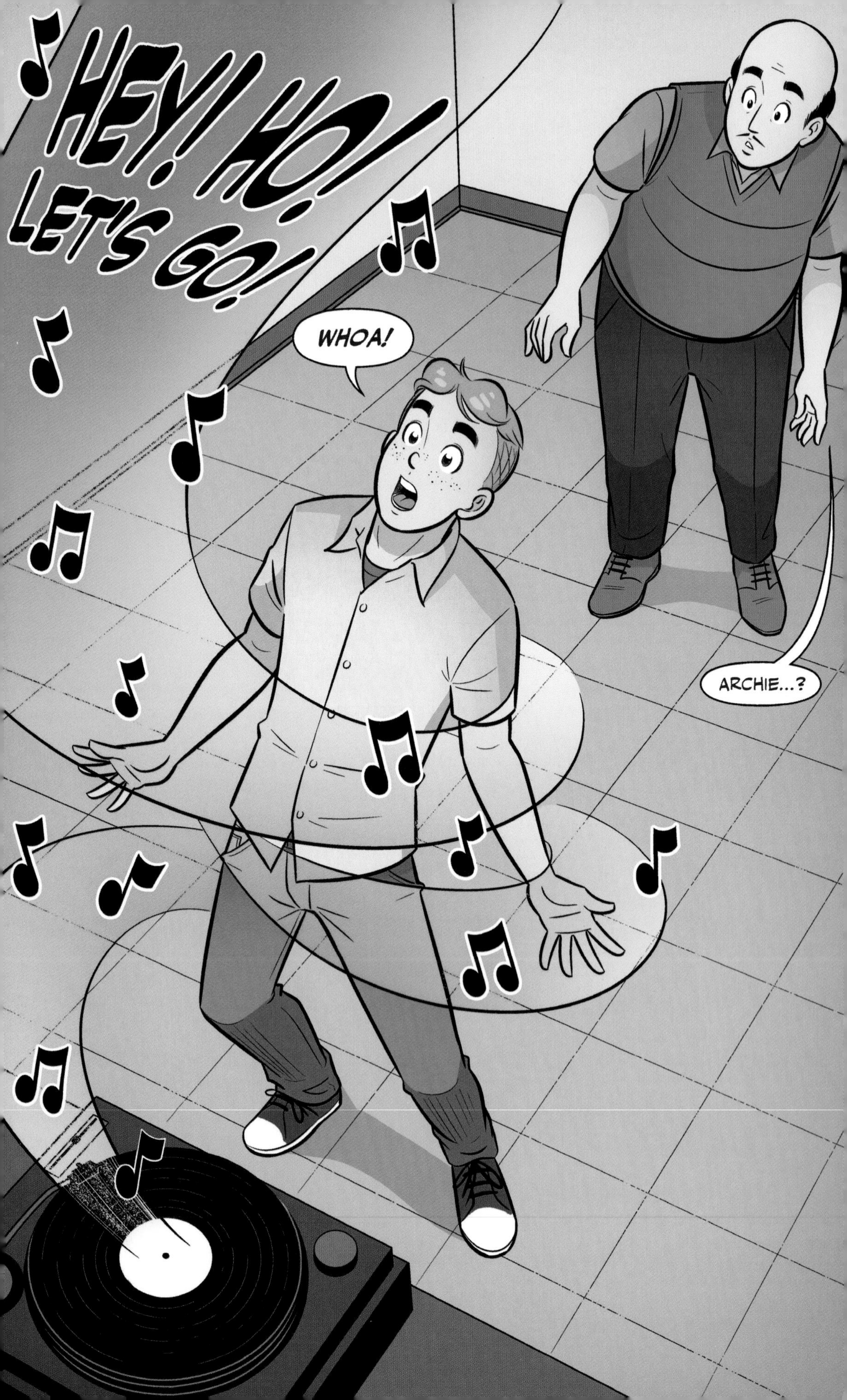
HEY! HO! LET'S GO!
WHOA!
ARCHIE...?

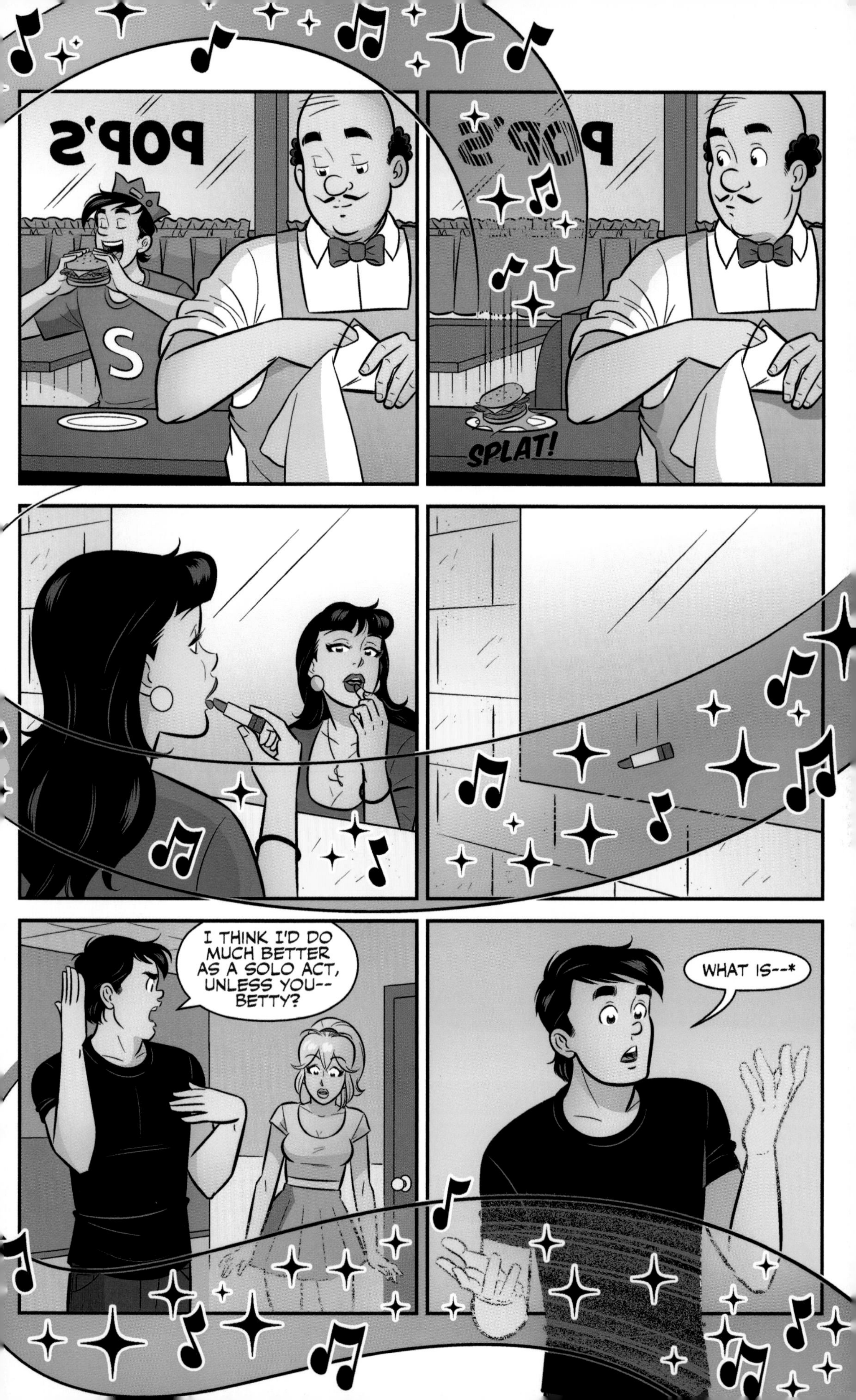
POP'S
POP'S
SPLAT!
I THINK I'D DO MUCH BETTER AS A SOLO ACT, UNLESS YOU-- BETTY?
WHAT IS--*

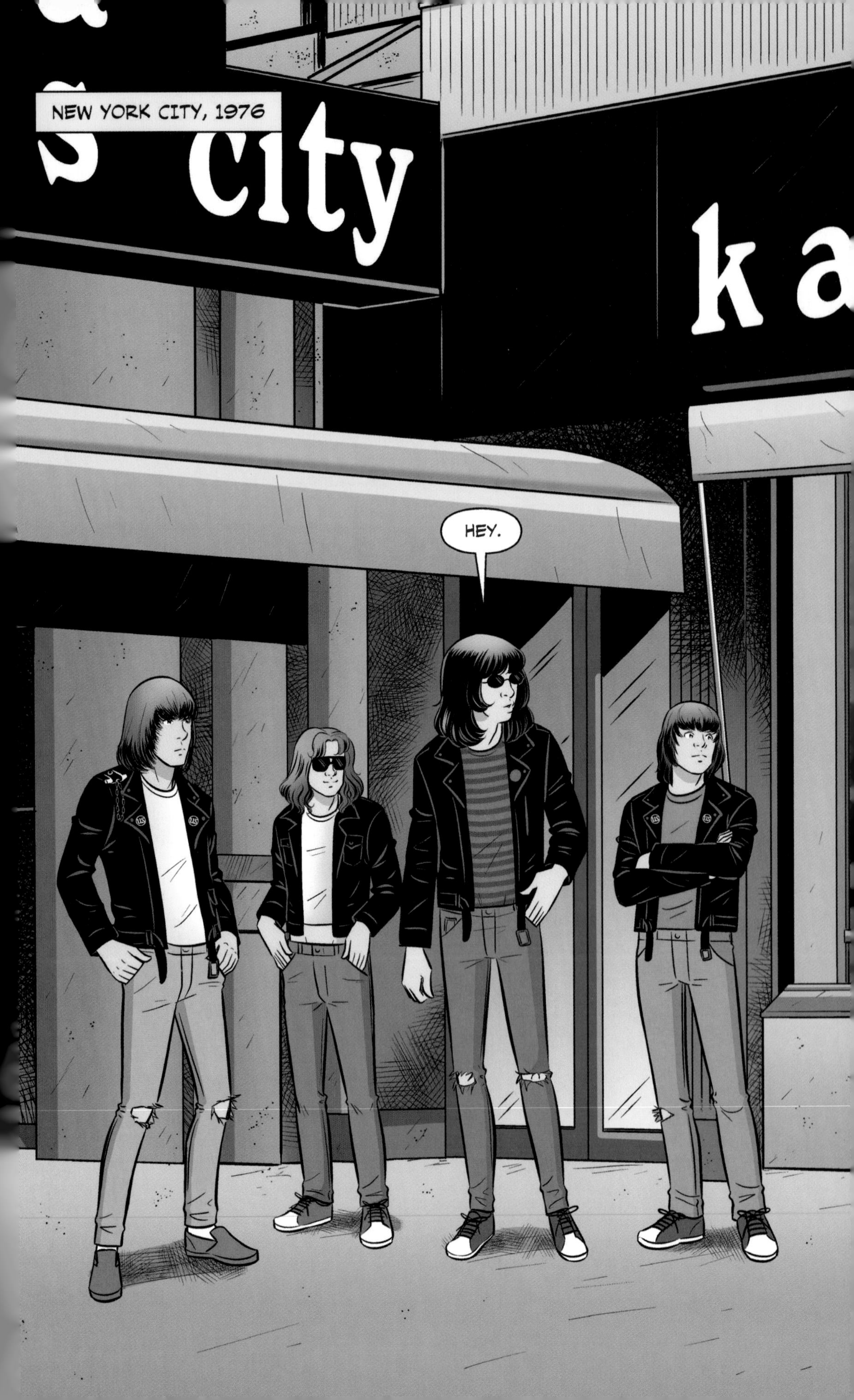
NEW YORK CITY, 1976
S city
ka
HEY.

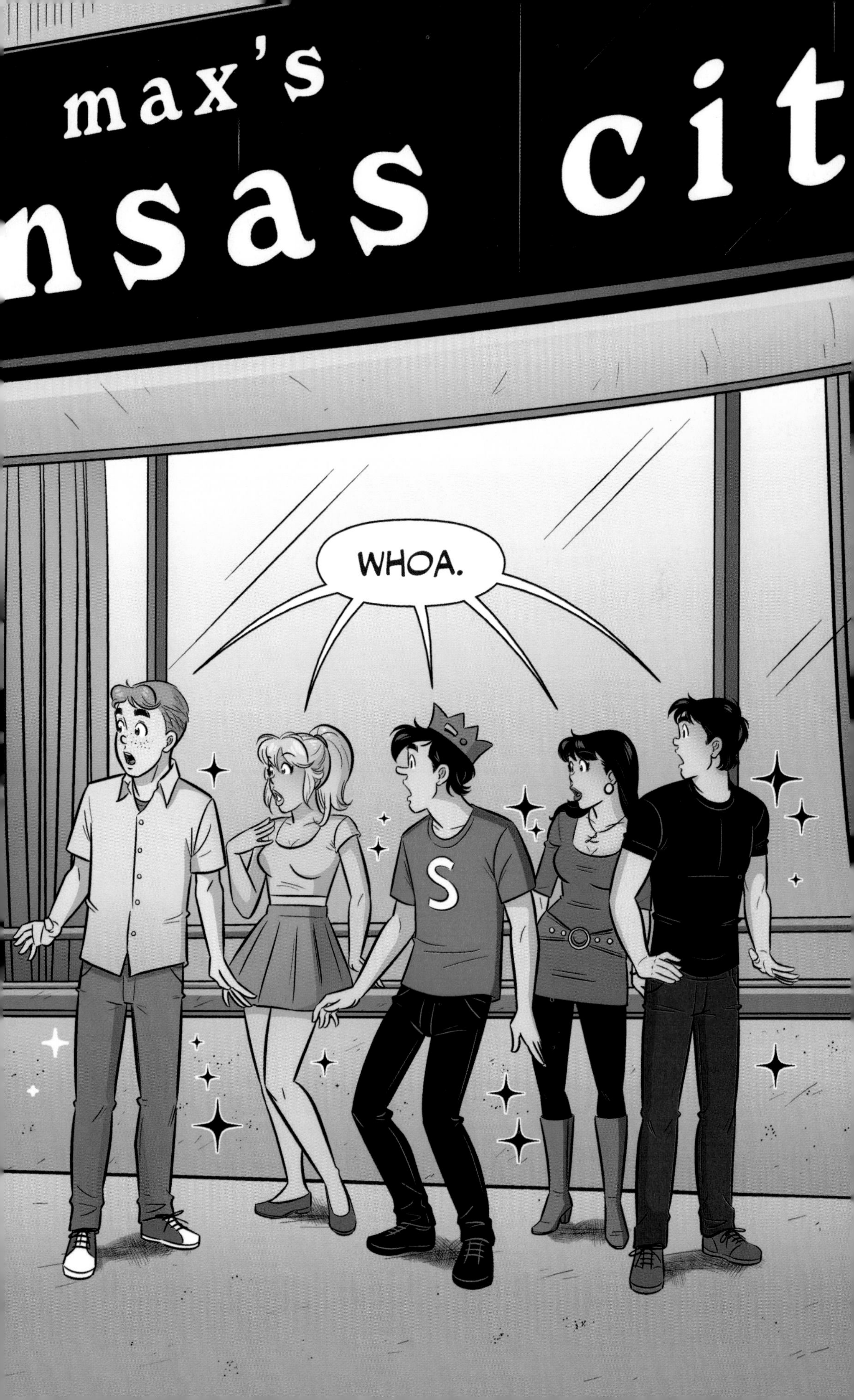
max's
nsas cit
WHOA.

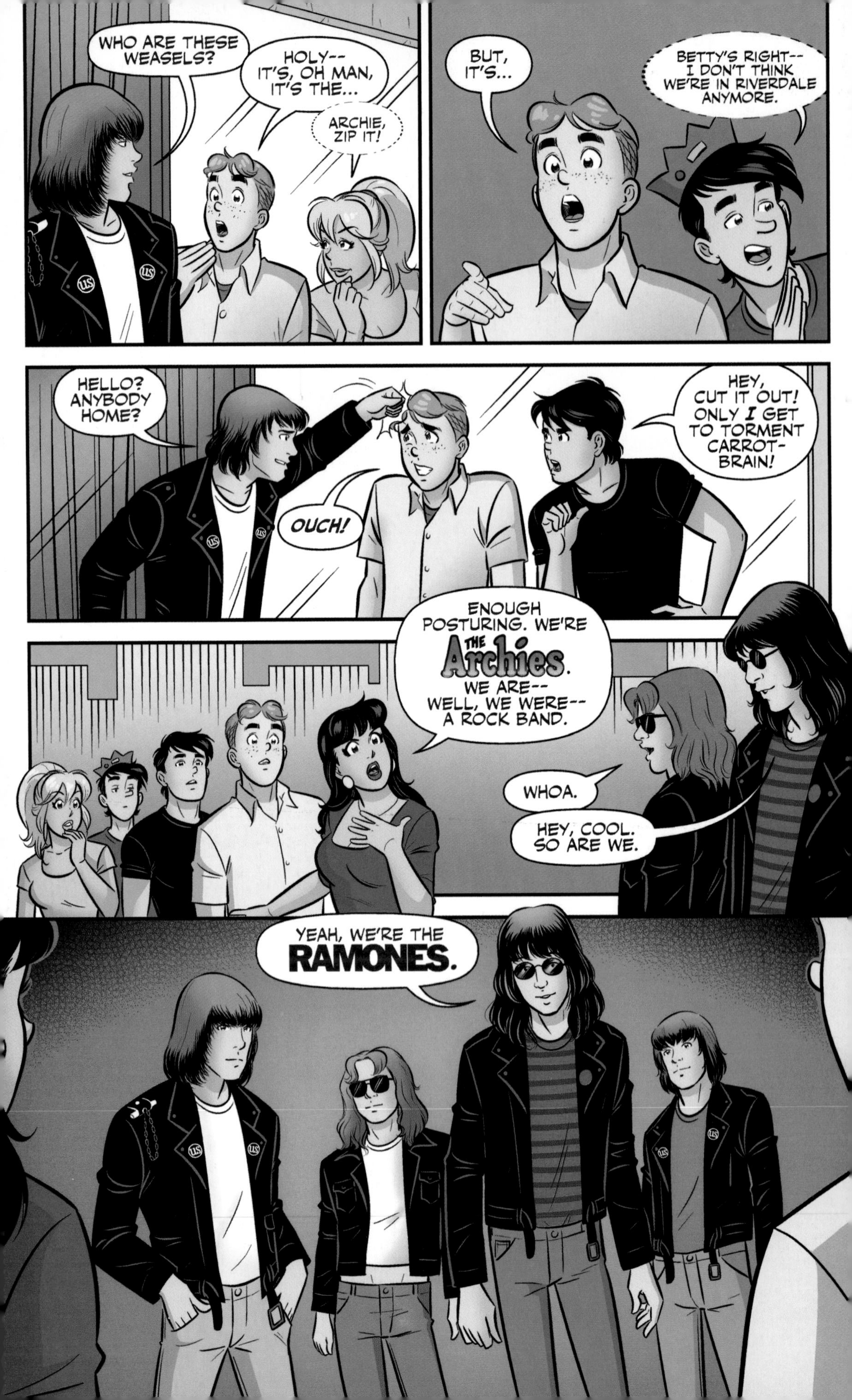
WHO ARE THESE WEASELS?
HOLY-- IT'S, OH MAN, IT'S THE...
ARCHIE, ZIP IT!
BUT, IT'S...
BETTY'S RIGHT-- I DON'T THINK WE'RE IN RIVERDALE ANYMORE.
HELLO? ANYBODY HOME?
OUCH!
HEY, CUT IT OUT! ONLY I GET TO TORMENT CARROT-BRAIN!
ENOUGH POSTURING. WE'RE THE Archies. WE ARE-- WELL, WE WERE-- A ROCK BAND.
WHOA.
HEY, COOL. SO ARE WE.
YEAH, WE'RE THE RAMONES.

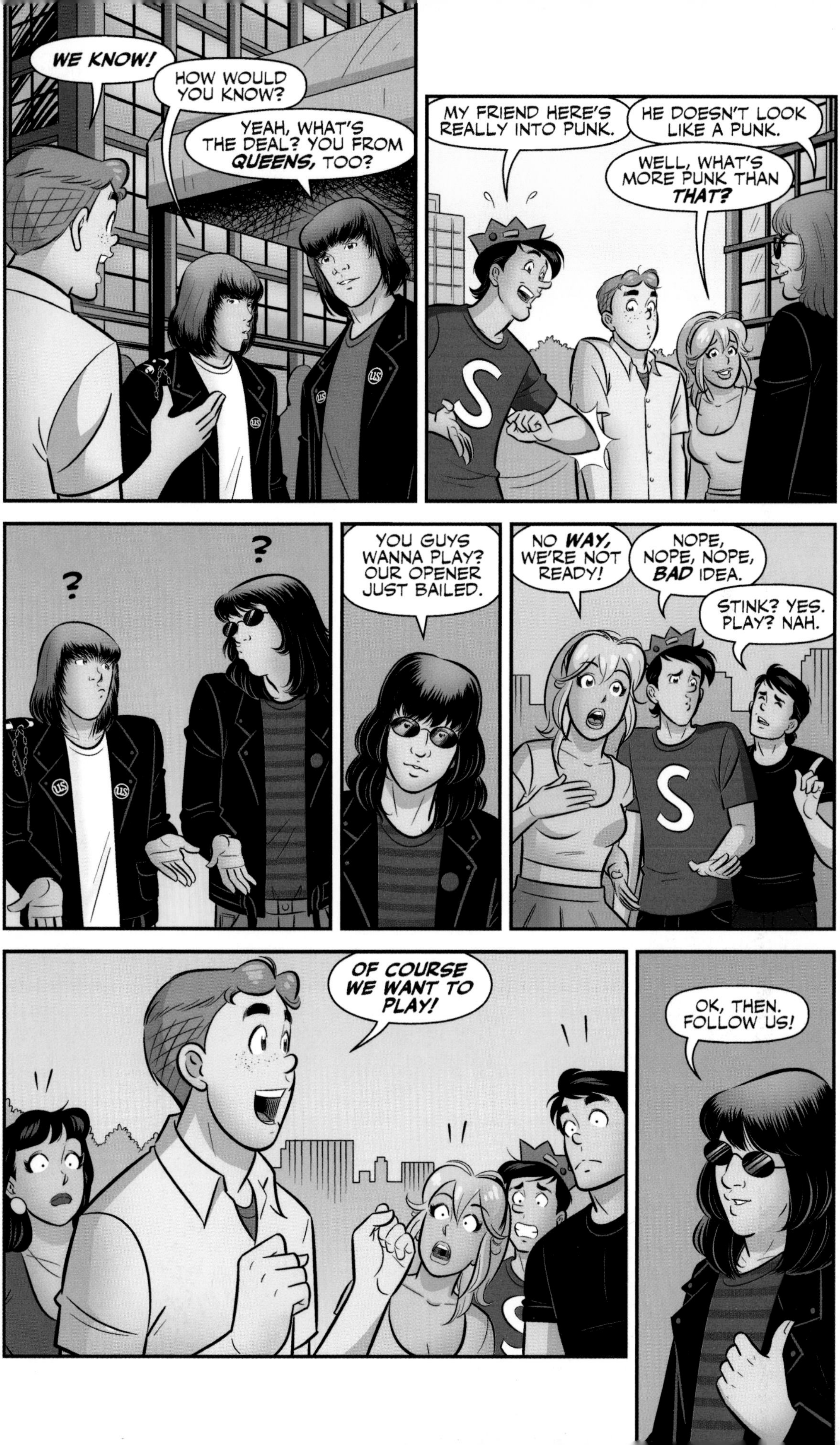
WE KNOW!
HOW WOULD YOU KNOW?
YEAH, WHAT'S THE DEAL? YOU FROM QUEENS, TOO?
MY FRIEND HERE'S REALLY INTO PUNK.
HE DOESN'T LOOK LIKE A PUNK.
WELL, WHAT'S MORE PUNK THAN THAT?
?
?
YOU GUYS WANNA PLAY? OUR OPENER JUST BAILED.
NO WAY, WE'RE NOT READY!
NOPE, NOPE, NOPE, BAD IDEA.
STINK? YES. PLAY? NAH.
OF COURSE WE WANT TO PLAY!
OK, THEN. FOLLOW US!

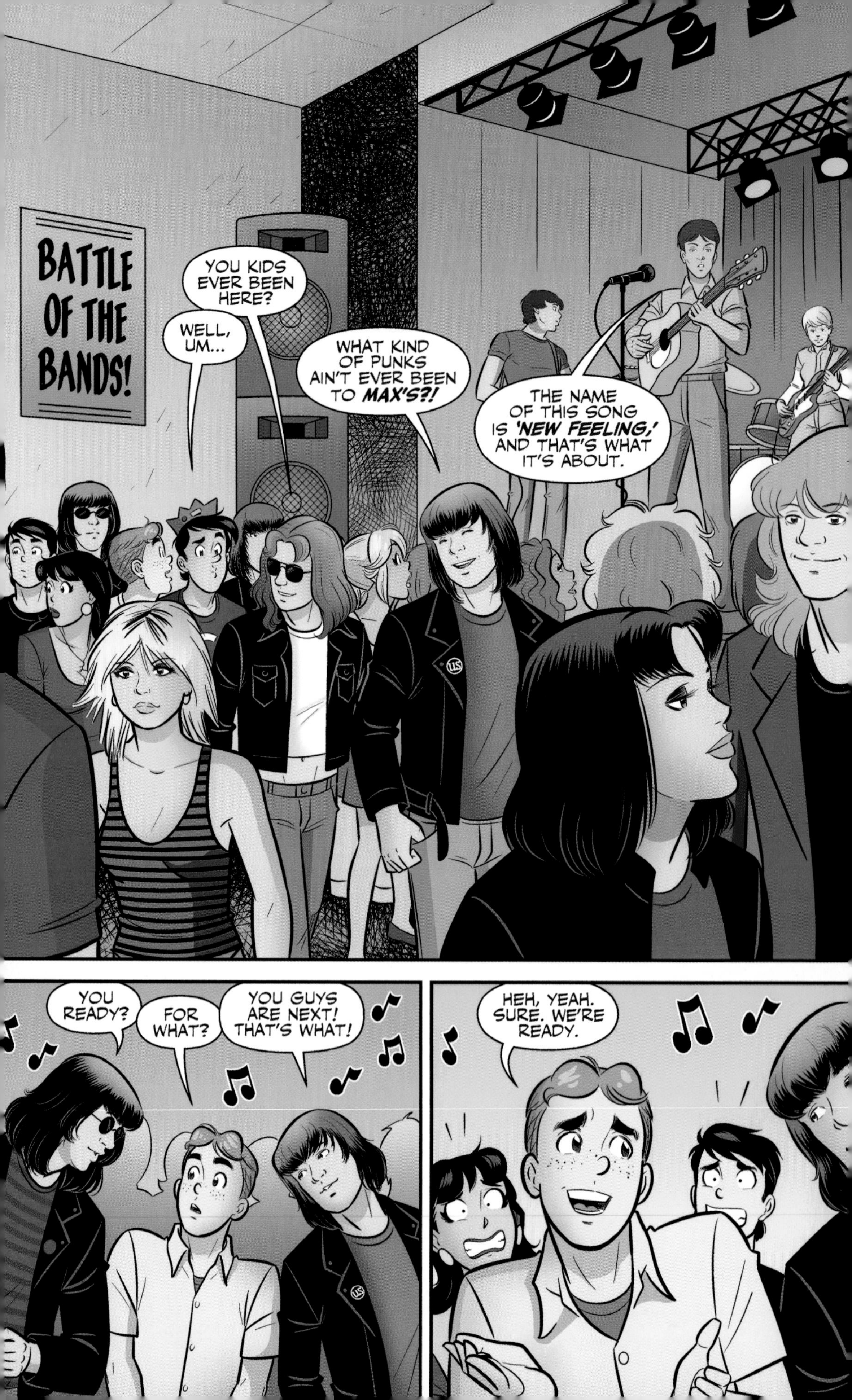
BATTLE OF THE BANDS!
YOU KIDS EVER BEEN HERE?
WELL, UM...
WHAT KIND OF PUNKS AIN'T EVER BEEN TO ***MAX'S?!***
THE NAME OF THIS SONG IS ***'NEW FEELING,'*** AND THAT'S WHAT IT'S ABOUT.
YOU READY?
FOR WHAT?
YOU GUYS ARE NEXT! THAT'S WHAT!
HEH, YEAH. SURE. WE'RE READY.

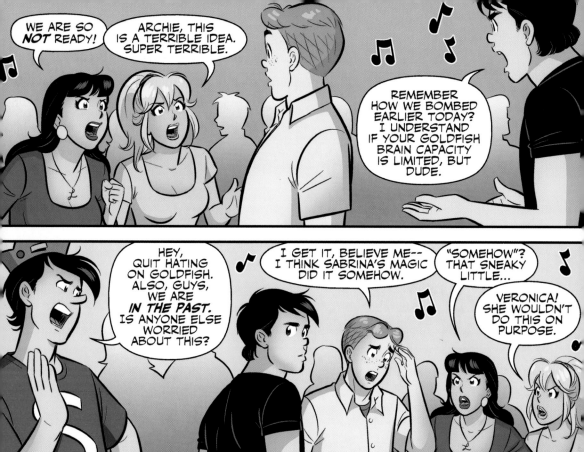

WE ARE SO **NOT** READY!

ARCHIE, THIS IS A TERRIBLE IDEA. SUPER TERRIBLE.

REMEMBER HOW WE BOMBED EARLIER TODAY? I UNDERSTAND IF YOUR GOLDFISH BRAIN CAPACITY IS LIMITED, BUT DUDE.

HEY, QUIT HATING ON GOLDFISH. ALSO, GUYS, WE ARE **IN THE PAST.** IS ANYONE ELSE WORRIED ABOUT THIS?

I GET IT, BELIEVE ME-- I THINK SABRINA'S MAGIC DID IT SOMEHOW.

"SOMEHOW"? THAT SNEAKY LITTLE...

VERONICA! SHE WOULDN'T DO THIS ON PURPOSE.

ON PURPOSE OR NOT, **WE ARE IN THE PAST.** LIKE, NOT TODAY. I SHUDDER TO THINK ABOUT HOW BURGERS WERE MADE.

THIS! THIS IS IT!

WHAT? SHINY PAPER GOT YOU DISTRACTED?

THIS IS THE RECORD! I PUT THIS ON BACKSTAGE AND IT SENT US HERE.

THAT'S OUR TICKET HOME!

BETTY, I'M AMAZED AT YOUR DEDUCTIVE SKILLS.

GRAND PRIZE

RAMONES

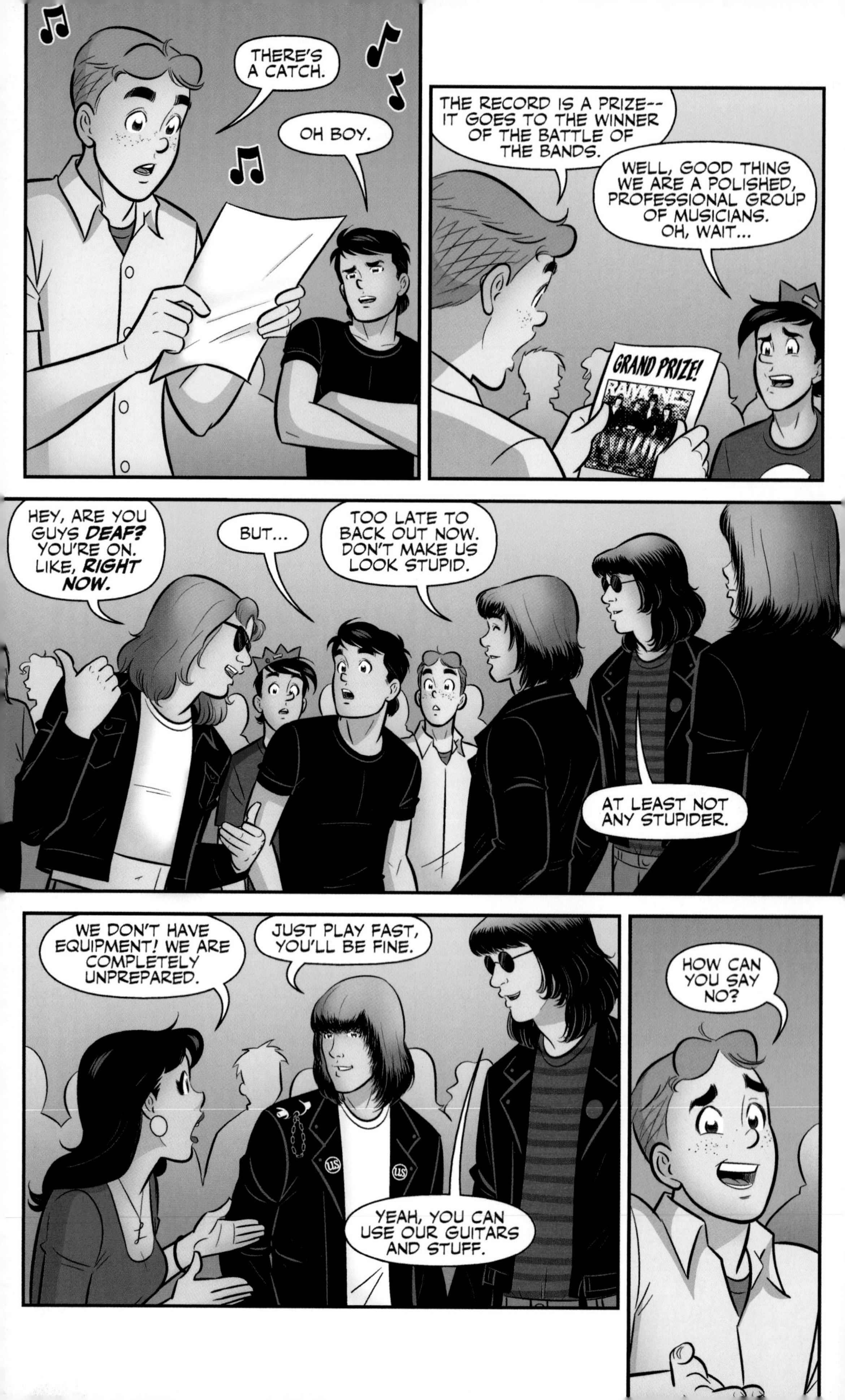
THERE'S A CATCH.
OH BOY.
THE RECORD IS A PRIZE-- IT GOES TO THE WINNER OF THE BATTLE OF THE BANDS.
WELL, GOOD THING WE ARE A POLISHED, PROFESSIONAL GROUP OF MUSICIANS. OH, WAIT...
GRAND PRIZE!
RAMONES
HEY, ARE YOU GUYS DEAF? YOU'RE ON. LIKE, RIGHT NOW.
BUT...
TOO LATE TO BACK OUT NOW. DON'T MAKE US LOOK STUPID.
AT LEAST NOT ANY STUPIDER.
WE DON'T HAVE EQUIPMENT! WE ARE COMPLETELY UNPREPARED.
JUST PLAY FAST, YOU'LL BE FINE.
YEAH, YOU CAN USE OUR GUITARS AND STUFF.
HOW CAN YOU SAY NO?

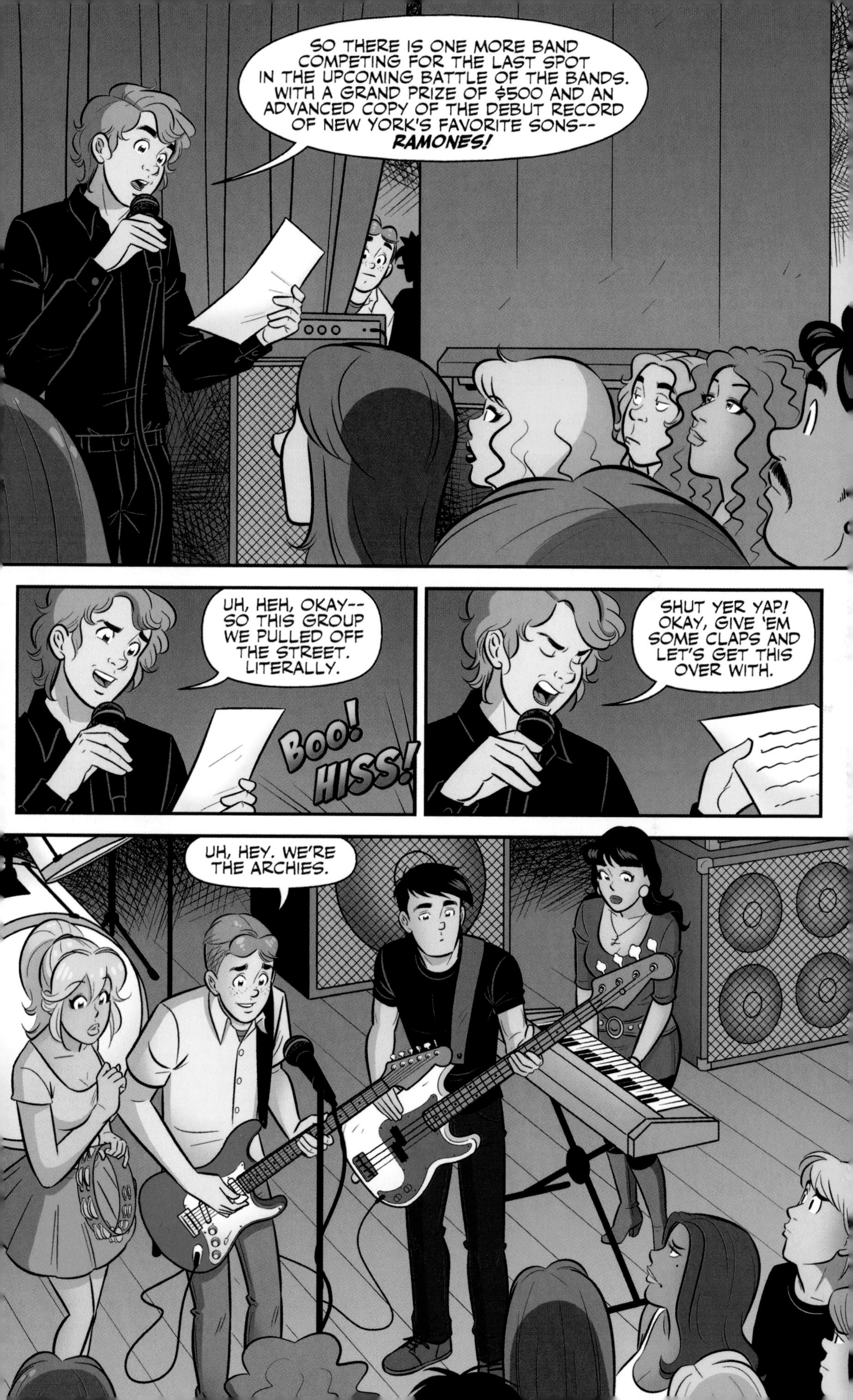
SO THERE IS ONE MORE BAND COMPETING FOR THE LAST SPOT IN THE UPCOMING BATTLE OF THE BANDS. WITH A GRAND PRIZE OF $500 AND AN ADVANCED COPY OF THE DEBUT RECORD OF NEW YORK'S FAVORITE SONS-- RAMONES!
UH, HEH, OKAY-- SO THIS GROUP WE PULLED OFF THE STREET. LITERALLY.
BOO! HISS!
SHUT YER YAP! OKAY, GIVE 'EM SOME CLAPS AND LET'S GET THIS OVER WITH.
UH, HEY. WE'RE THE ARCHIES.

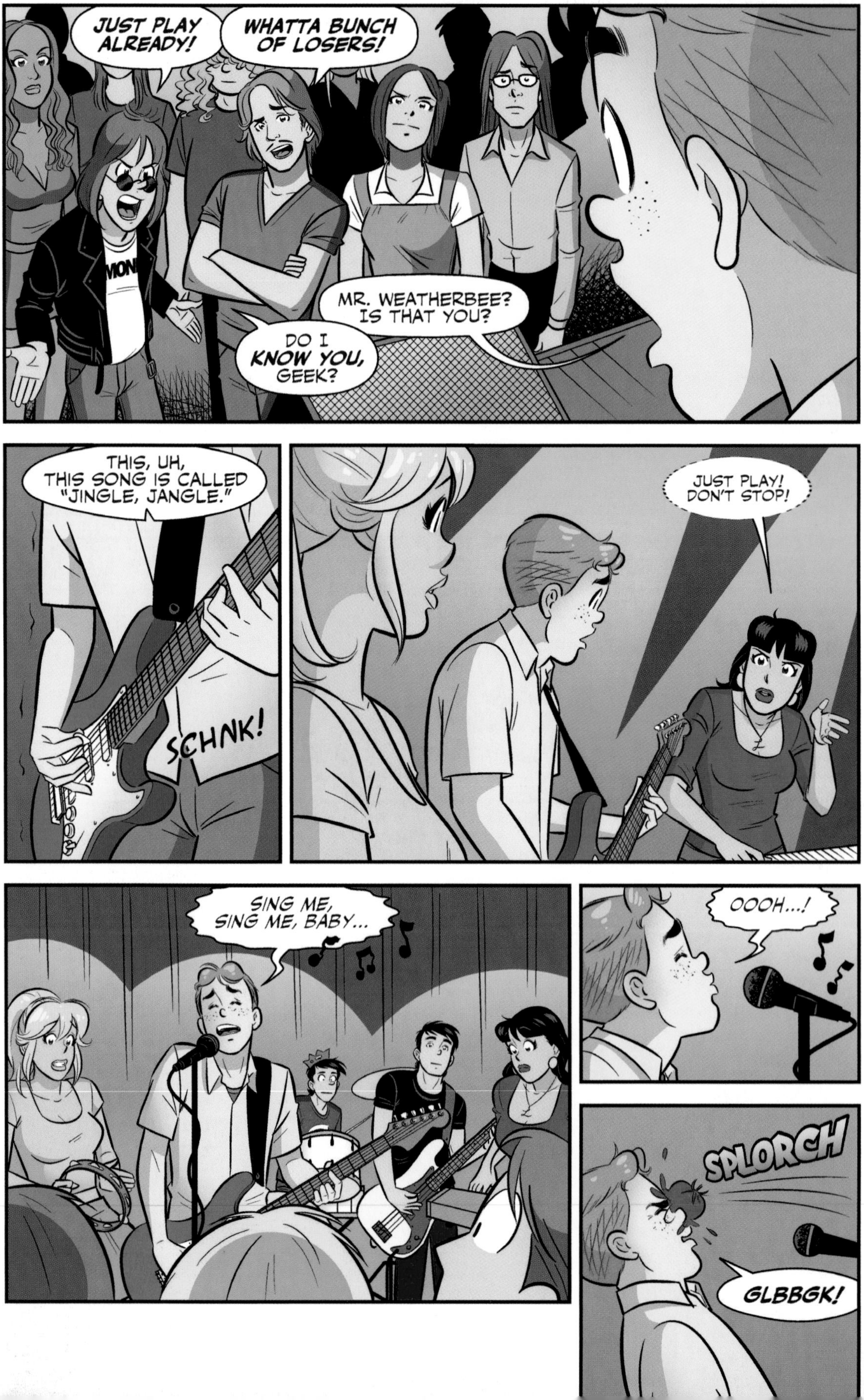
JUST PLAY ALREADY!
WHATTA BUNCH OF LOSERS!
MR. WEATHERBEE? IS THAT YOU?
DO I KNOW YOU, GEEK?
THIS, UH, THIS SONG IS CALLED "JINGLE, JANGLE."
SCHNK!
JUST PLAY! DON'T STOP!
SING ME, SING ME, BABY...
OOOH...!
SPLORCH
GLBBGK!

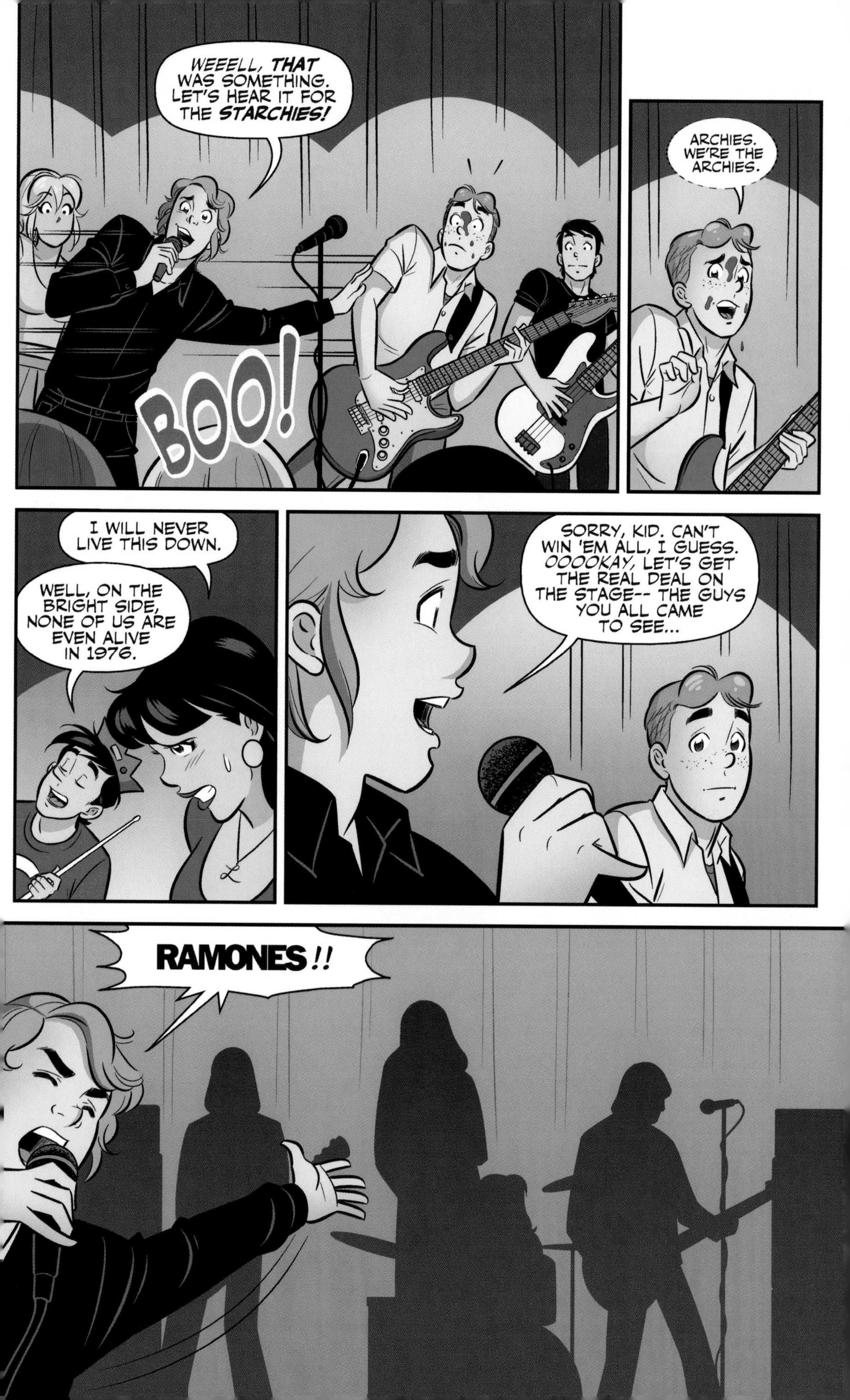
WEEELL, THAT WAS SOMETHING. LET'S HEAR IT FOR THE STARCHIES!
BOO!
ARCHIES. WE'RE THE ARCHIES.
I WILL NEVER LIVE THIS DOWN.
WELL, ON THE BRIGHT SIDE, NONE OF US ARE EVEN ALIVE IN 1976.
SORRY, KID. CAN'T WIN 'EM ALL, I GUESS. OOOOKAY, LET'S GET THE REAL DEAL ON THE STAGE-- THE GUYS YOU ALL CAME TO SEE...
RAMONES!!

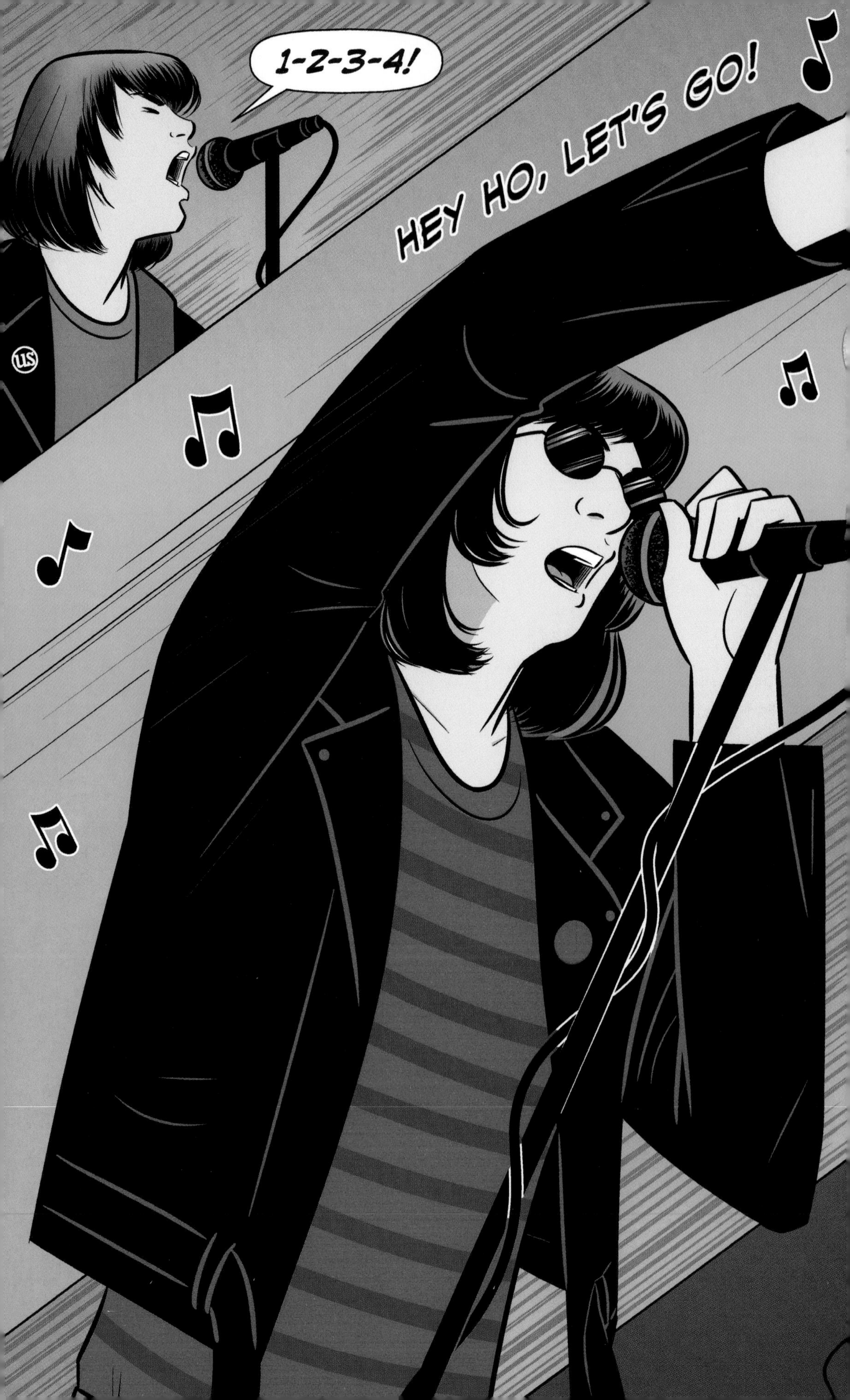
1-2-3-4!
HEY HO, LET'S GO!

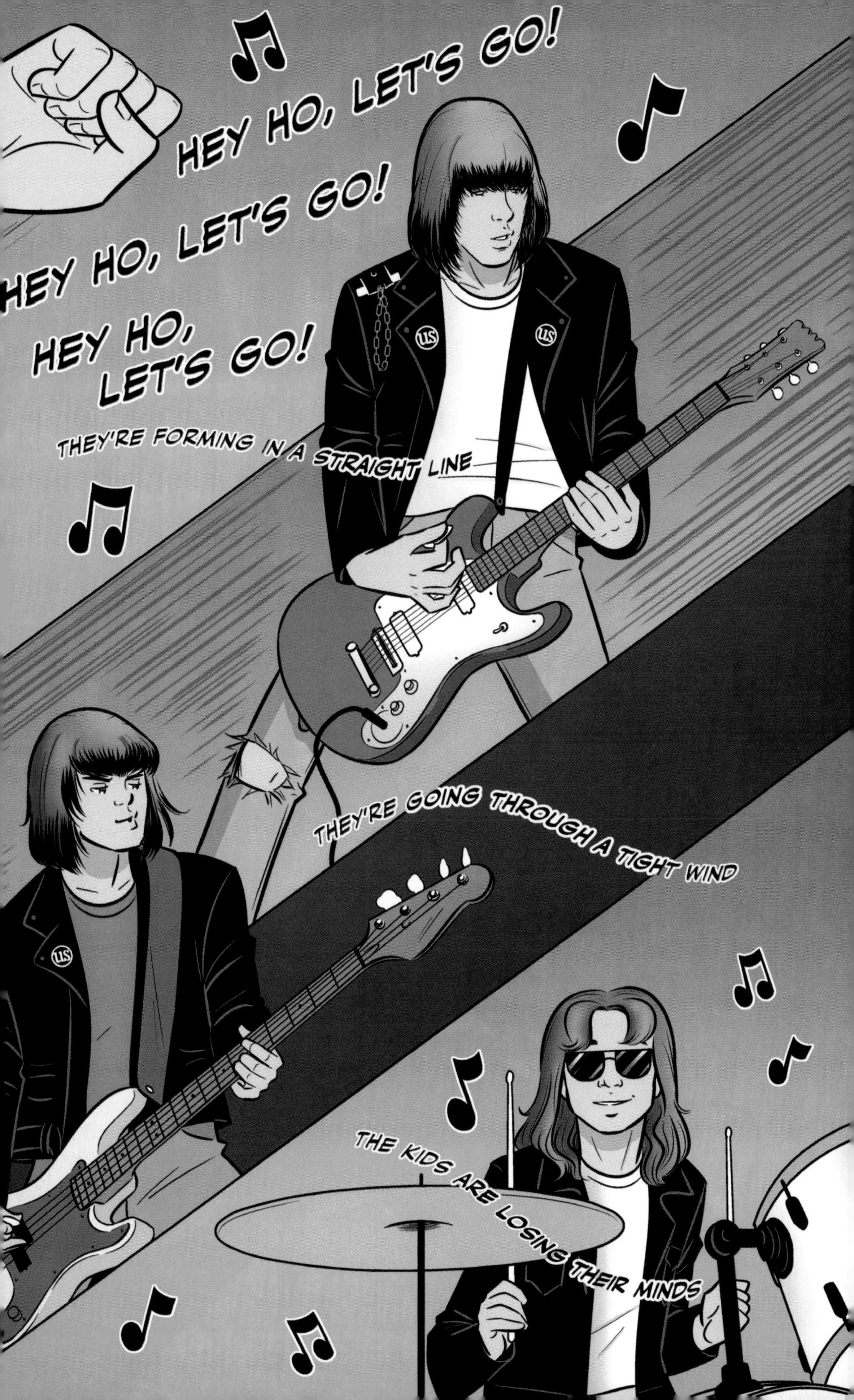
HEY HO, LET'S GO!
HEY HO, LET'S GO!
HEY HO, LET'S GO!
THEY'RE FORMING IN A STRAIGHT LINE
THEY'RE GOING THROUGH A TIGHT WIND
THE KIDS ARE LOSING THEIR MINDS

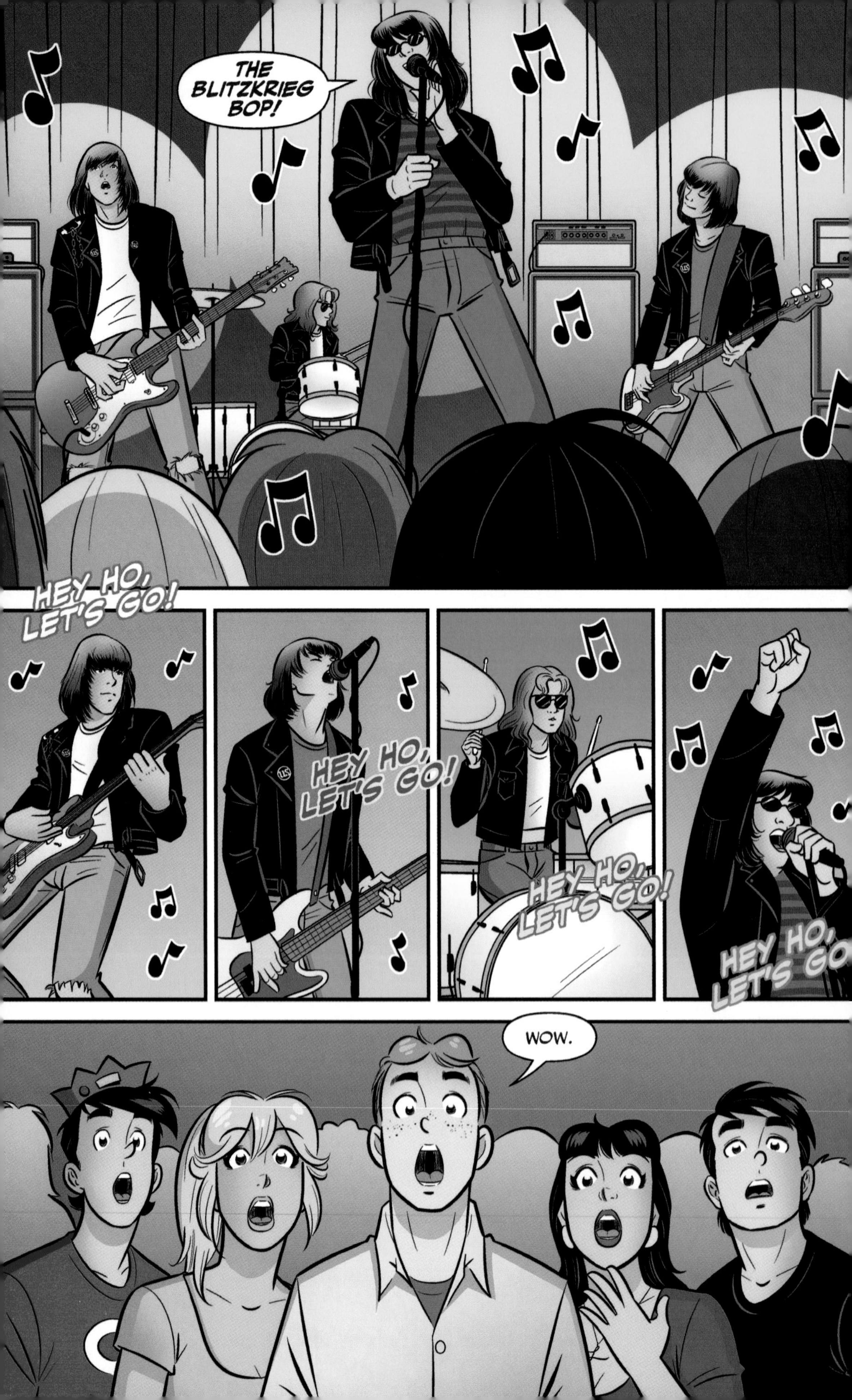
THE BLITZKRIEG BOP!
HEY HO, LET'S GO!
HEY HO, LET'S GO!
HEY HO, LET'S GO!
HEY HO, LET'S GO
WOW.

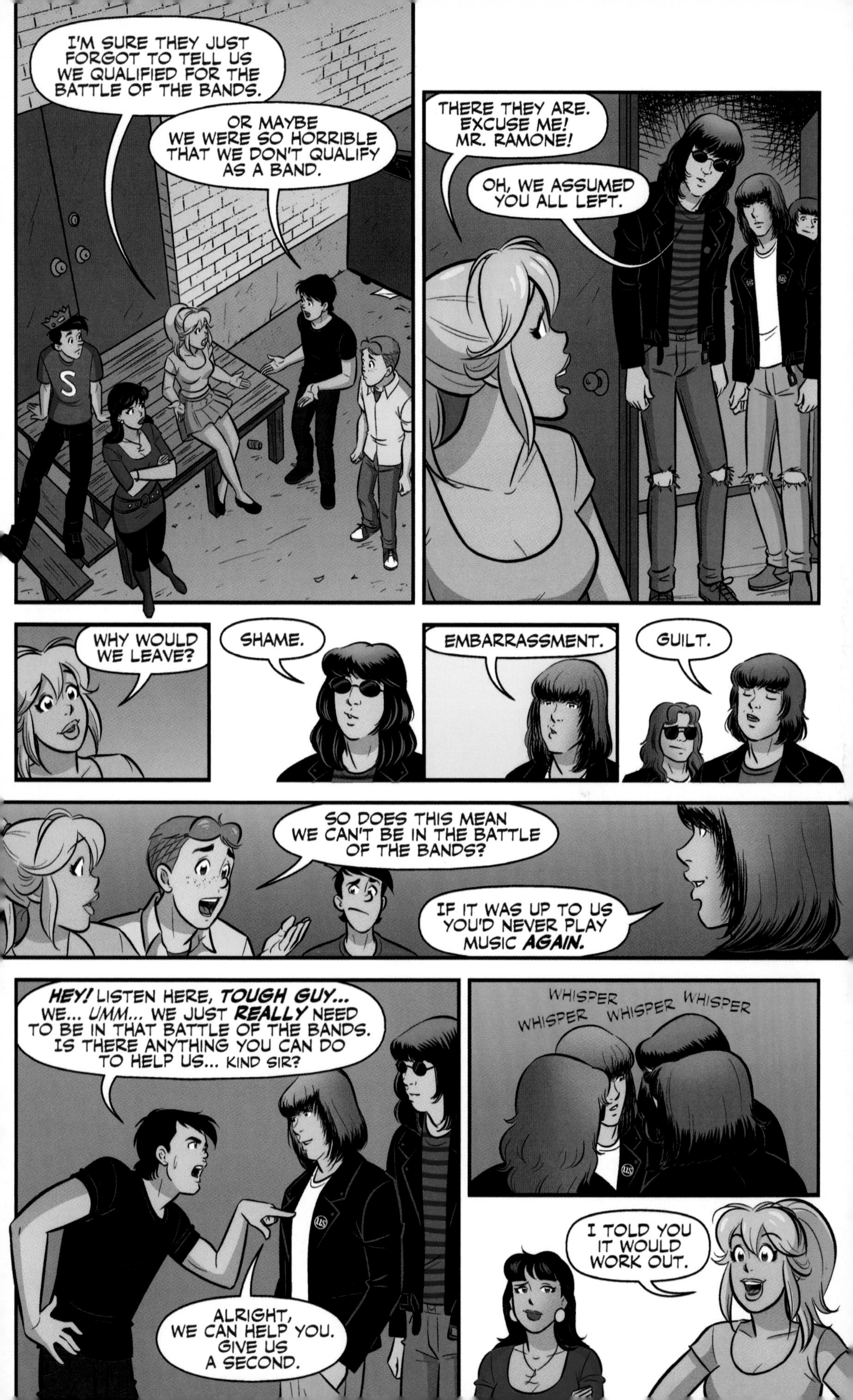
I'M SURE THEY JUST FORGOT TO TELL US WE QUALIFIED FOR THE BATTLE OF THE BANDS.
OR MAYBE WE WERE SO HORRIBLE THAT WE DON'T QUALIFY AS A BAND.
THERE THEY ARE. EXCUSE ME! MR. RAMONE!
OH, WE ASSUMED YOU ALL LEFT.
WHY WOULD WE LEAVE?
SHAME.
EMBARRASSMENT.
GUILT.
SO DOES THIS MEAN WE CAN'T BE IN THE BATTLE OF THE BANDS?
IF IT WAS UP TO US YOU'D NEVER PLAY MUSIC AGAIN.
HEY! LISTEN HERE, TOUGH GUY... WE... UMM... WE JUST REALLY NEED TO BE IN THAT BATTLE OF THE BANDS. IS THERE ANYTHING YOU CAN DO TO HELP US... KIND SIR?
ALRIGHT, WE CAN HELP YOU. GIVE US A SECOND.
WHISPER WHISPER WHISPER WHISPER
I TOLD YOU IT WOULD WORK OUT.

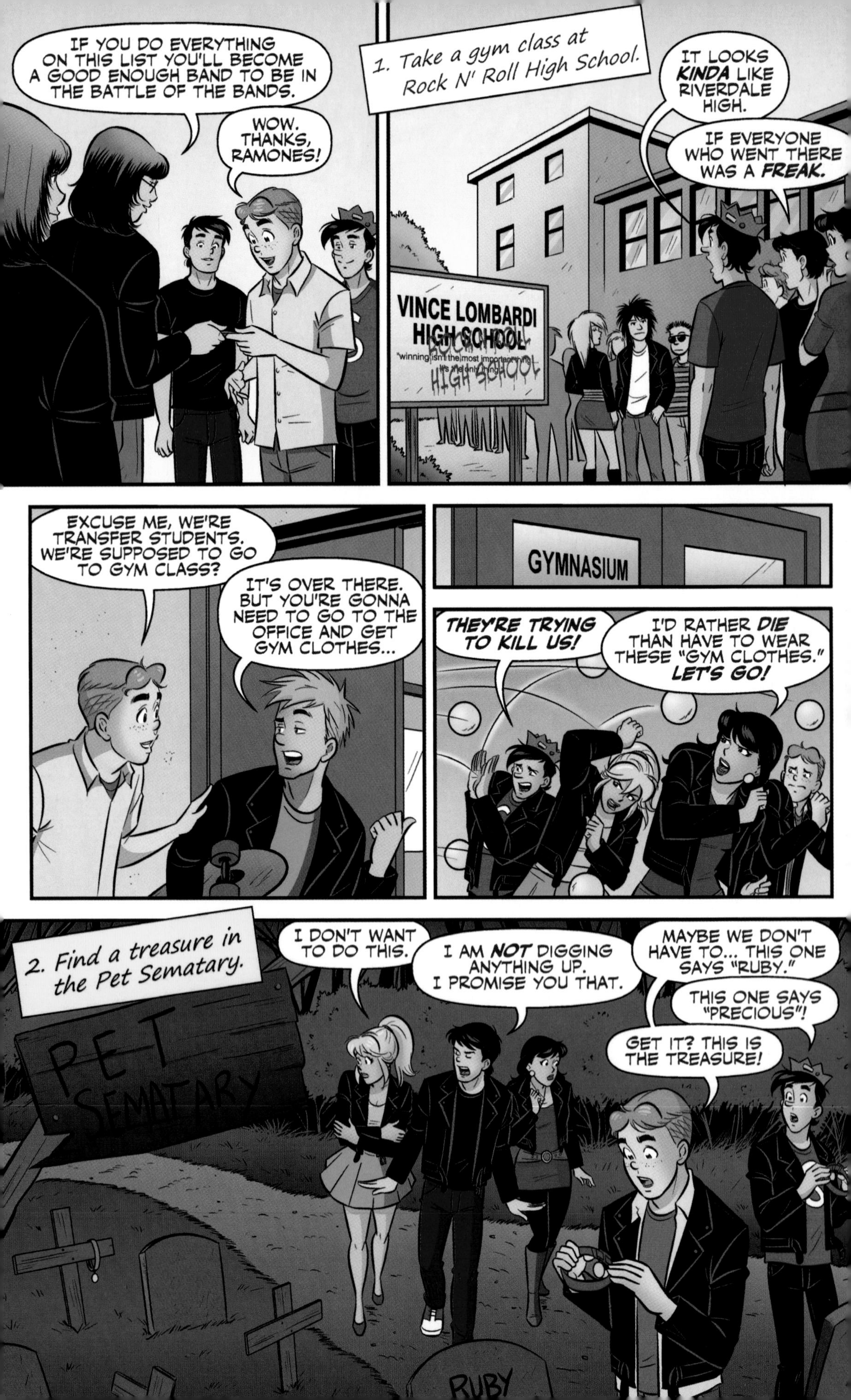
IF YOU DO EVERYTHING ON THIS LIST YOU'LL BECOME A GOOD ENOUGH BAND TO BE IN THE BATTLE OF THE BANDS.
WOW. THANKS, RAMONES!
1. Take a gym class at Rock N' Roll High School.
IT LOOKS KINDA LIKE RIVERDALE HIGH.
IF EVERYONE WHO WENT THERE WAS A FREAK.
VINCE LOMBARDI HIGH SCHOOL
HIGH SCHOOL
EXCUSE ME, WE'RE TRANSFER STUDENTS. WE'RE SUPPOSED TO GO TO GYM CLASS?
IT'S OVER THERE. BUT YOU'RE GONNA NEED TO GO TO THE OFFICE AND GET GYM CLOTHES...
GYMNASIUM
THEY'RE TRYING TO KILL US!
I'D RATHER DIE THAN HAVE TO WEAR THESE "GYM CLOTHES." LET'S GO!
2. Find a treasure in the Pet Sematary.
PET SEMATARY
I DON'T WANT TO DO THIS.
I AM NOT DIGGING ANYTHING UP. I PROMISE YOU THAT.
MAYBE WE DON'T HAVE TO... THIS ONE SAYS "RUBY."
THIS ONE SAYS "PRECIOUS"!
GET IT? THIS IS THE TREASURE!
RUBY

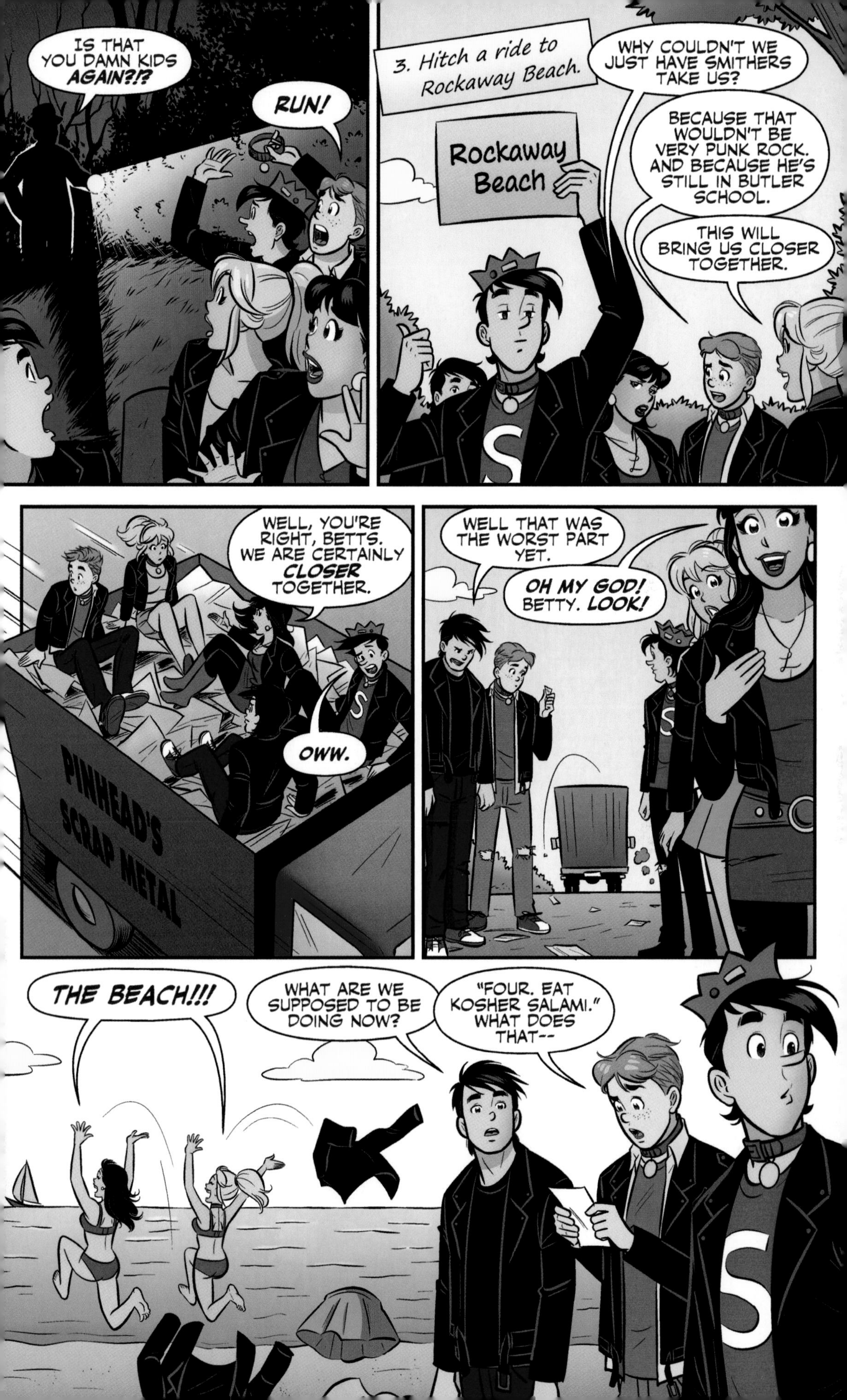
IS THAT YOU DAMN KIDS AGAIN?!?
RUN!
3. Hitch a ride to Rockaway Beach.
Rockaway Beach
WHY COULDN'T WE JUST HAVE SMITHERS TAKE US?
BECAUSE THAT WOULDN'T BE VERY PUNK ROCK. AND BECAUSE HE'S STILL IN BUTLER SCHOOL.
THIS WILL BRING US CLOSER TOGETHER.
WELL, YOU'RE RIGHT, BETTS. WE ARE CERTAINLY CLOSER TOGETHER.
OWW.
PINHEAD'S SCRAP METAL
WELL THAT WAS THE WORST PART YET.
OH MY GOD! BETTY. LOOK!
THE BEACH!!!
WHAT ARE WE SUPPOSED TO BE DOING NOW?
"FOUR. EAT KOSHER SALAMI." WHAT DOES THAT--

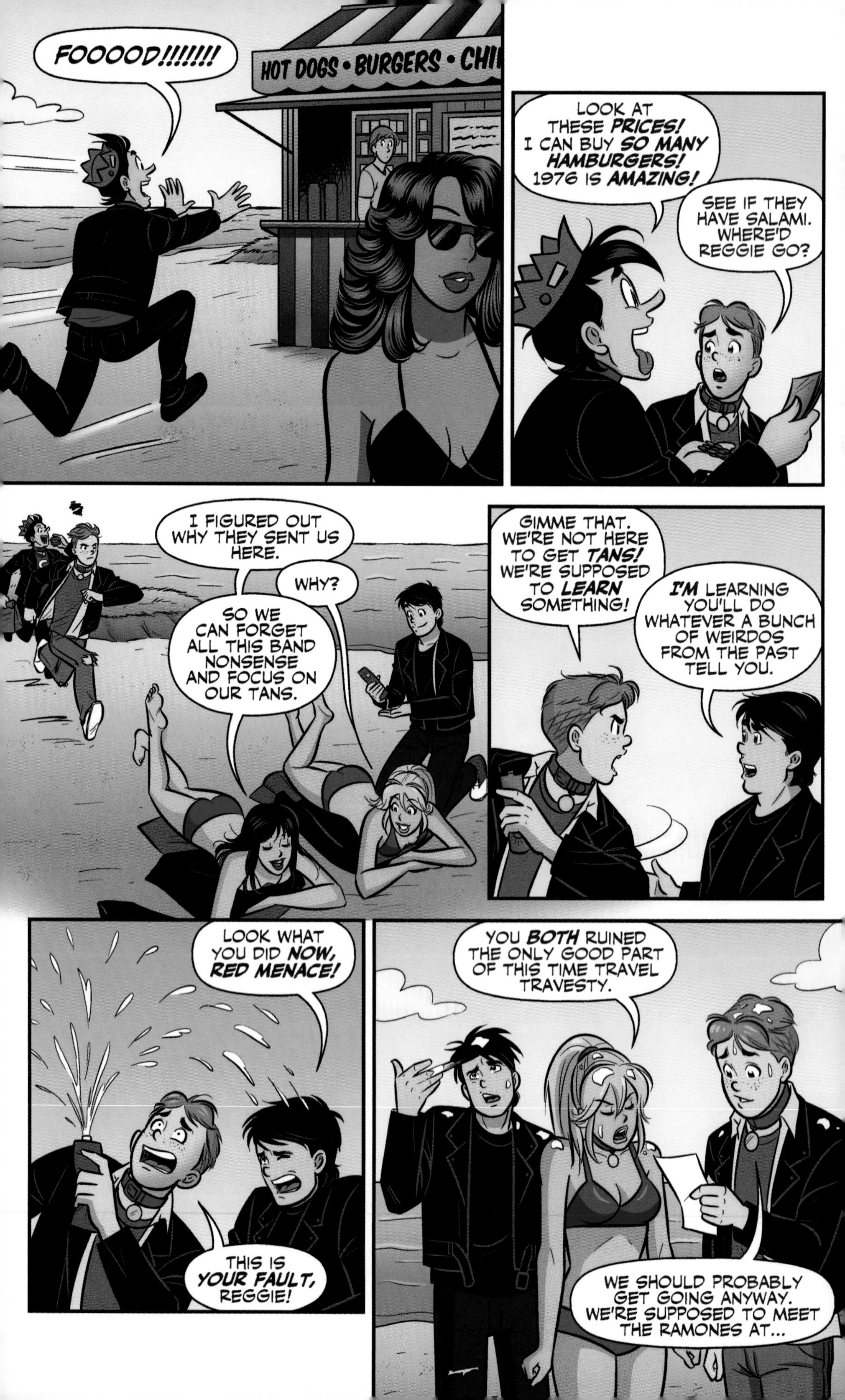
FOOOOD!!!!!!!
HOT DOGS • BURGERS • CHI
LOOK AT THESE PRICES! I CAN BUY SO MANY HAMBURGERS! 1976 IS AMAZING!
SEE IF THEY HAVE SALAMI. WHERE'D REGGIE GO?
I FIGURED OUT WHY THEY SENT US HERE.
WHY?
SO WE CAN FORGET ALL THIS BAND NONSENSE AND FOCUS ON OUR TANS.
GIMME THAT. WE'RE NOT HERE TO GET TANS! WE'RE SUPPOSED TO LEARN SOMETHING!
I'M LEARNING YOU'LL DO WHATEVER A BUNCH OF WEIRDOS FROM THE PAST TELL YOU.
LOOK WHAT YOU DID NOW, RED MENACE!
THIS IS YOUR FAULT, REGGIE!
YOU BOTH RUINED THE ONLY GOOD PART OF THIS TIME TRAVEL TRAVESTY.
WE SHOULD PROBABLY GET GOING ANYWAY. WE'RE SUPPOSED TO MEET THE RAMONES AT...

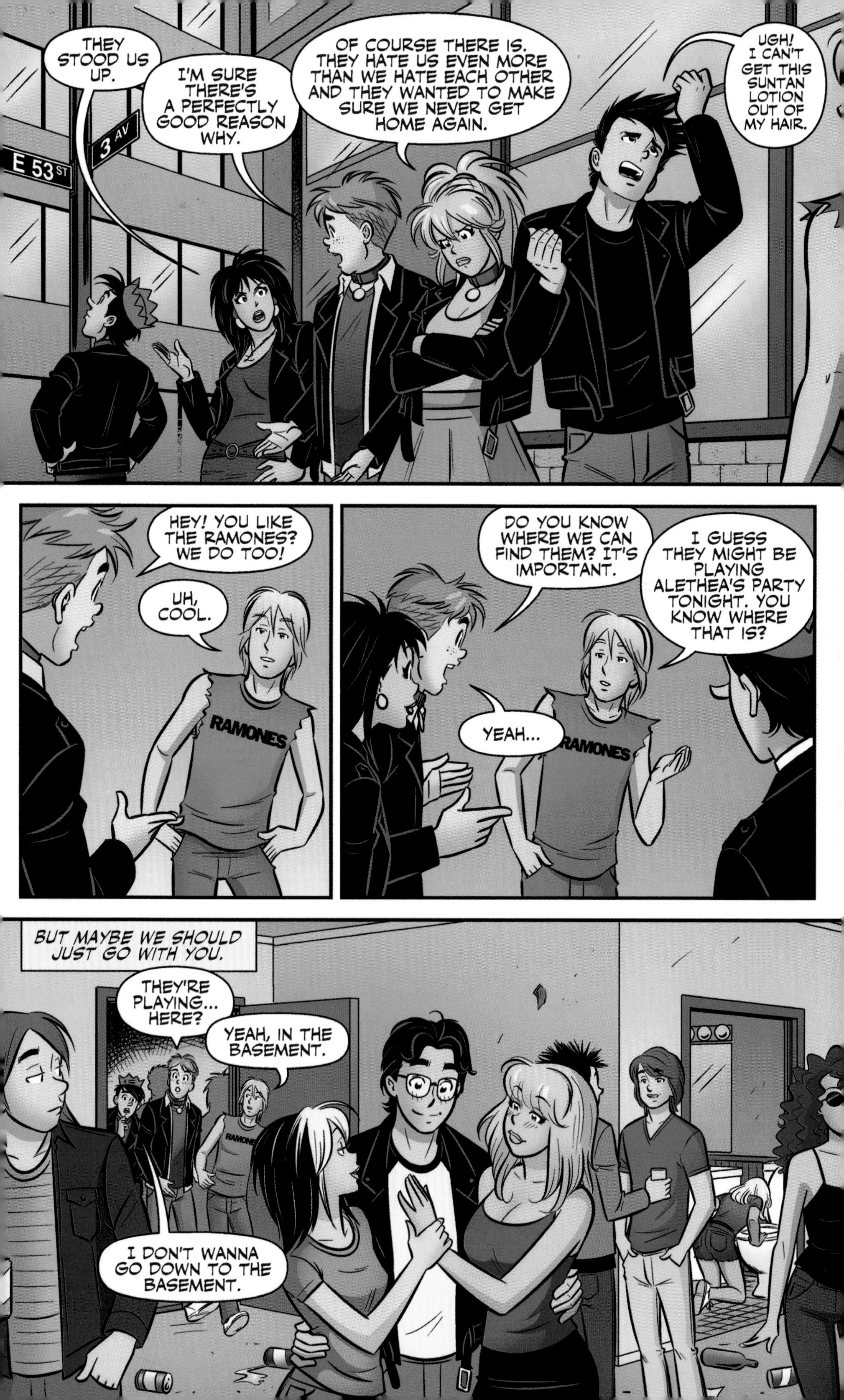
THEY STOOD US UP.
I'M SURE THERE'S A PERFECTLY GOOD REASON WHY.
OF COURSE THERE IS. THEY HATE US EVEN MORE THAN WE HATE EACH OTHER AND THEY WANTED TO MAKE SURE WE NEVER GET HOME AGAIN.
UGH! I CAN'T GET THIS SUNTAN LOTION OUT OF MY HAIR.
E 53 ST
3 AV
HEY! YOU LIKE THE RAMONES? WE DO TOO!
UH, COOL.
RAMONES
DO YOU KNOW WHERE WE CAN FIND THEM? IT'S IMPORTANT.
I GUESS THEY MIGHT BE PLAYING ALETHEA'S PARTY TONIGHT. YOU KNOW WHERE THAT IS?
YEAH...
RAMONES
BUT MAYBE WE SHOULD JUST GO WITH YOU.
THEY'RE PLAYING... HERE?
YEAH, IN THE BASEMENT.
RAMONES
I DON'T WANNA GO DOWN TO THE BASEMENT.

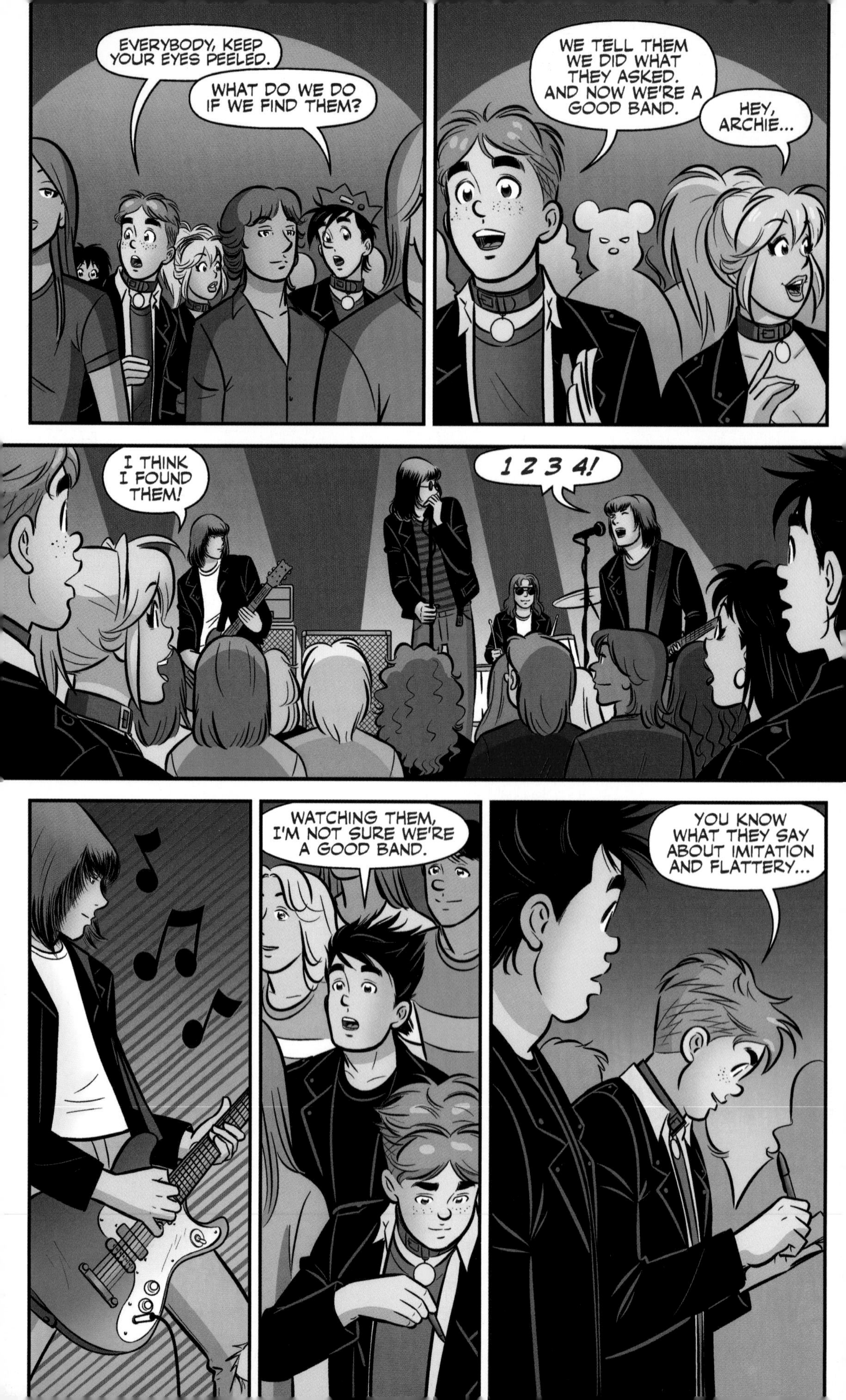

EVERYBODY, KEEP YOUR EYES PEELED.
WHAT DO WE DO IF WE FIND THEM?
WE TELL THEM WE DID WHAT THEY ASKED. AND NOW WE'RE A GOOD BAND.
HEY, ARCHIE...
I THINK I FOUND THEM!
1 2 3 4!
WATCHING THEM, I'M NOT SURE WE'RE A GOOD BAND.
YOU KNOW WHAT THEY SAY ABOUT IMITATION AND FLATTERY...

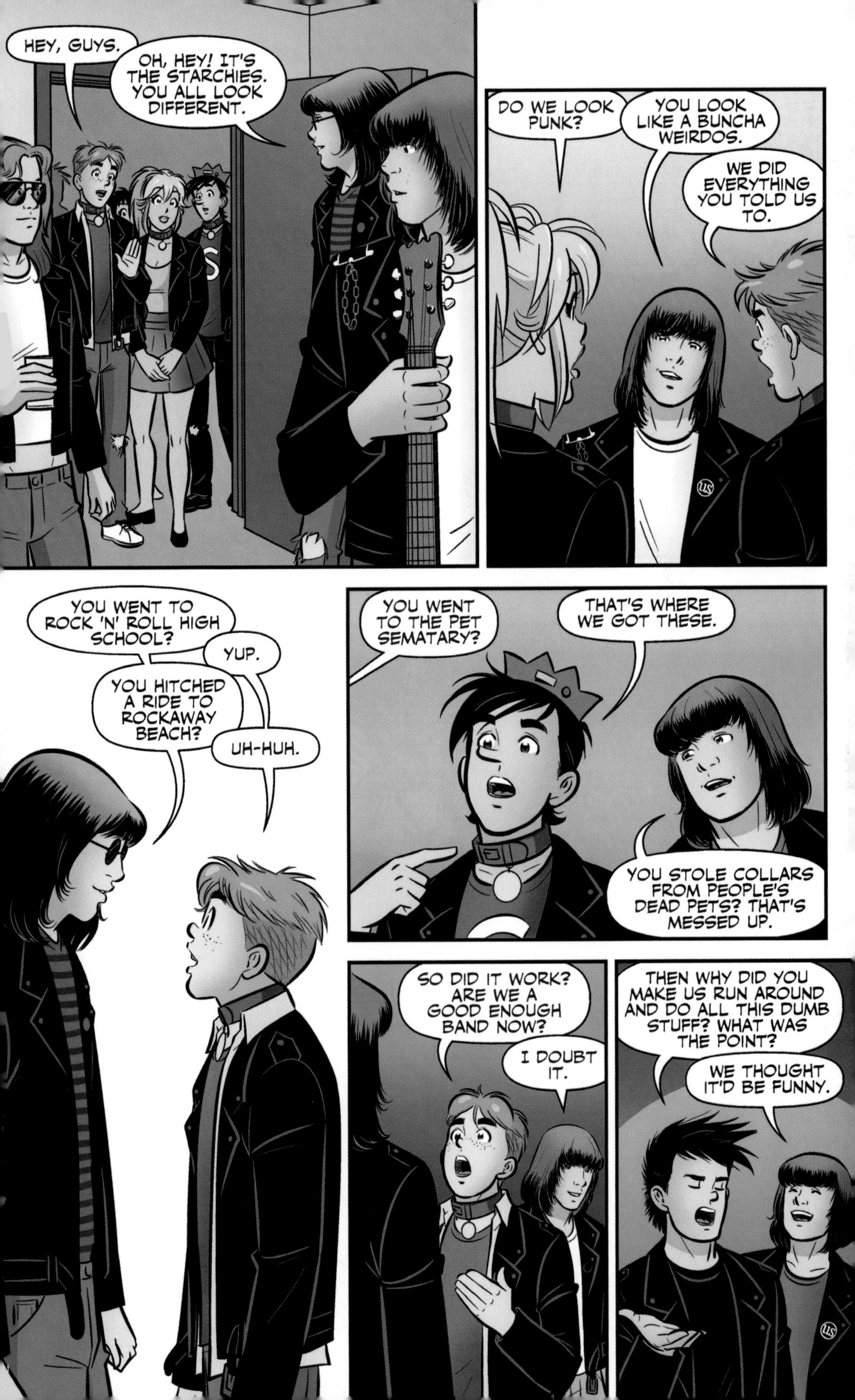
HEY, GUYS.
OH, HEY! IT'S THE STARCHIES. YOU ALL LOOK DIFFERENT.
DO WE LOOK PUNK?
YOU LOOK LIKE A BUNCHA WEIRDOS.
WE DID EVERYTHING YOU TOLD US TO.
YOU WENT TO ROCK 'N' ROLL HIGH SCHOOL?
YUP.
YOU HITCHED A RIDE TO ROCKAWAY BEACH?
UH-HUH.
YOU WENT TO THE PET SEMATARY?
THAT'S WHERE WE GOT THESE.
YOU STOLE COLLARS FROM PEOPLE'S DEAD PETS? THAT'S MESSED UP.
SO DID IT WORK? ARE WE A GOOD ENOUGH BAND NOW?
I DOUBT IT.
THEN WHY DID YOU MAKE US RUN AROUND AND DO ALL THIS DUMB STUFF? WHAT WAS THE POINT?
WE THOUGHT IT'D BE FUNNY.

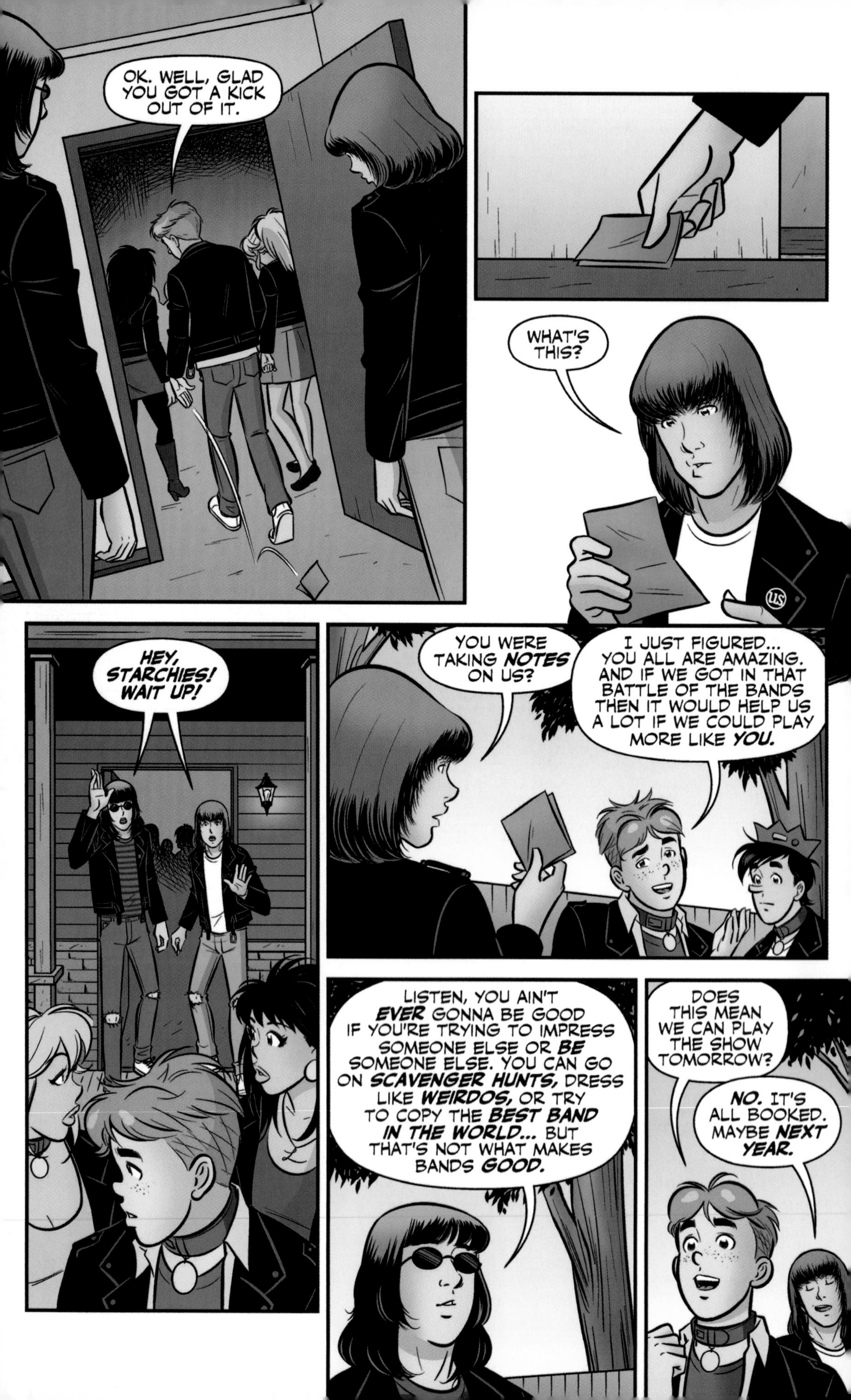
OK. WELL, GLAD YOU GOT A KICK OUT OF IT.
WHAT'S THIS?
HEY, STARCHIES! WAIT UP!
YOU WERE TAKING NOTES ON US?
I JUST FIGURED... YOU ALL ARE AMAZING. AND IF WE GOT IN THAT BATTLE OF THE BANDS THEN IT WOULD HELP US A LOT IF WE COULD PLAY MORE LIKE YOU.
LISTEN, YOU AIN'T EVER GONNA BE GOOD IF YOU'RE TRYING TO IMPRESS SOMEONE ELSE OR BE SOMEONE ELSE. YOU CAN GO ON SCAVENGER HUNTS, DRESS LIKE WEIRDOS, OR TRY TO COPY THE BEST BAND IN THE WORLD... BUT THAT'S NOT WHAT MAKES BANDS GOOD.
DOES THIS MEAN WE CAN PLAY THE SHOW TOMORROW?
NO. IT'S ALL BOOKED. MAYBE NEXT YEAR.

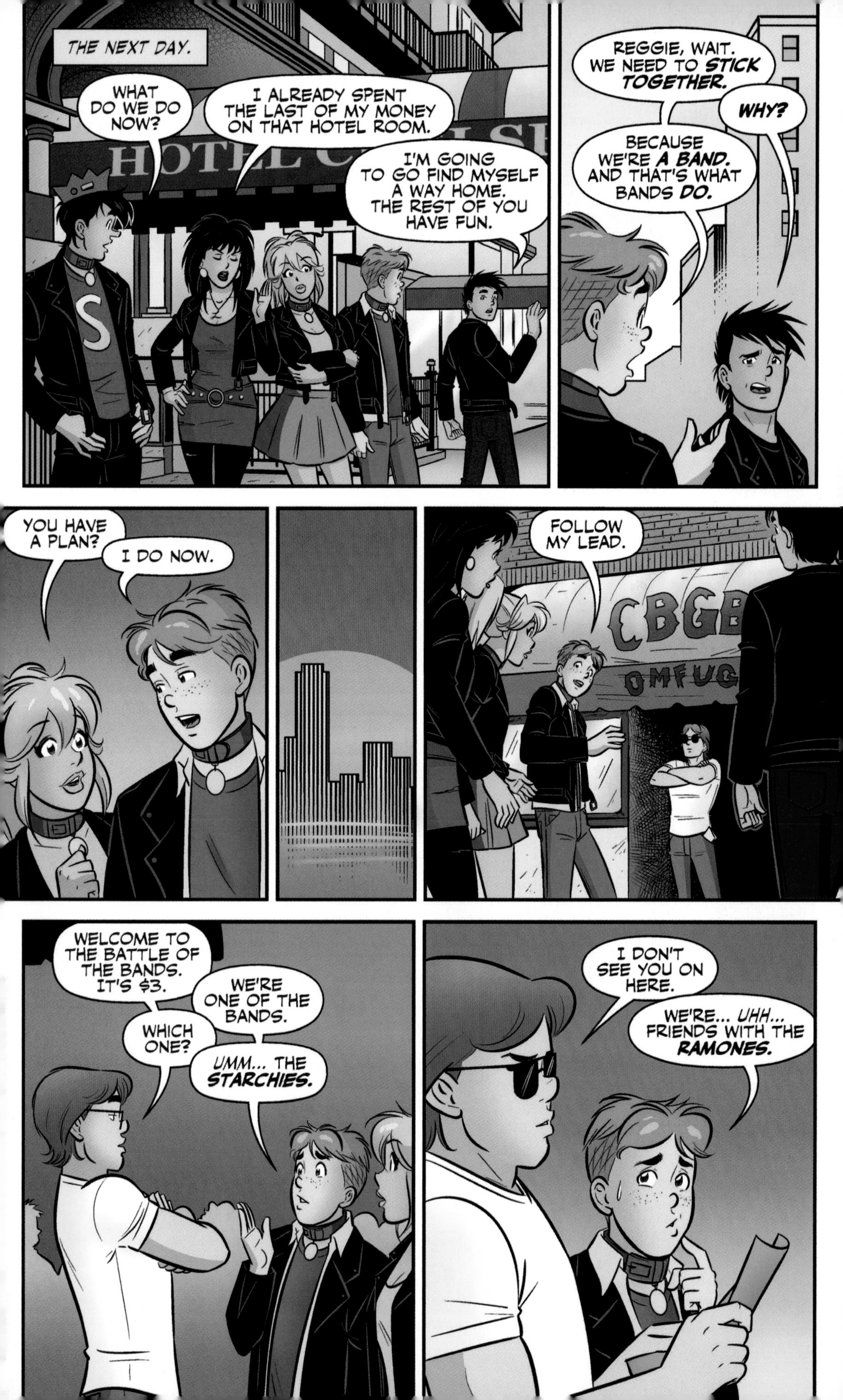
THE NEXT DAY.
WHAT DO WE DO NOW?
I ALREADY SPENT THE LAST OF MY MONEY ON THAT HOTEL ROOM.
I'M GOING TO GO FIND MYSELF A WAY HOME. THE REST OF YOU HAVE FUN.
HOTEL
REGGIE, WAIT. WE NEED TO STICK TOGETHER.
WHY?
BECAUSE WE'RE A BAND. AND THAT'S WHAT BANDS DO.
YOU HAVE A PLAN?
I DO NOW.
FOLLOW MY LEAD.
CBGB
OMFUG
WELCOME TO THE BATTLE OF THE BANDS. IT'S $3.
WE'RE ONE OF THE BANDS.
WHICH ONE?
UMM... THE STARCHIES.
I DON'T SEE YOU ON HERE.
WE'RE... UHH... FRIENDS WITH THE RAMONES.

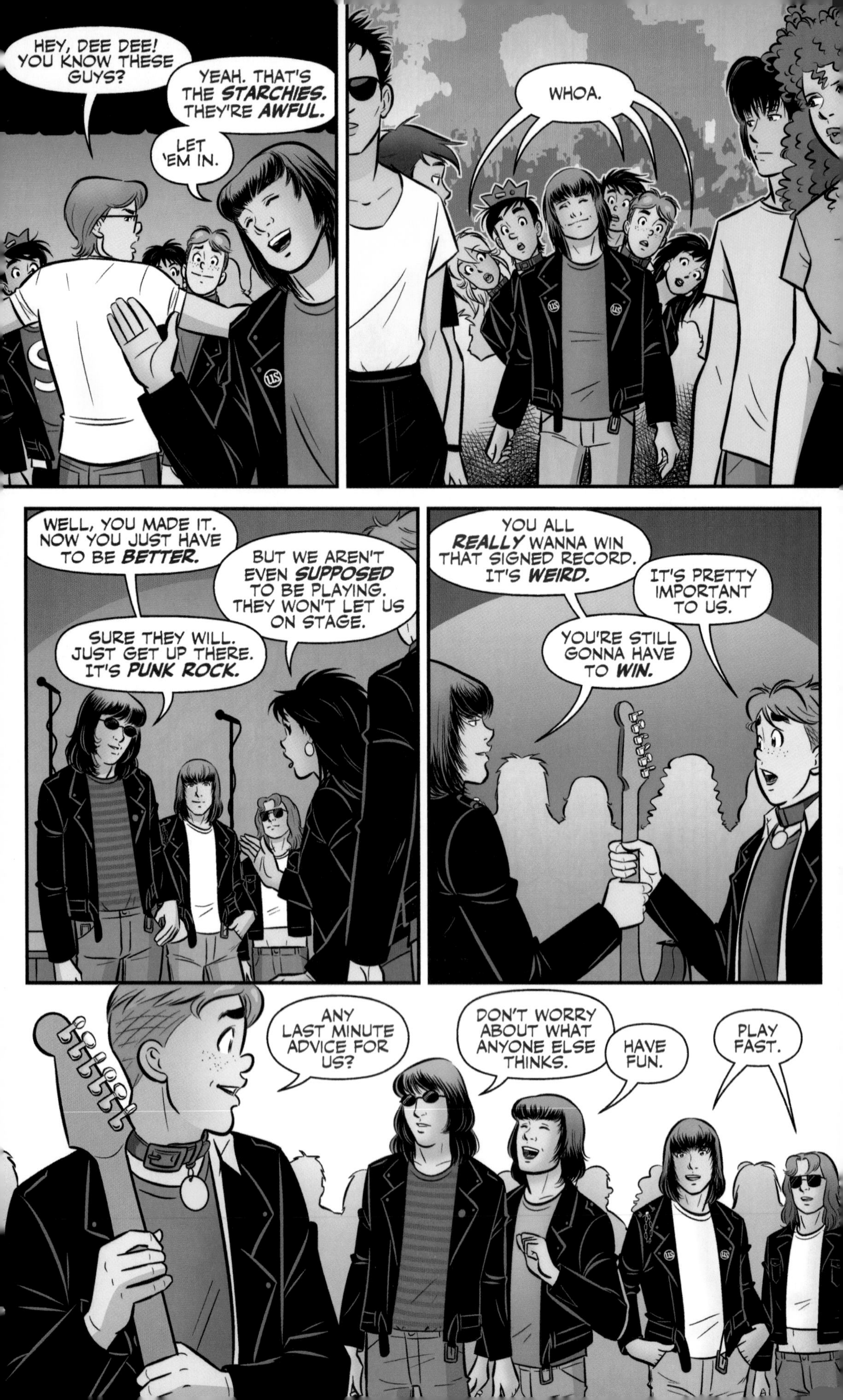
HEY, DEE DEE! YOU KNOW THESE GUYS?
YEAH. THAT'S THE STARCHIES. THEY'RE AWFUL.
LET 'EM IN.
WHOA.
WELL, YOU MADE IT. NOW YOU JUST HAVE TO BE BETTER.
BUT WE AREN'T EVEN SUPPOSED TO BE PLAYING. THEY WON'T LET US ON STAGE.
SURE THEY WILL. JUST GET UP THERE. IT'S PUNK ROCK.
YOU ALL REALLY WANNA WIN THAT SIGNED RECORD. IT'S WEIRD.
IT'S PRETTY IMPORTANT TO US.
YOU'RE STILL GONNA HAVE TO WIN.
ANY LAST MINUTE ADVICE FOR US?
DON'T WORRY ABOUT WHAT ANYONE ELSE THINKS.
HAVE FUN.
PLAY FAST.

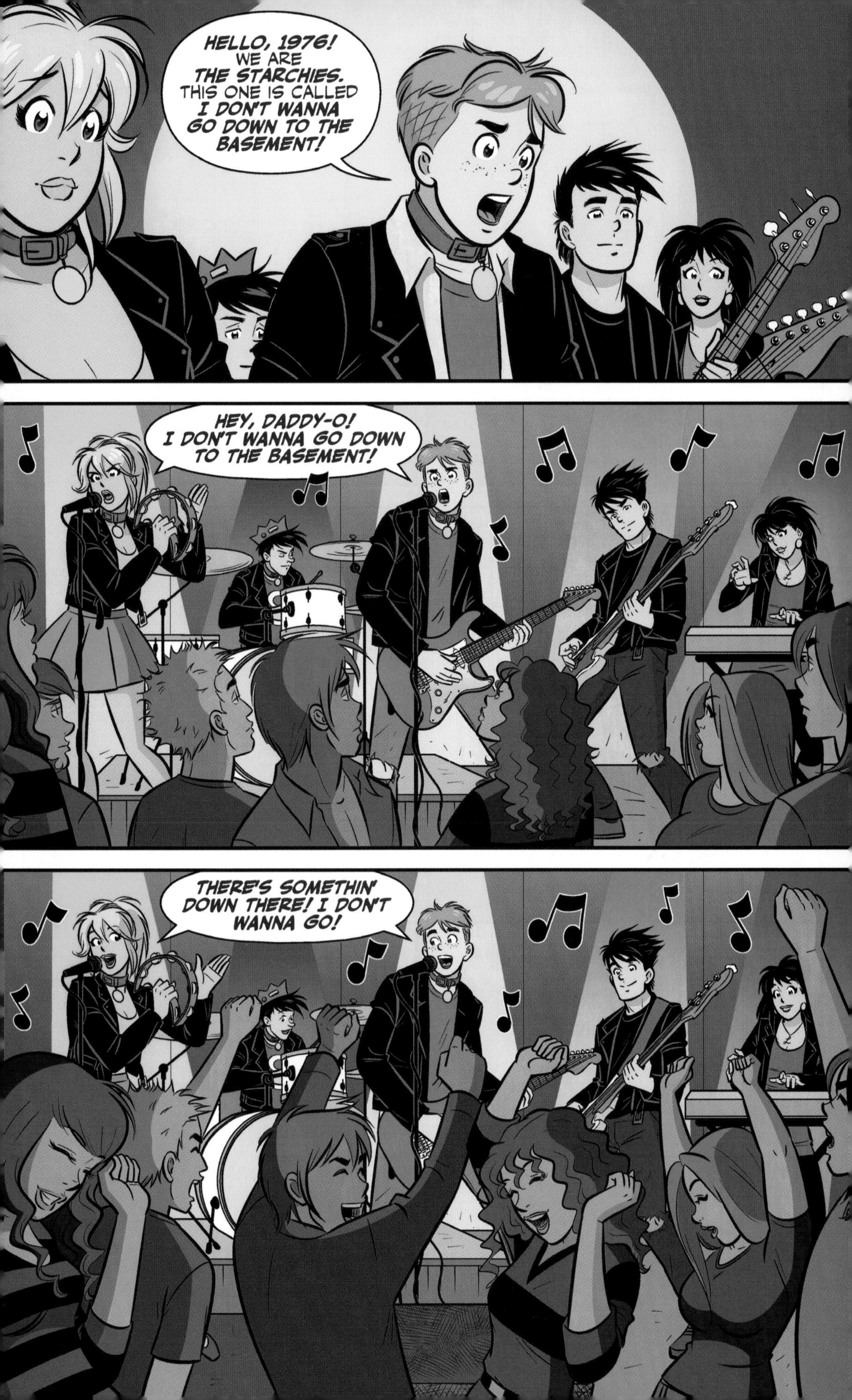
HELLO, 1976! WE ARE THE STARCHIES. THIS ONE IS CALLED I DON'T WANNA GO DOWN TO THE BASEMENT!
HEY, DADDY-O! I DON'T WANNA GO DOWN TO THE BASEMENT!
THERE'S SOMETHIN' DOWN THERE! I DON'T WANNA GO!

WELL, *THAT* WAS FUN. GIVE IT UP FOR ALL THE BANDS. I THINK WE CAN ALL AGREE THAT ONE BAND *REALLY* STOLE THE SHOW THOUGH.

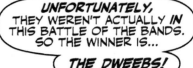

UNFORTUNATELY, THEY WEREN'T ACTUALLY *IN* THIS BATTLE OF THE BANDS. SO THE WINNER IS...

THE DWEEBS!

OK! OK! IT'S THE *STARCHIES!* AND HERE TO GIVE THEM THEIR PRIZE...

CONGRATS TO *THE STARCHIES!* THEY REALLY *ROCKED IT* TONIGHT. I BET IN 40 YEARS, PEOPLE ARE STILL GONNA BE TALKING ABOUT THEM.

HERE'S THE RECORD. YOU GUYS EARNED IT.

SORTA.

THANKS, JOEY. WE COULDN'T HAVE DONE IT WITHOUT YOU GUYS.

SORTA.

I HOPE THIS CAN--*

GOOD LUCK, STARCHIES! DON'T FORGET TO HAVE FUN.

AND PLAY FASTER.

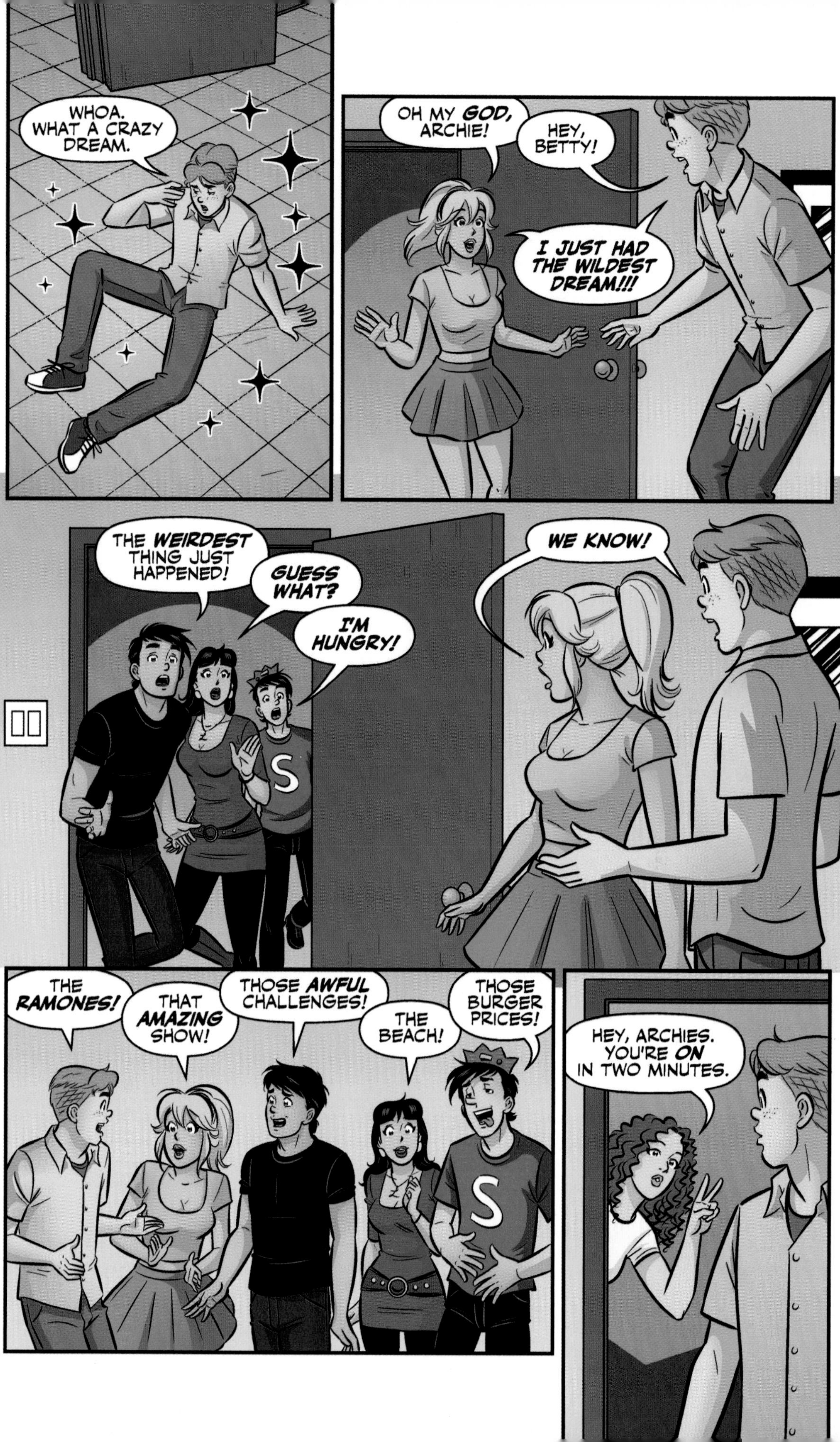
WHOA. WHAT A CRAZY DREAM.
OH MY GOD, ARCHIE!
HEY, BETTY!
I JUST HAD THE WILDEST DREAM!!!
THE WEIRDEST THING JUST HAPPENED!
GUESS WHAT?
I'M HUNGRY!
WE KNOW!
THE RAMONES!
THAT AMAZING SHOW!
THOSE AWFUL CHALLENGES!
THE BEACH!
THOSE BURGER PRICES!
HEY, ARCHIES. YOU'RE ON IN TWO MINUTES.

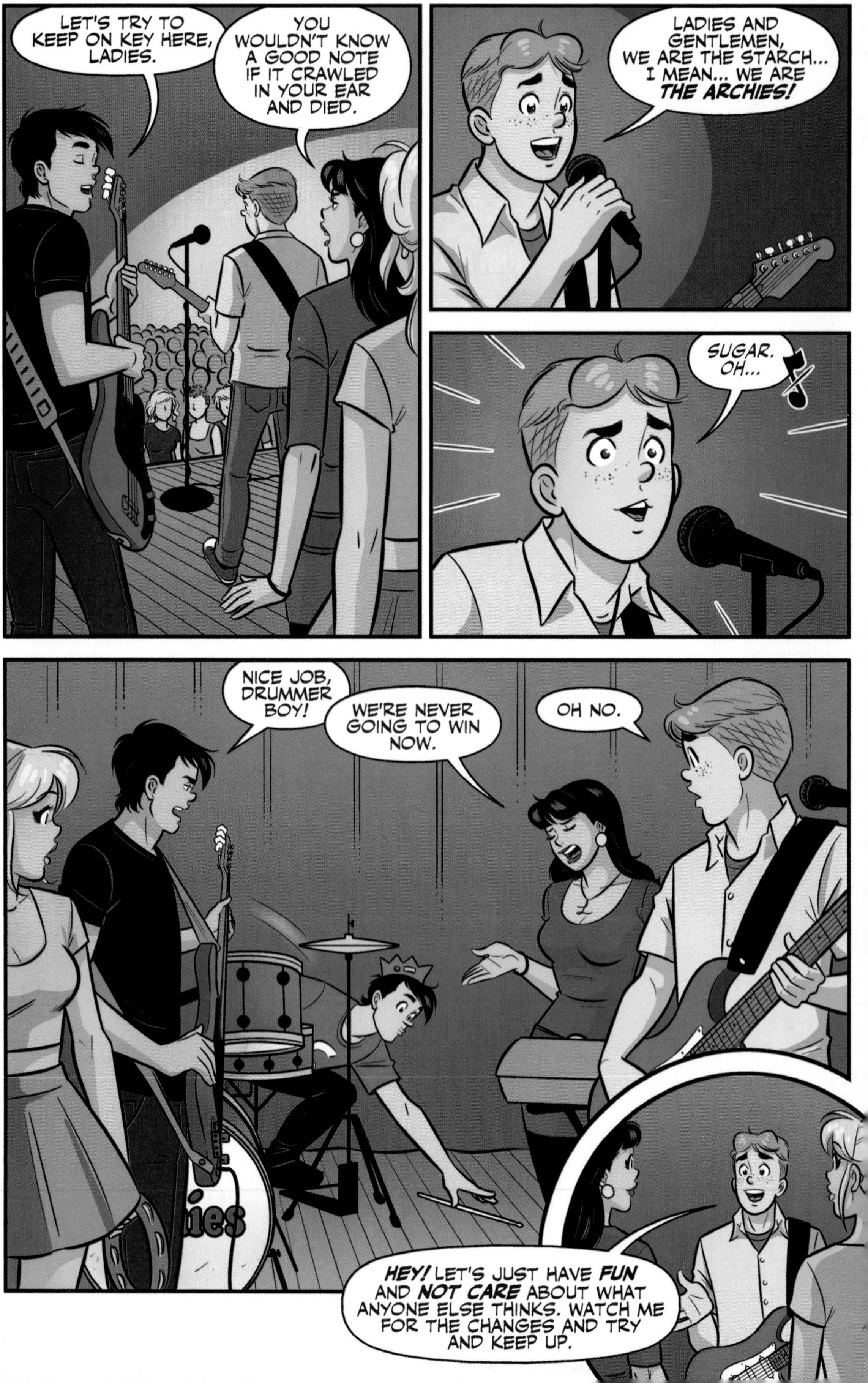
LET'S TRY TO KEEP ON KEY HERE, LADIES.
YOU WOULDN'T KNOW A GOOD NOTE IF IT CRAWLED IN YOUR EAR AND DIED.
LADIES AND GENTLEMEN, WE ARE THE STARCH... I MEAN... WE ARE **THE ARCHIES!**
SUGAR. OH...
NICE JOB, DRUMMER BOY!
WE'RE NEVER GOING TO WIN NOW.
OH NO.
HEY! LET'S JUST HAVE **FUN** AND **NOT CARE** ABOUT WHAT ANYONE ELSE THINKS. WATCH ME FOR THE CHANGES AND TRY AND KEEP UP.

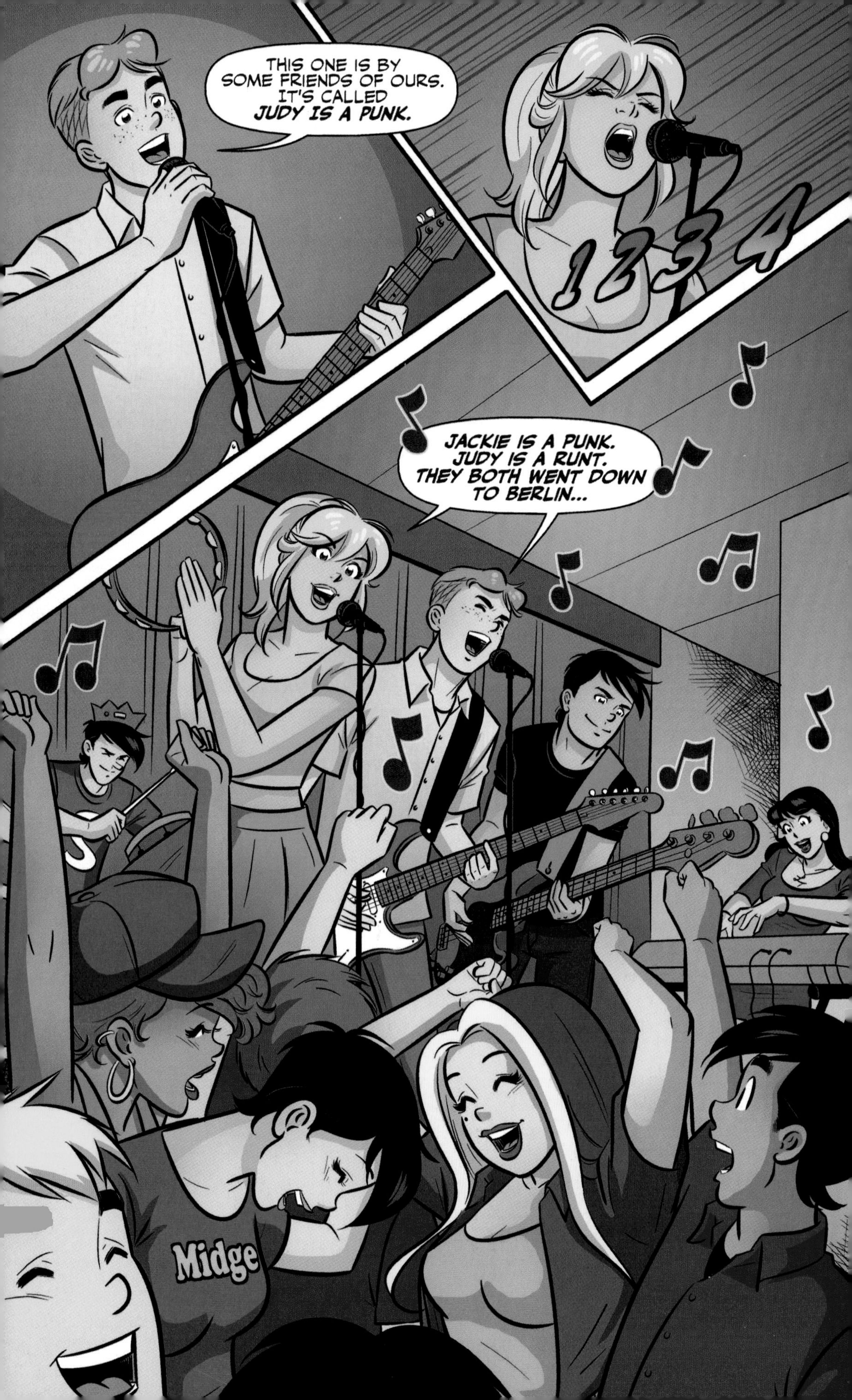
THIS ONE IS BY SOME FRIENDS OF OURS. IT'S CALLED JUDY IS A PUNK.
1 2 3 4
JACKIE IS A PUNK. JUDY IS A RUNT. THEY BOTH WENT DOWN TO BERLIN...
Midge

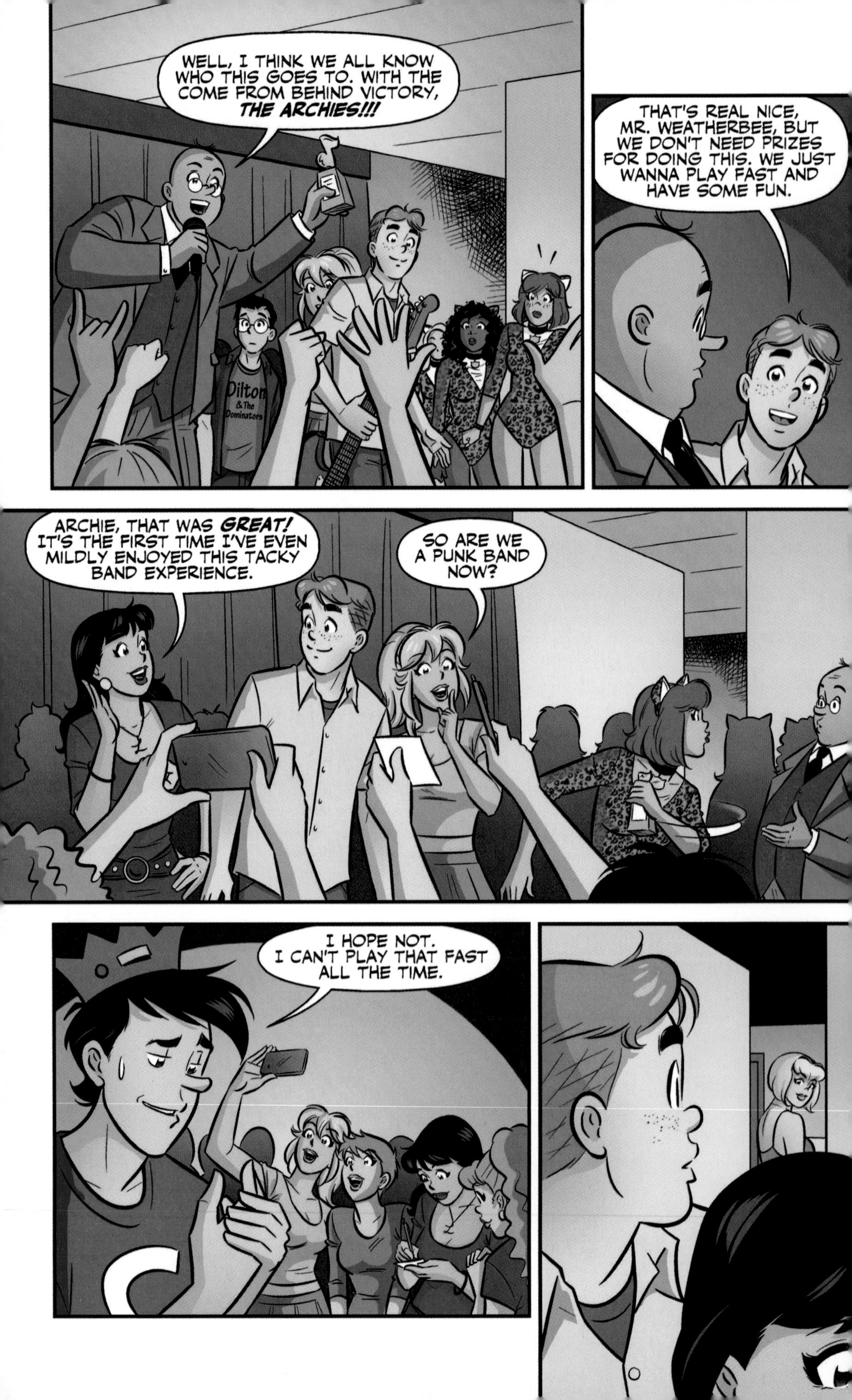
WELL, I THINK WE ALL KNOW WHO THIS GOES TO. WITH THE COME FROM BEHIND VICTORY, ***THE ARCHIES!!!***
Dilton & The Dominators
THAT'S REAL NICE, MR. WEATHERBEE, BUT WE DON'T NEED PRIZES FOR DOING THIS. WE JUST WANNA PLAY FAST AND HAVE SOME FUN.
ARCHIE, THAT WAS ***GREAT!*** IT'S THE FIRST TIME I'VE EVEN MILDLY ENJOYED THIS TACKY BAND EXPERIENCE.
SO ARE WE A PUNK BAND NOW?
I HOPE NOT. I CAN'T PLAY THAT FAST ALL THE TIME.

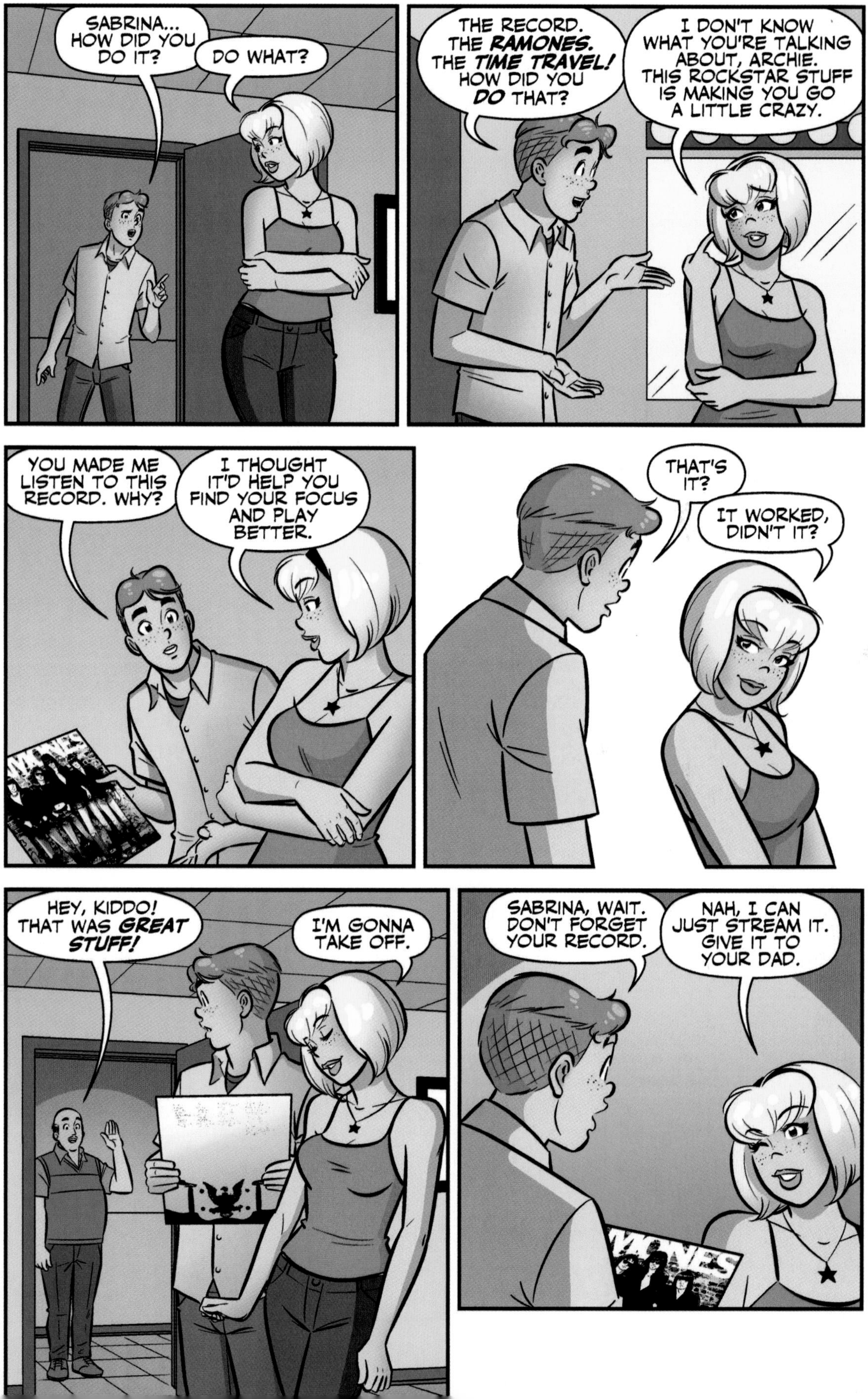
SABRINA... HOW DID YOU DO IT?
DO WHAT?
THE RECORD. THE RAMONES. THE TIME TRAVEL! HOW DID YOU DO THAT?
I DON'T KNOW WHAT YOU'RE TALKING ABOUT, ARCHIE. THIS ROCKSTAR STUFF IS MAKING YOU GO A LITTLE CRAZY.
YOU MADE ME LISTEN TO THIS RECORD. WHY?
I THOUGHT IT'D HELP YOU FIND YOUR FOCUS AND PLAY BETTER.
THAT'S IT?
IT WORKED, DIDN'T IT?
HEY, KIDDO! THAT WAS GREAT STUFF!
I'M GONNA TAKE OFF.
SABRINA, WAIT. DON'T FORGET YOUR RECORD.
NAH, I CAN JUST STREAM IT. GIVE IT TO YOUR DAD.

YOU ALL WERE **GREAT** UP THERE! IT FELT LIKE I WAS WATCHING THE **REAL** RAMONES! I HAVEN'T FELT THAT SINCE BACK IN THE DAY.

THANKS, DAD.

ARCHIE, THE CROWD WANTS AN ENCORE.

I...UHH... I GOT YOU THIS.

THIS IS A FIRST PRESSING! AND IT'S SIGNED! THAT'S AMAZING. YOU DON'T WANT THIS FOR YOURSELF?

NO. I DON'T NEED A SIGNED RECORD.

I'M JUST HAPPY I GET TO PLAY ON STAGE WITH MY FRIENDS.

NOW GO. DON'T KEEP YOUR PUBLIC WAITING. GET OUT THERE.

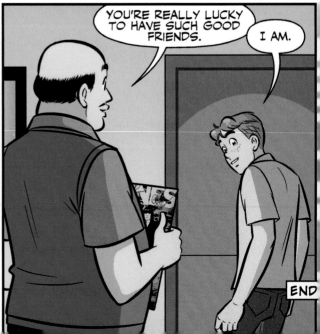

YOU'RE REALLY LUCKY TO HAVE SUCH GOOD FRIENDS.

I AM.

END

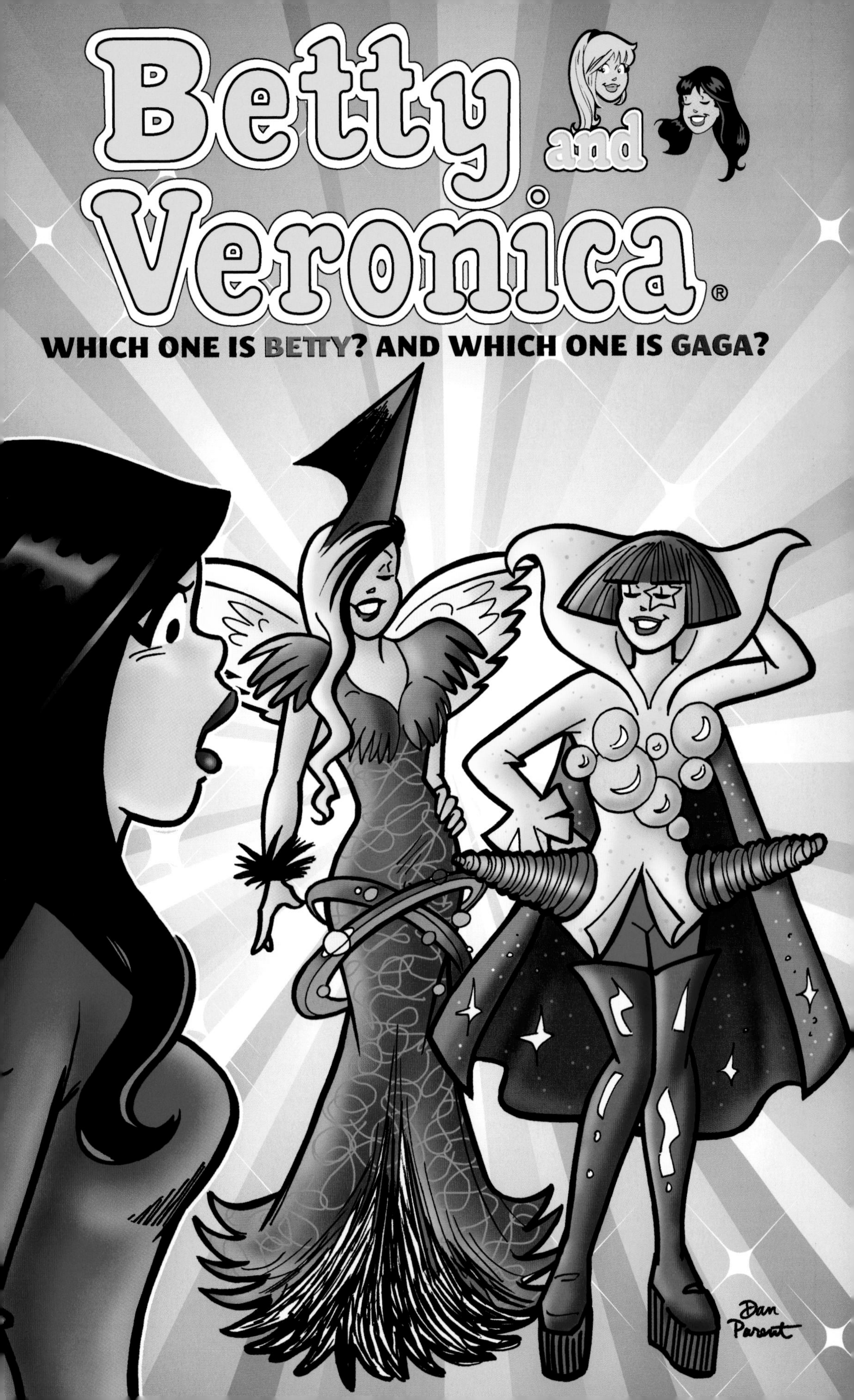
Betty and Veronica®
WHICH ONE IS BETTY? AND WHICH ONE IS GAGA?
Dan Parent

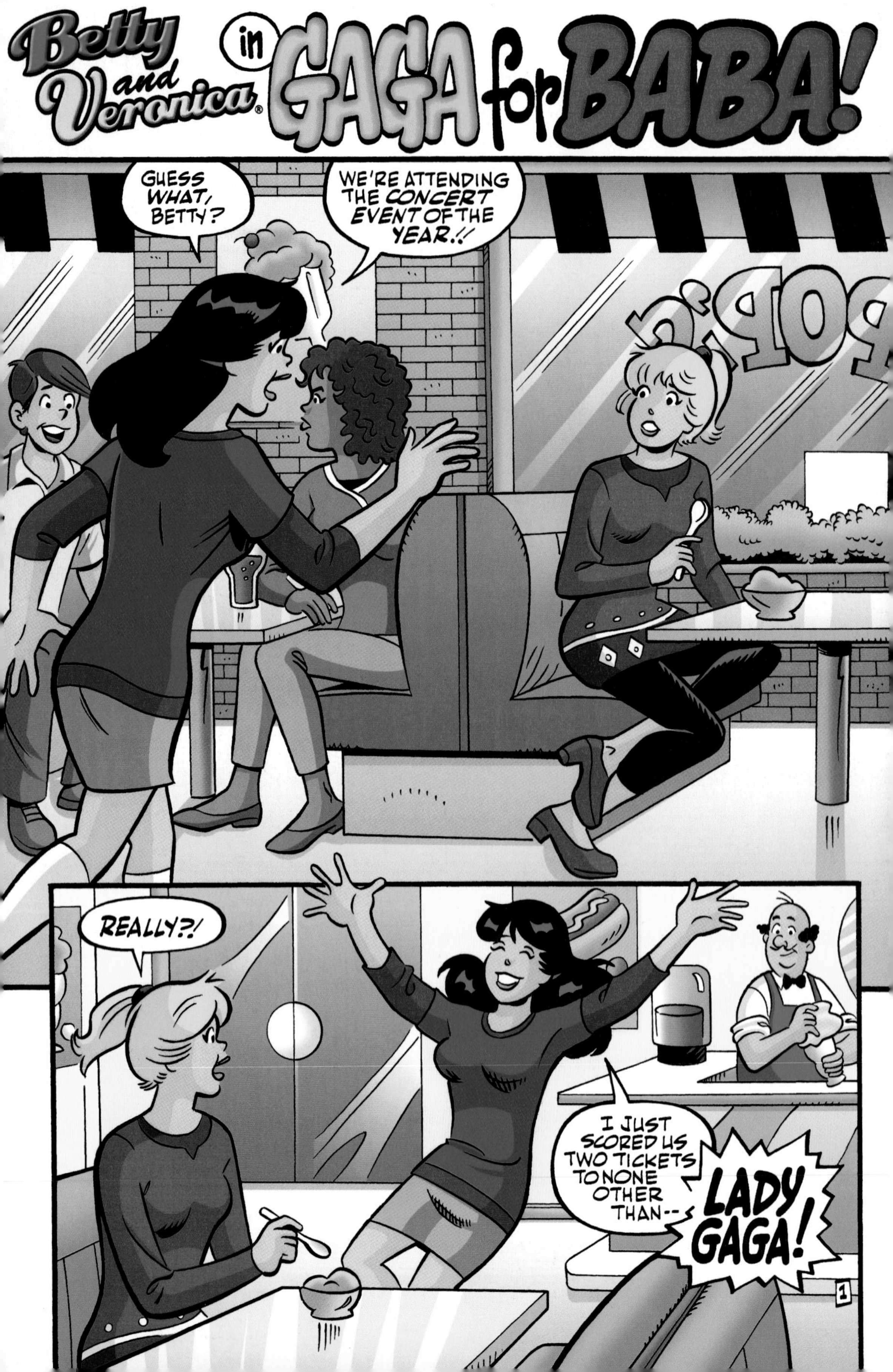
Betty and Veronica in GAGA for BABA!
GUESS WHAT, BETTY?
WE'RE ATTENDING THE CONCERT EVENT OF THE YEAR!!
POP'S
REALLY?!
I JUST SCORED US TWO TICKETS TO NONE OTHER THAN--
LADY GAGA!
1

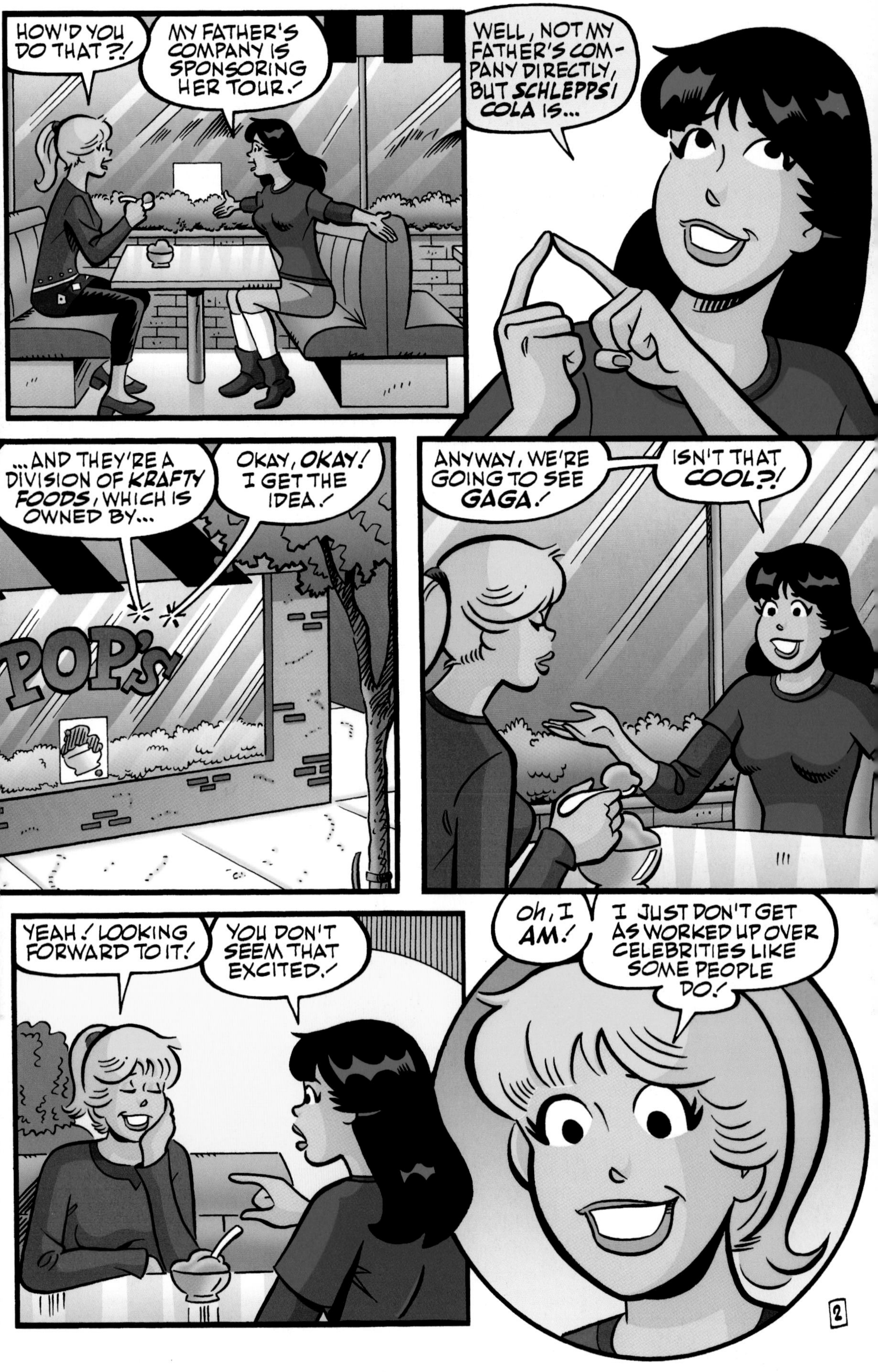
HOW'D YOU DO THAT?!
MY FATHER'S COMPANY IS SPONSORING HER TOUR!
WELL, NOT MY FATHER'S COMPANY DIRECTLY, BUT SCHLEPPSI COLA IS...
...AND THEY'RE A DIVISION OF KRAFTY FOODS, WHICH IS OWNED BY...
OKAY, OKAY! I GET THE IDEA!
POP'S
ANYWAY, WE'RE GOING TO SEE GAGA!
ISN'T THAT COOL?!
YEAH! LOOKING FORWARD TO IT!
YOU DON'T SEEM THAT EXCITED!
Oh, I AM!
I JUST DON'T GET AS WORKED UP OVER CELEBRITIES LIKE SOME PEOPLE DO!

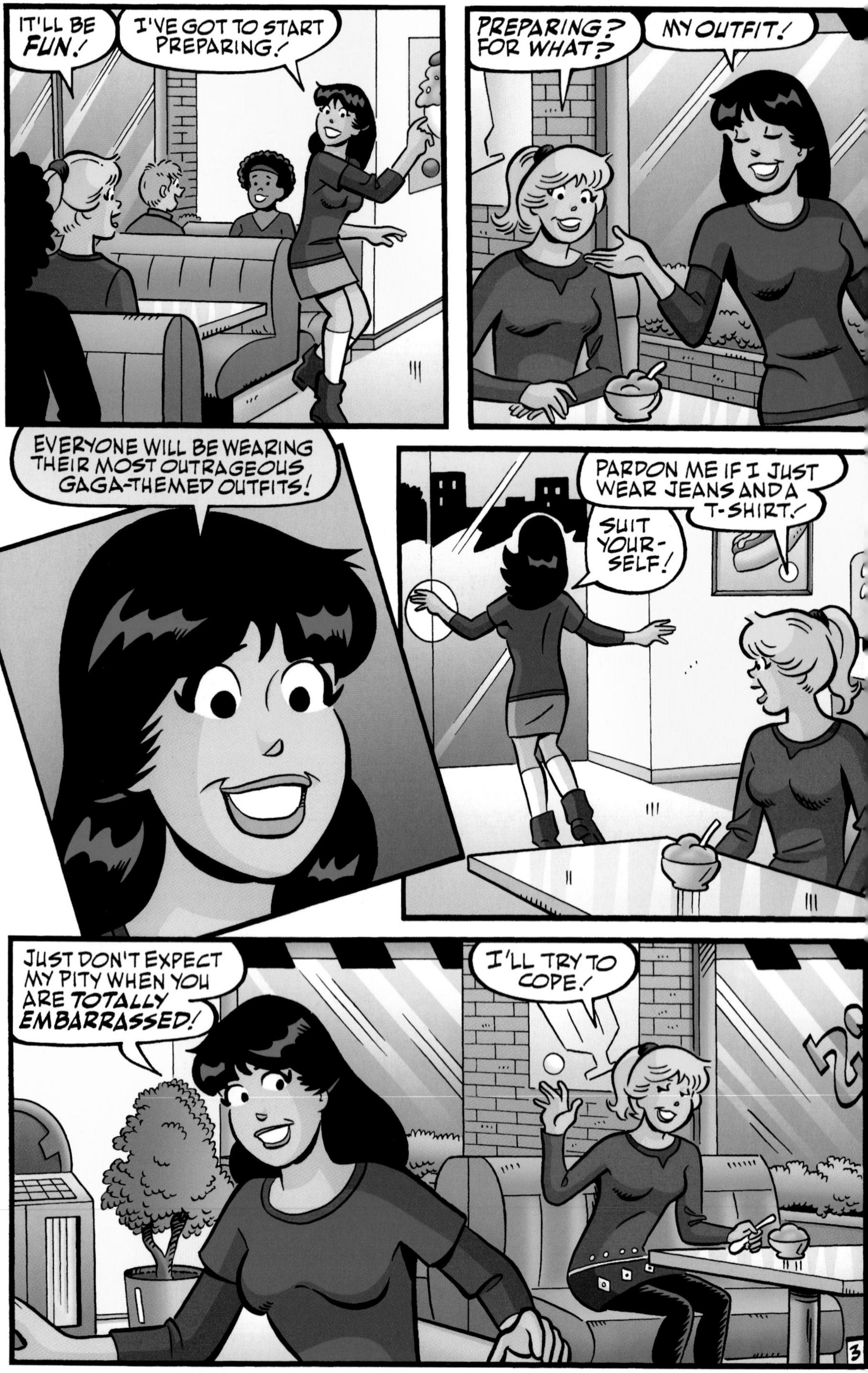
IT'LL BE FUN!
I'VE GOT TO START PREPARING!
PREPARING? FOR WHAT?
MY OUTFIT!
EVERYONE WILL BE WEARING THEIR MOST OUTRAGEOUS GAGA-THEMED OUTFITS!
PARDON ME IF I JUST WEAR JEANS AND A T-SHIRT!
SUIT YOURSELF!
JUST DON'T EXPECT MY PITY WHEN YOU ARE TOTALLY EMBARRASSED!
I'LL TRY TO COPE!

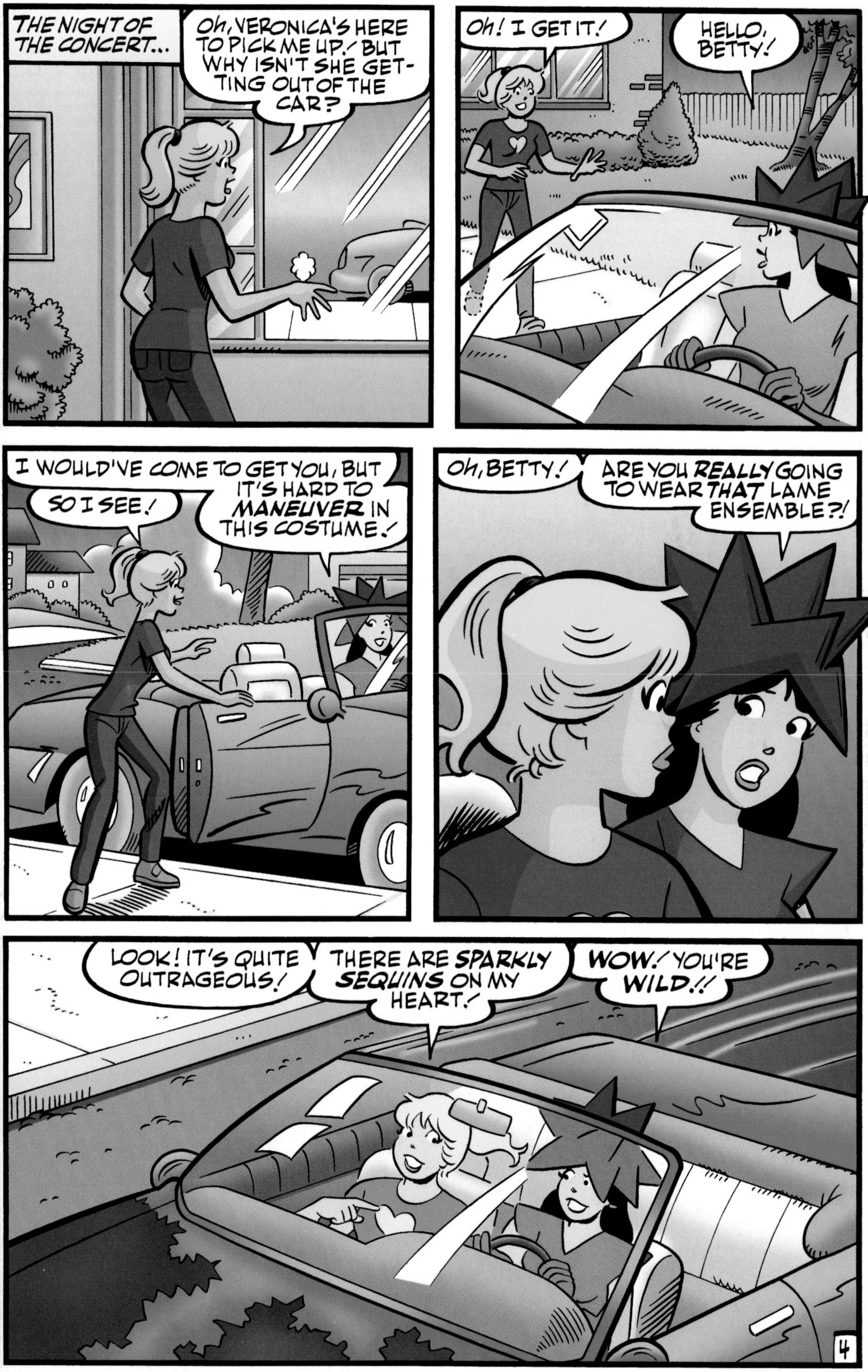
THE NIGHT OF THE CONCERT...
Oh, VERONICA'S HERE TO PICK ME UP! BUT WHY ISN'T SHE GETTING OUT OF THE CAR?
Oh! I GET IT!
HELLO, BETTY!
I WOULD'VE COME TO GET YOU, BUT IT'S HARD TO MANEUVER IN THIS COSTUME!
SO I SEE!
Oh, BETTY!
ARE YOU REALLY GOING TO WEAR THAT LAME ENSEMBLE?!
LOOK! IT'S QUITE OUTRAGEOUS!
THERE ARE SPARKLY SEQUINS ON MY HEART!
WOW! YOU'RE WILD!!
4

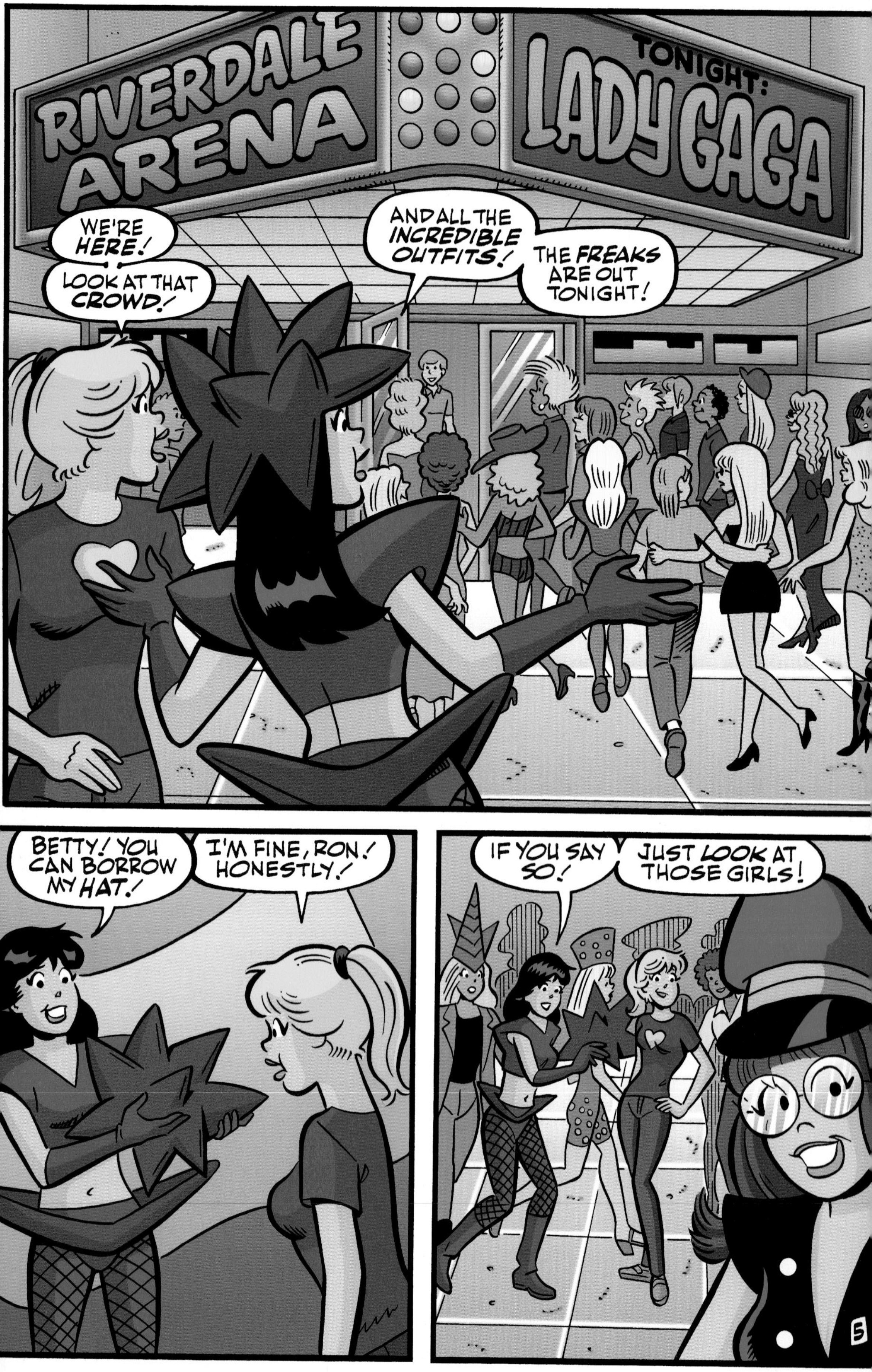
RIVERDALE ARENA
TONIGHT: LADY GAGA
WE'RE HERE!
LOOK AT THAT CROWD!
AND ALL THE INCREDIBLE OUTFITS!
THE FREAKS ARE OUT TONIGHT!
BETTY! YOU CAN BORROW MY HAT!
I'M FINE, RON! HONESTLY!
IF YOU SAY SO!
JUST LOOK AT THOSE GIRLS!

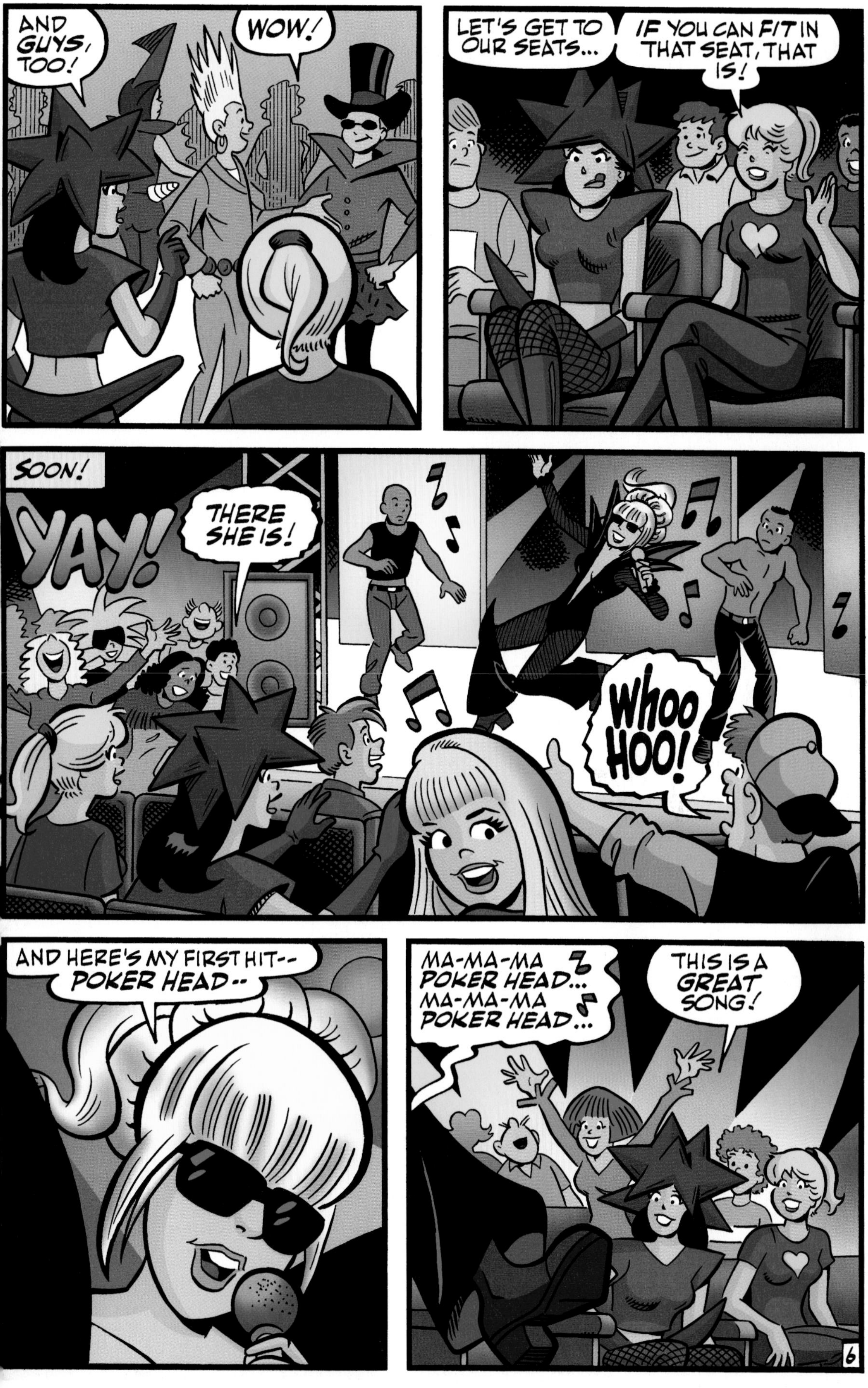
AND GUYS, TOO!
WOW!
LET'S GET TO OUR SEATS...
IF YOU CAN FIT IN THAT SEAT, THAT IS!
SOON!
YAY!
THERE SHE IS!
Whoo HOO!
AND HERE'S MY FIRST HIT-- POKER HEAD--
MA-MA-MA POKER HEAD... MA-MA-MA POKER HEAD...
THIS IS A GREAT SONG!
6

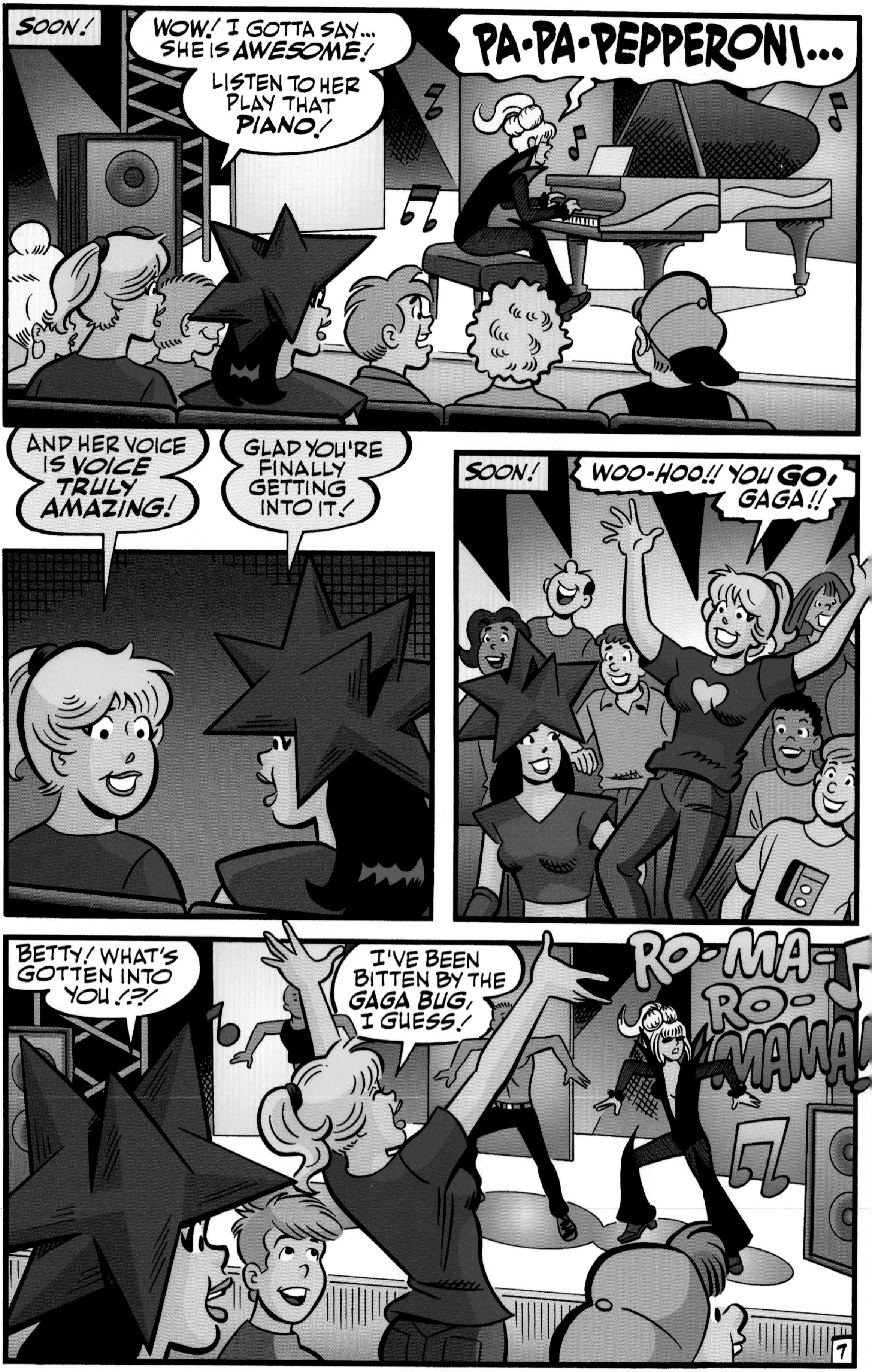
SOON!
WOW! I GOTTA SAY... SHE IS AWESOME!
LISTEN TO HER PLAY THAT PIANO!
PA-PA-PEPPERONI...
AND HER VOICE IS VOICE TRULY AMAZING!
GLAD YOU'RE FINALLY GETTING INTO IT!
SOON!
WOO-HOO!! YOU GO, GAGA!!
BETTY! WHAT'S GOTTEN INTO YOU!?!
I'VE BEEN BITTEN BY THE GAGA BUG, I GUESS!
RO-MA-RO-MAMA!

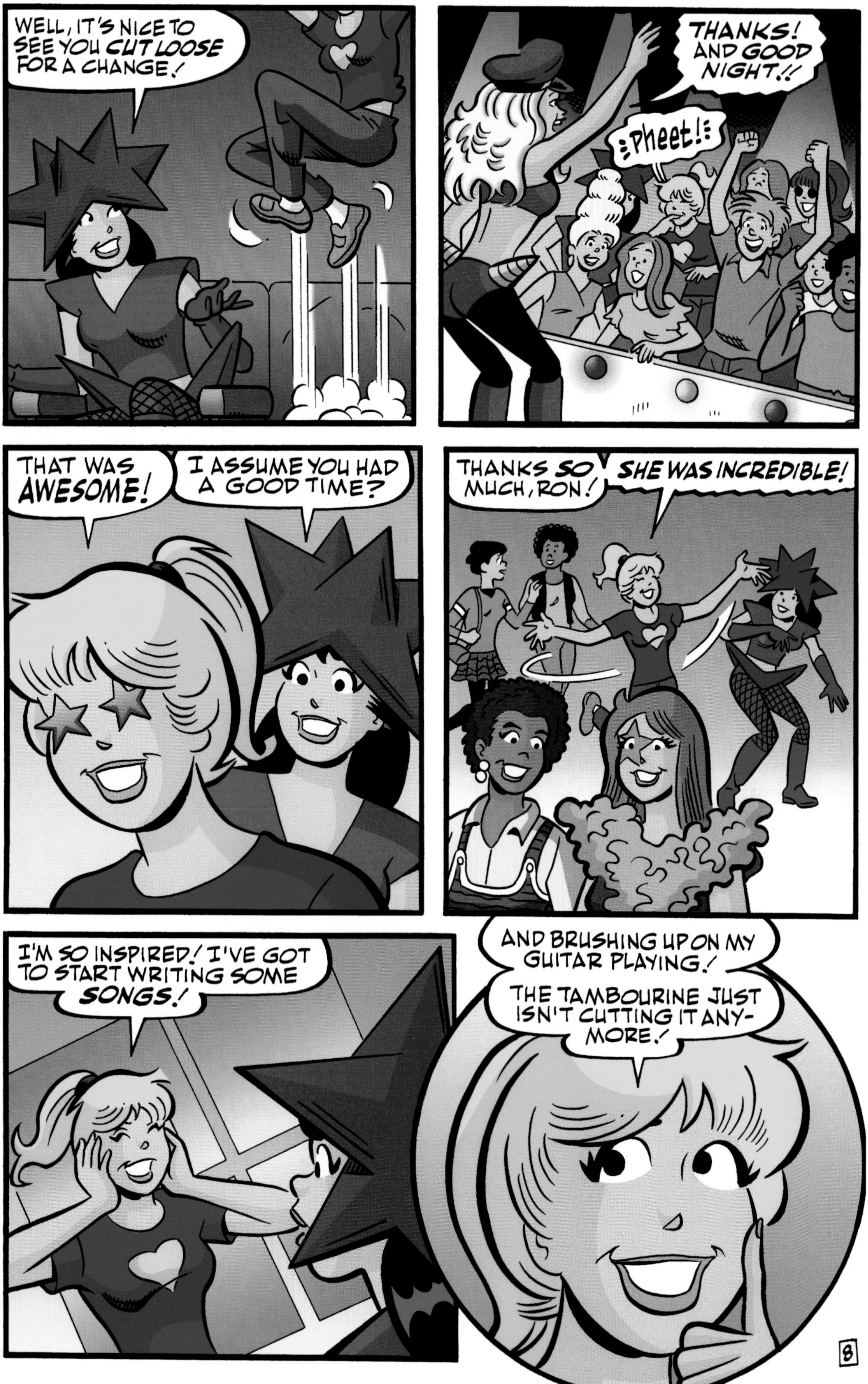
WELL, IT'S NICE TO SEE YOU CUT LOOSE FOR A CHANGE!
THANKS! AND GOOD NIGHT!!
PHEET!
THAT WAS AWESOME!
I ASSUME YOU HAD A GOOD TIME?
THANKS SO MUCH, RON!
SHE WAS INCREDIBLE!
I'M SO INSPIRED! I'VE GOT TO START WRITING SOME SONGS!
AND BRUSHING UP ON MY GUITAR PLAYING!
THE TAMBOURINE JUST ISN'T CUTTING IT ANY-MORE!

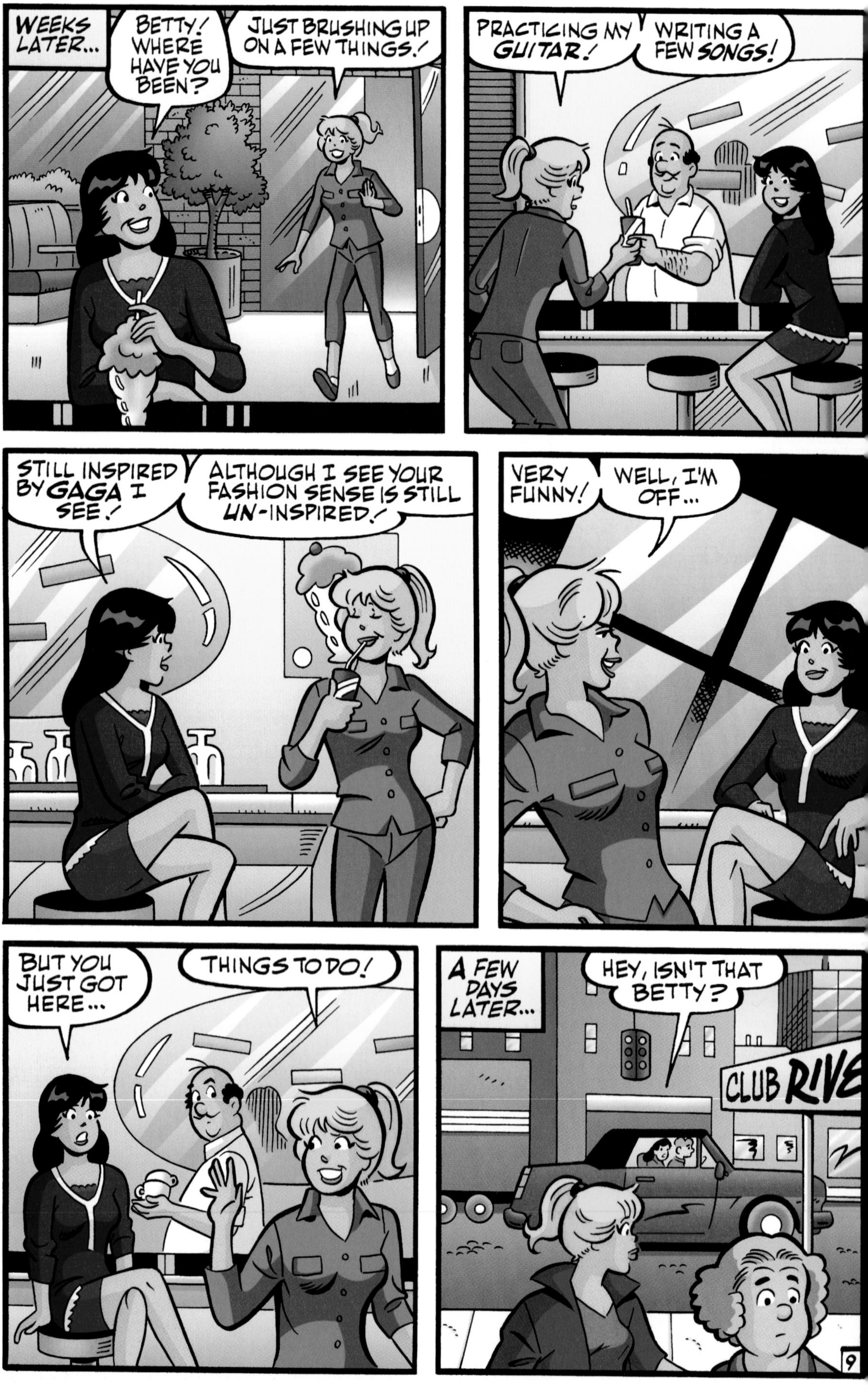
WEEKS LATER...
BETTY! WHERE HAVE YOU BEEN?
JUST BRUSHING UP ON A FEW THINGS!
PRACTICING MY GUITAR!
WRITING A FEW SONGS!
STILL INSPIRED BY GAGA I SEE!
ALTHOUGH I SEE YOUR FASHION SENSE IS STILL UN-INSPIRED!
VERY FUNNY!
WELL, I'M OFF...
BUT YOU JUST GOT HERE...
THINGS TO DO!
A FEW DAYS LATER...
HEY, ISN'T THAT BETTY?
CLUB RIVE
9

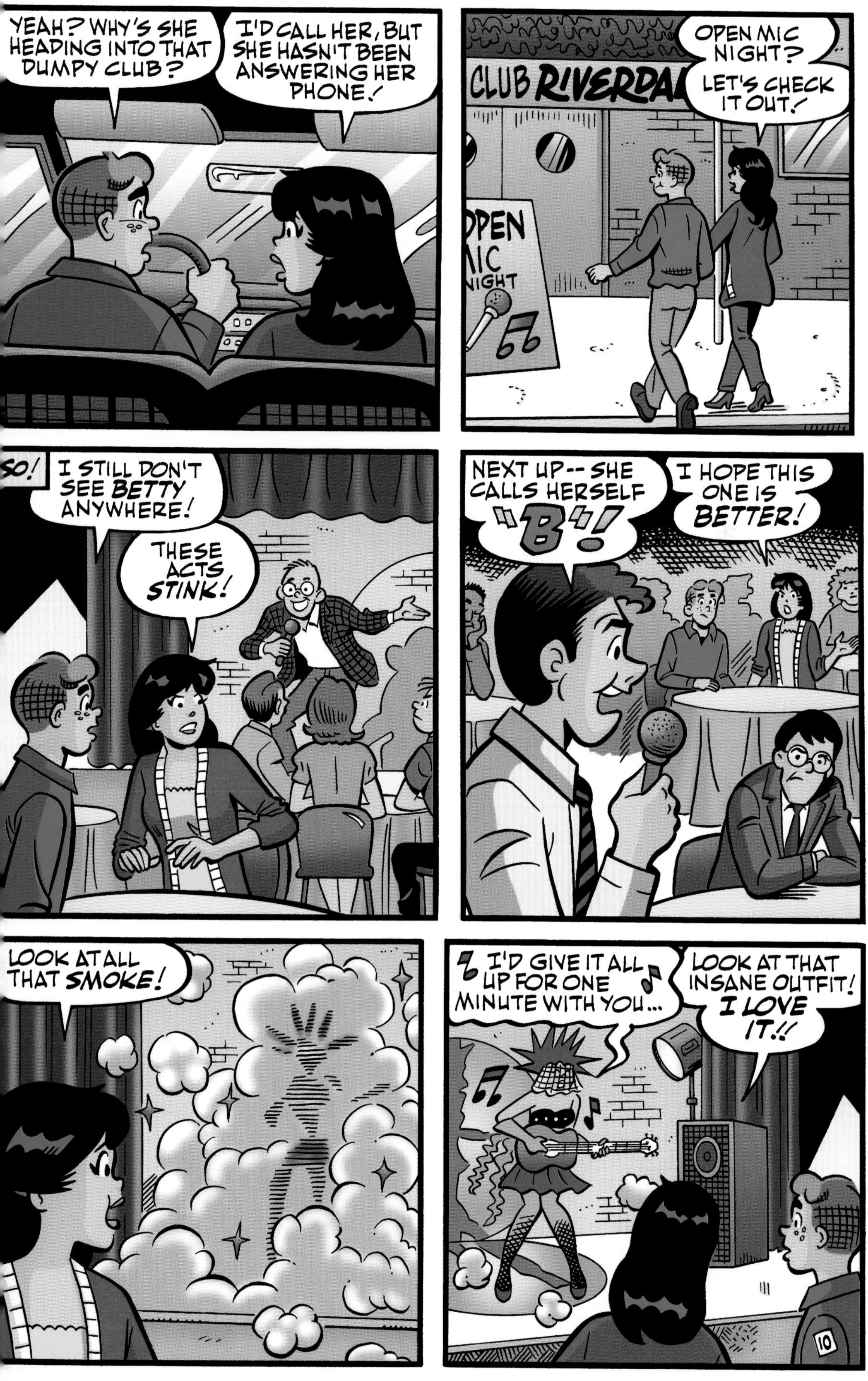
YEAH? WHY'S SHE HEADING INTO THAT DUMPY CLUB?
I'D CALL HER, BUT SHE HASN'T BEEN ANSWERING HER PHONE!
CLUB RIVERDA
OPEN MIC NIGHT?
LET'S CHECK IT OUT!
PEN IC IGHT
SO!
I STILL DON'T SEE BETTY ANYWHERE!
THESE ACTS STINK!
NEXT UP -- SHE CALLS HERSELF "B"!
I HOPE THIS ONE IS BETTER!
LOOK AT ALL THAT SMOKE!
I'D GIVE IT ALL UP FOR ONE MINUTE WITH YOU...
LOOK AT THAT INSANE OUTFIT! I LOVE IT!!
10

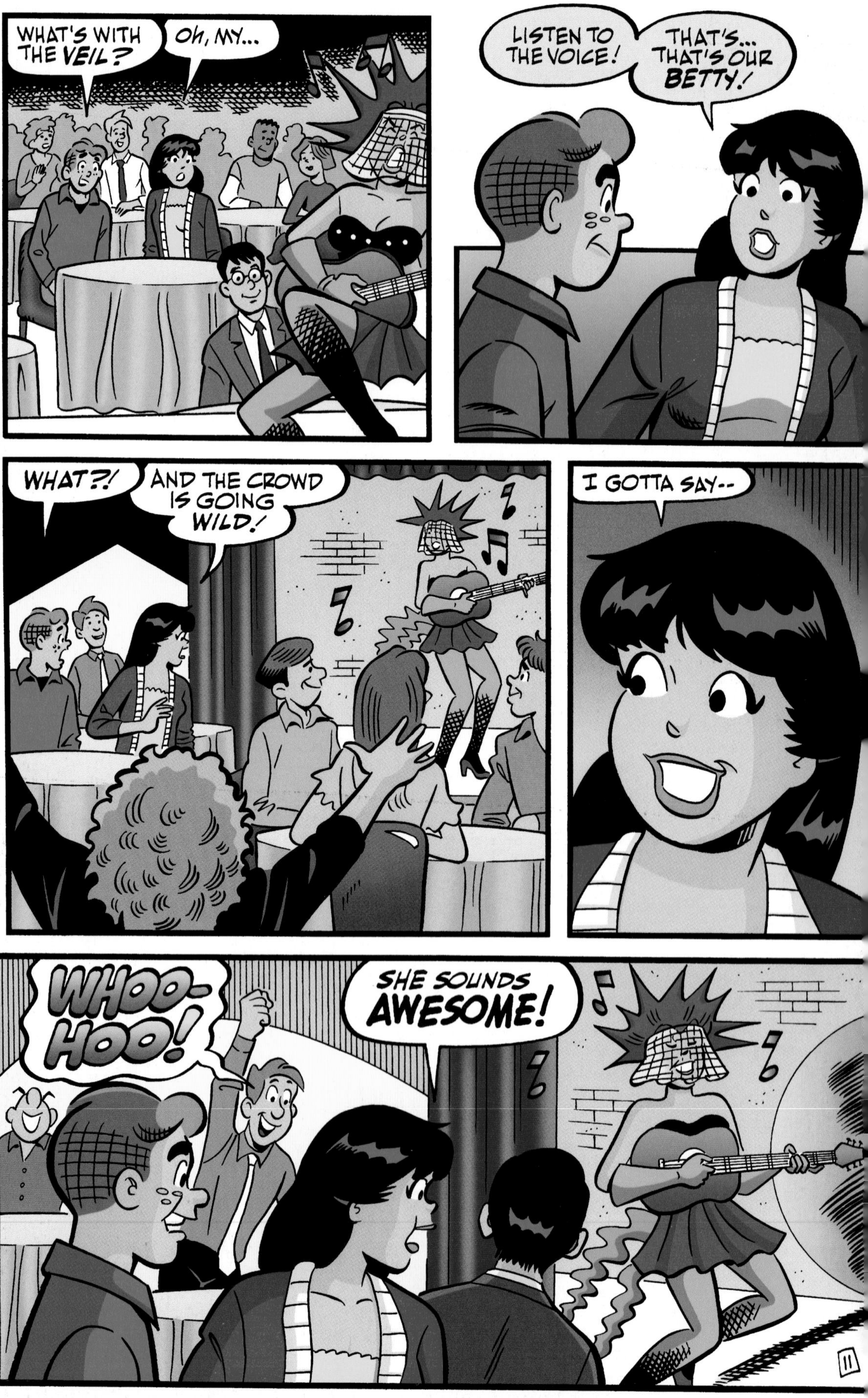

WHAT'S WITH THE VEIL?
Oh, MY...
LISTEN TO THE VOICE!
THAT'S... THAT'S OUR BETTY!
WHAT?!
AND THE CROWD IS GOING WILD!
I GOTTA SAY--
WHOO-HOO!
SHE SOUNDS AWESOME!
11

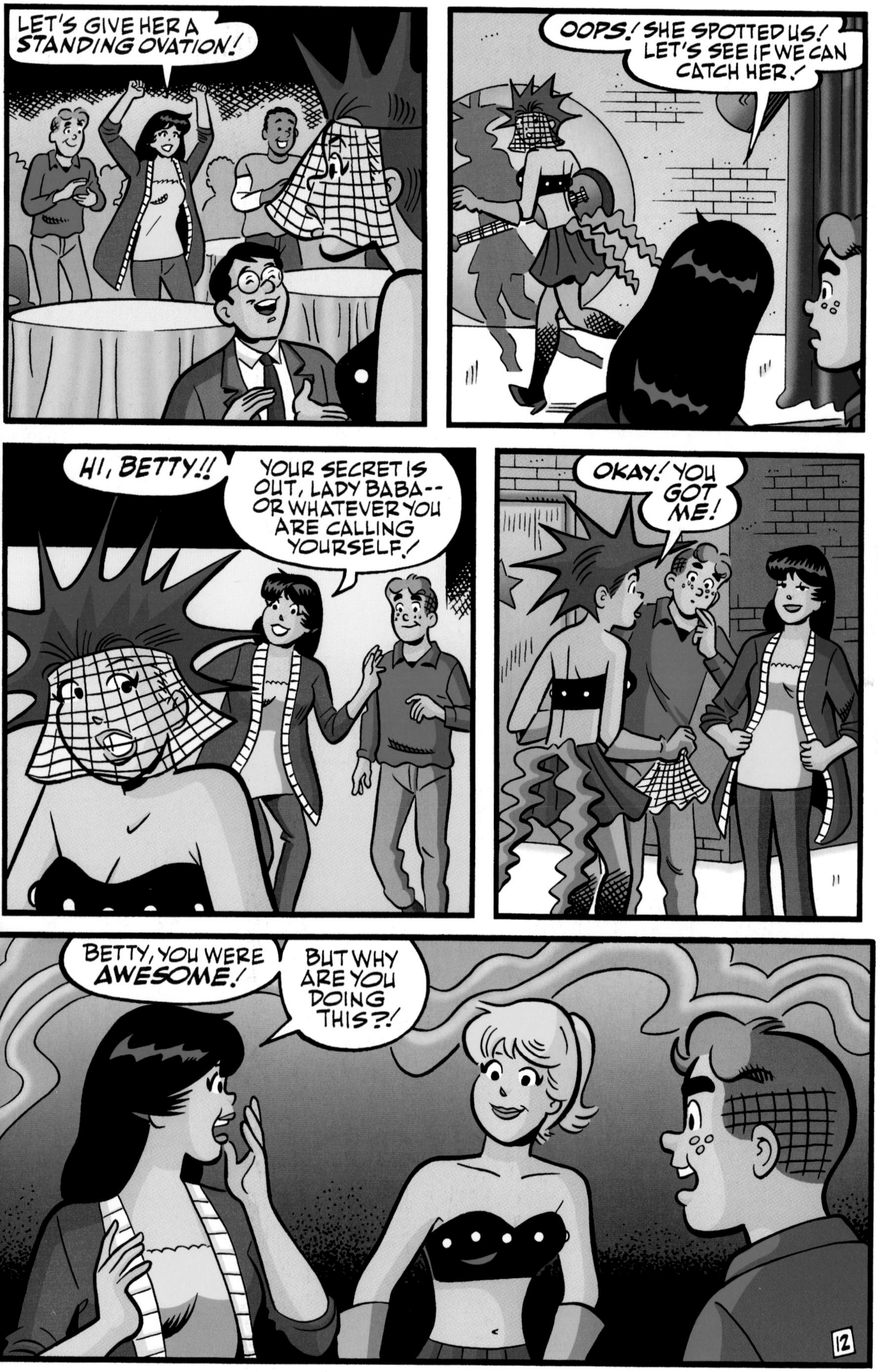
LET'S GIVE HER A STANDING OVATION!
OOPS! SHE SPOTTED US! LET'S SEE IF WE CAN CATCH HER!
HI, BETTY!!
YOUR SECRET IS OUT, LADY BABA-- OR WHATEVER YOU ARE CALLING YOURSELF!
OKAY! YOU GOT ME!
BETTY, YOU WERE AWESOME!
BUT WHY ARE YOU DOING THIS?!
12

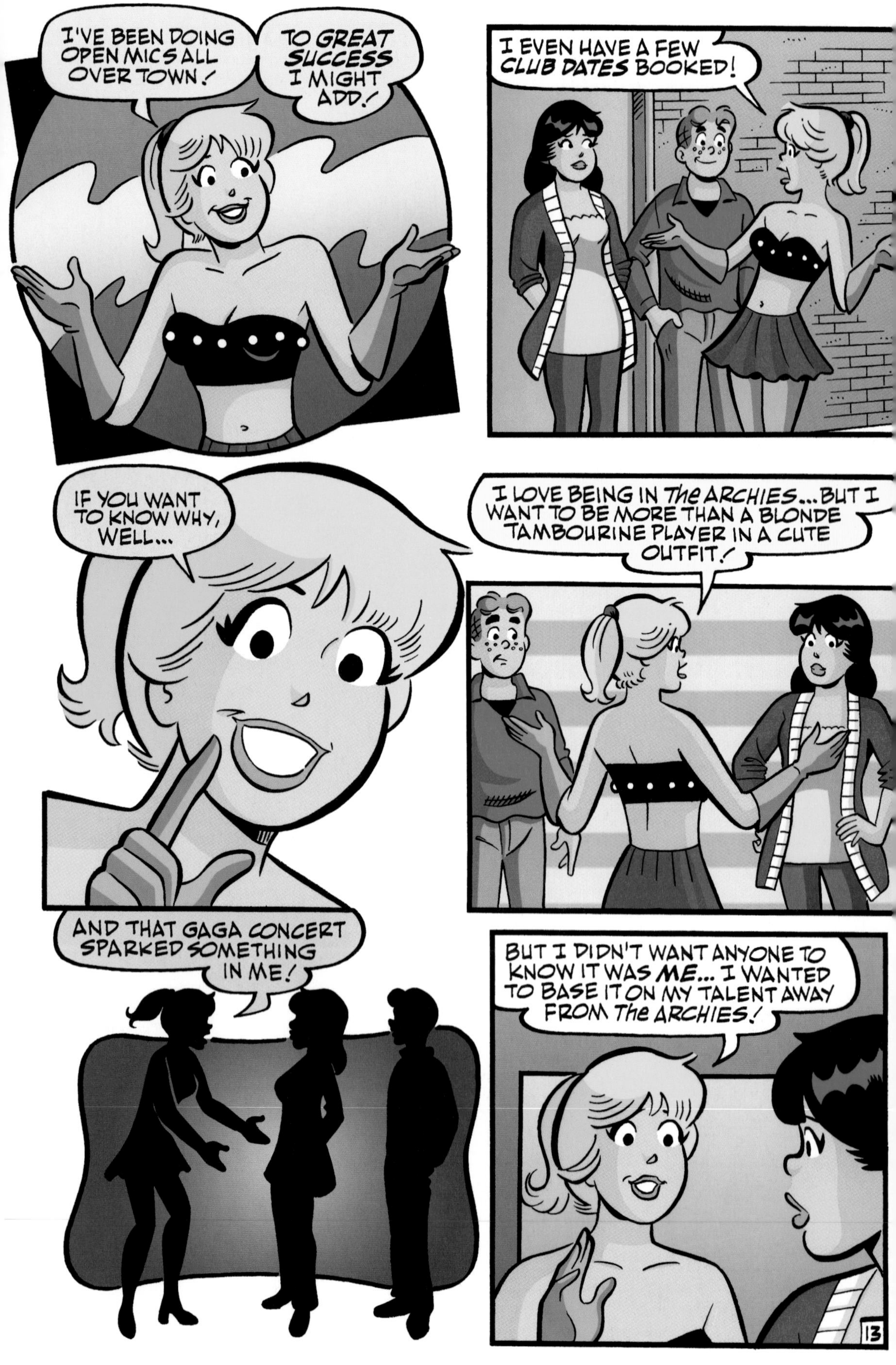
I'VE BEEN DOING OPEN MICS ALL OVER TOWN!
TO GREAT SUCCESS I MIGHT ADD!
I EVEN HAVE A FEW CLUB DATES BOOKED!
IF YOU WANT TO KNOW WHY, WELL...
I LOVE BEING IN The ARCHIES...BUT I WANT TO BE MORE THAN A BLONDE TAMBOURINE PLAYER IN A CUTE OUTFIT!
AND THAT GAGA CONCERT SPARKED SOMETHING IN ME!
BUT I DIDN'T WANT ANYONE TO KNOW IT WAS ME... I WANTED TO BASE IT ON MY TALENT AWAY FROM The ARCHIES!
13

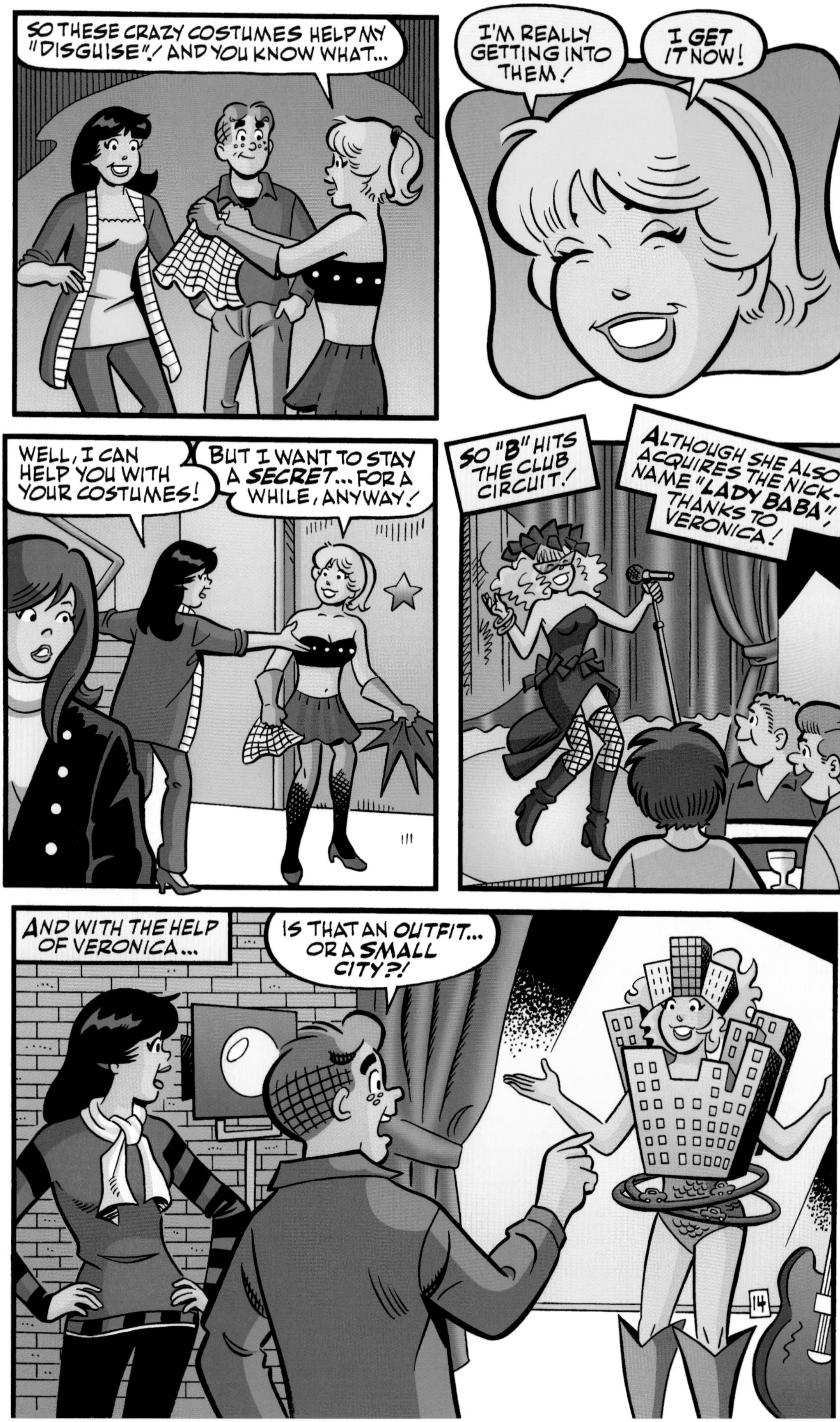
SO THESE CRAZY COSTUMES HELP MY "DISGUISE"! AND YOU KNOW WHAT...
I'M REALLY GETTING INTO THEM!
I GET IT NOW!
WELL, I CAN HELP YOU WITH YOUR COSTUMES!
BUT I WANT TO STAY A SECRET... FOR A WHILE, ANYWAY!
SO "B" HITS THE CLUB CIRCUIT!
ALTHOUGH SHE ALSO ACQUIRES THE NICK-NAME "LADY BABA", THANKS TO VERONICA!
AND WITH THE HELP OF VERONICA...
IS THAT AN OUTFIT... OR A SMALL CITY?!
14

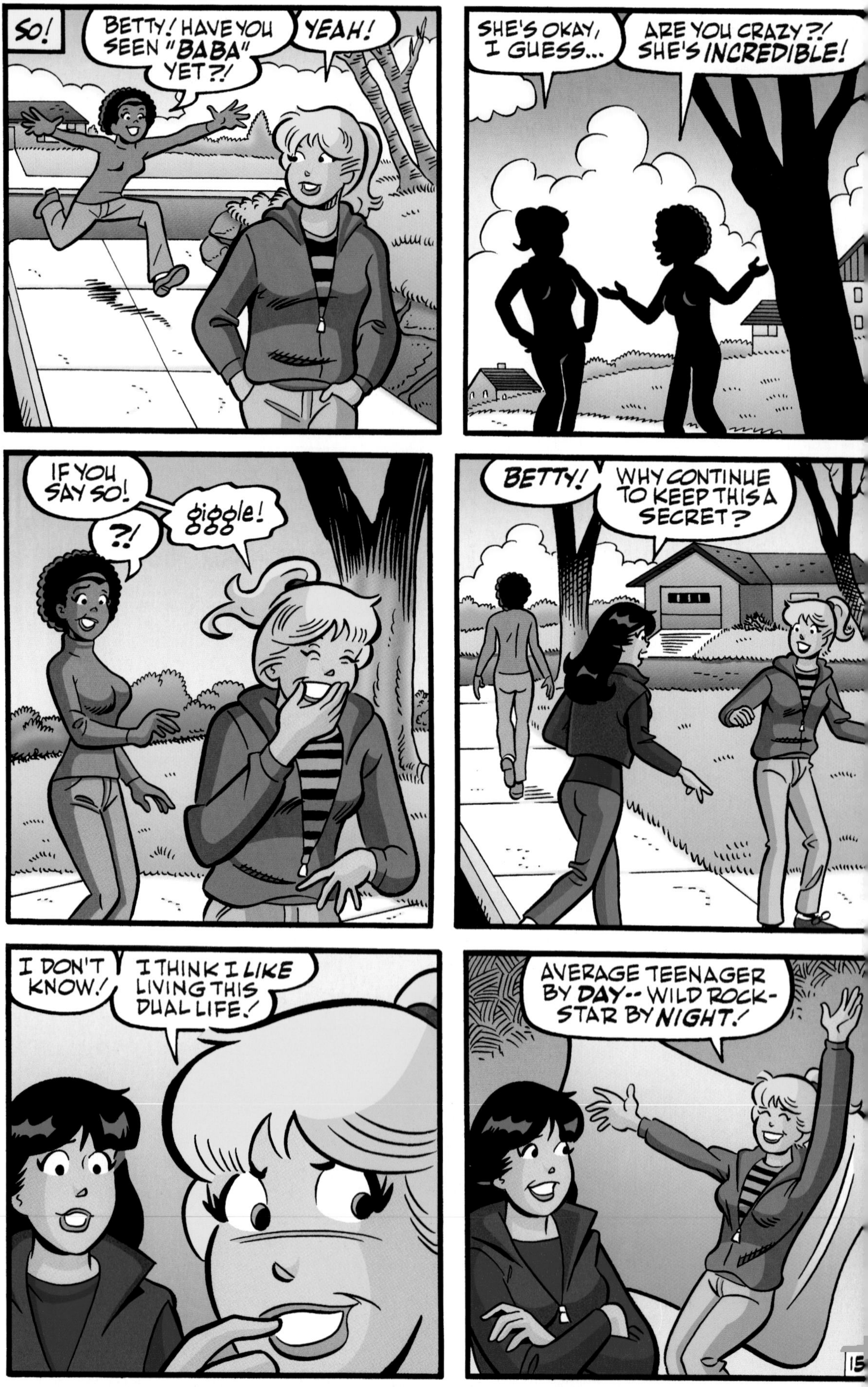
SO!
BETTY! HAVE YOU SEEN "BABA" YET?!
YEAH!
SHE'S OKAY, I GUESS...
ARE YOU CRAZY?! SHE'S INCREDIBLE!
IF YOU SAY SO!
?!
giggle!
BETTY!
WHY CONTINUE TO KEEP THIS A SECRET?
I DON'T KNOW!
I THINK I LIKE LIVING THIS DUAL LIFE!
AVERAGE TEENAGER BY DAY-- WILD ROCK-STAR BY NIGHT!

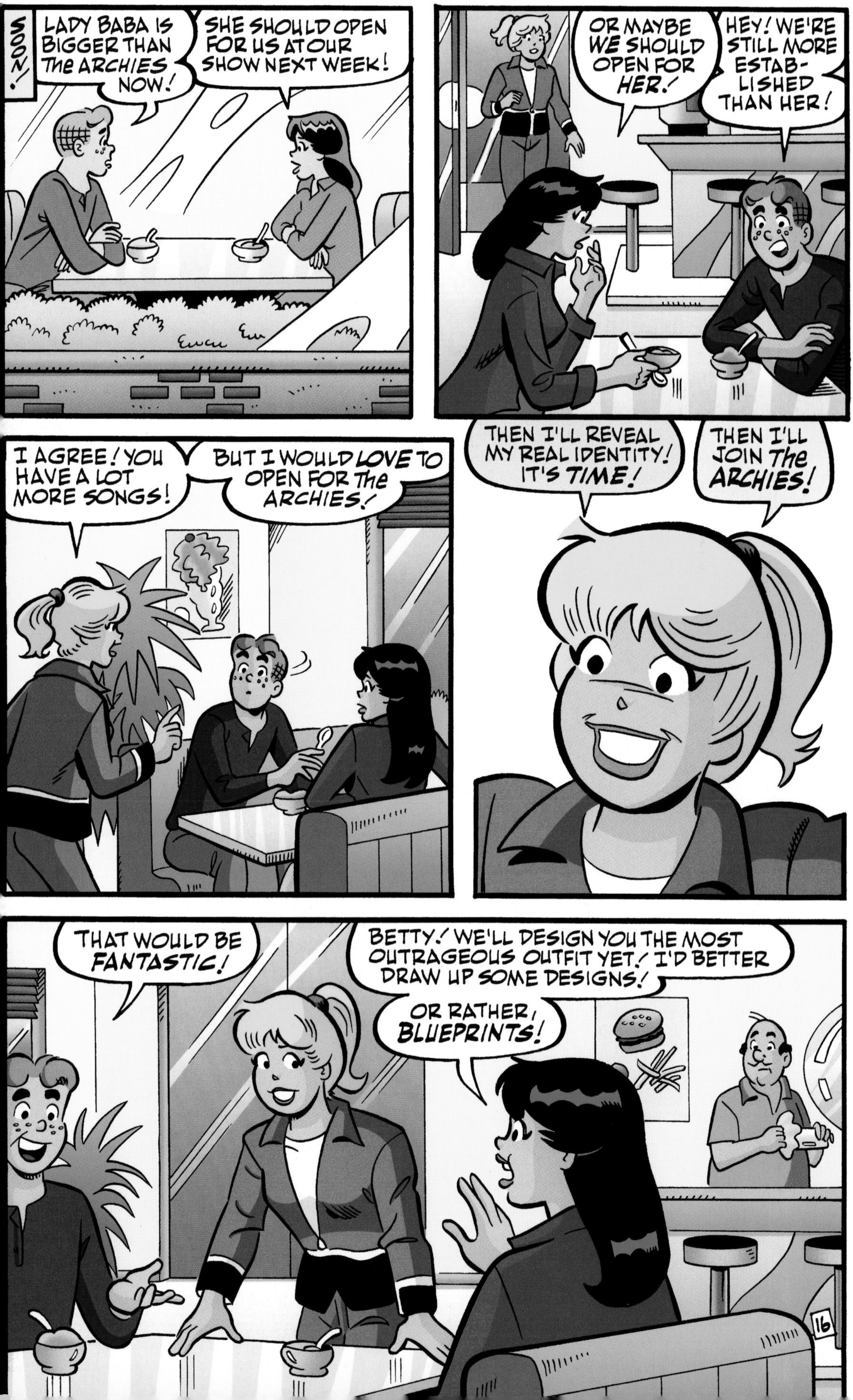
SOON!
LADY BABA IS BIGGER THAN The ARCHIES NOW!
SHE SHOULD OPEN FOR US AT OUR SHOW NEXT WEEK!
OR MAYBE WE SHOULD OPEN FOR HER!
HEY! WE'RE STILL MORE ESTAB-LISHED THAN HER!
I AGREE! YOU HAVE A LOT MORE SONGS!
BUT I WOULD LOVE TO OPEN FOR The ARCHIES!
THEN I'LL REVEAL MY REAL IDENTITY! IT'S TIME!
THEN I'LL JOIN The ARCHIES!
THAT WOULD BE FANTASTIC!
BETTY! WE'LL DESIGN YOU THE MOST OUTRAGEOUS OUTFIT YET! I'D BETTER DRAW UP SOME DESIGNS!
OR RATHER, BLUEPRINTS!
16

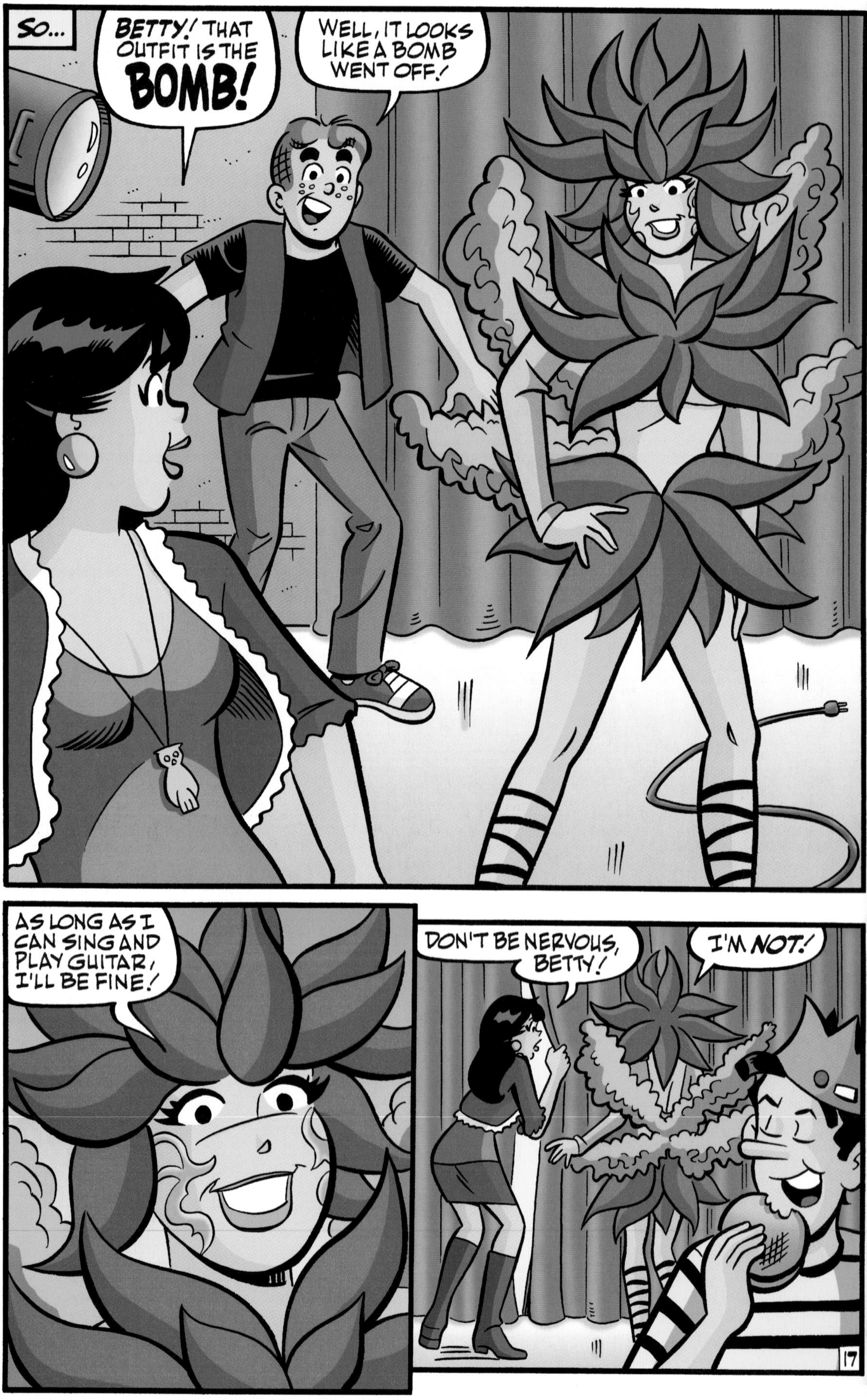
SO...
BETTY! THAT OUTFIT IS THE BOMB!
WELL, IT LOOKS LIKE A BOMB WENT OFF!
AS LONG AS I CAN SING AND PLAY GUITAR, I'LL BE FINE!
DON'T BE NERVOUS, BETTY!
I'M NOT!
17

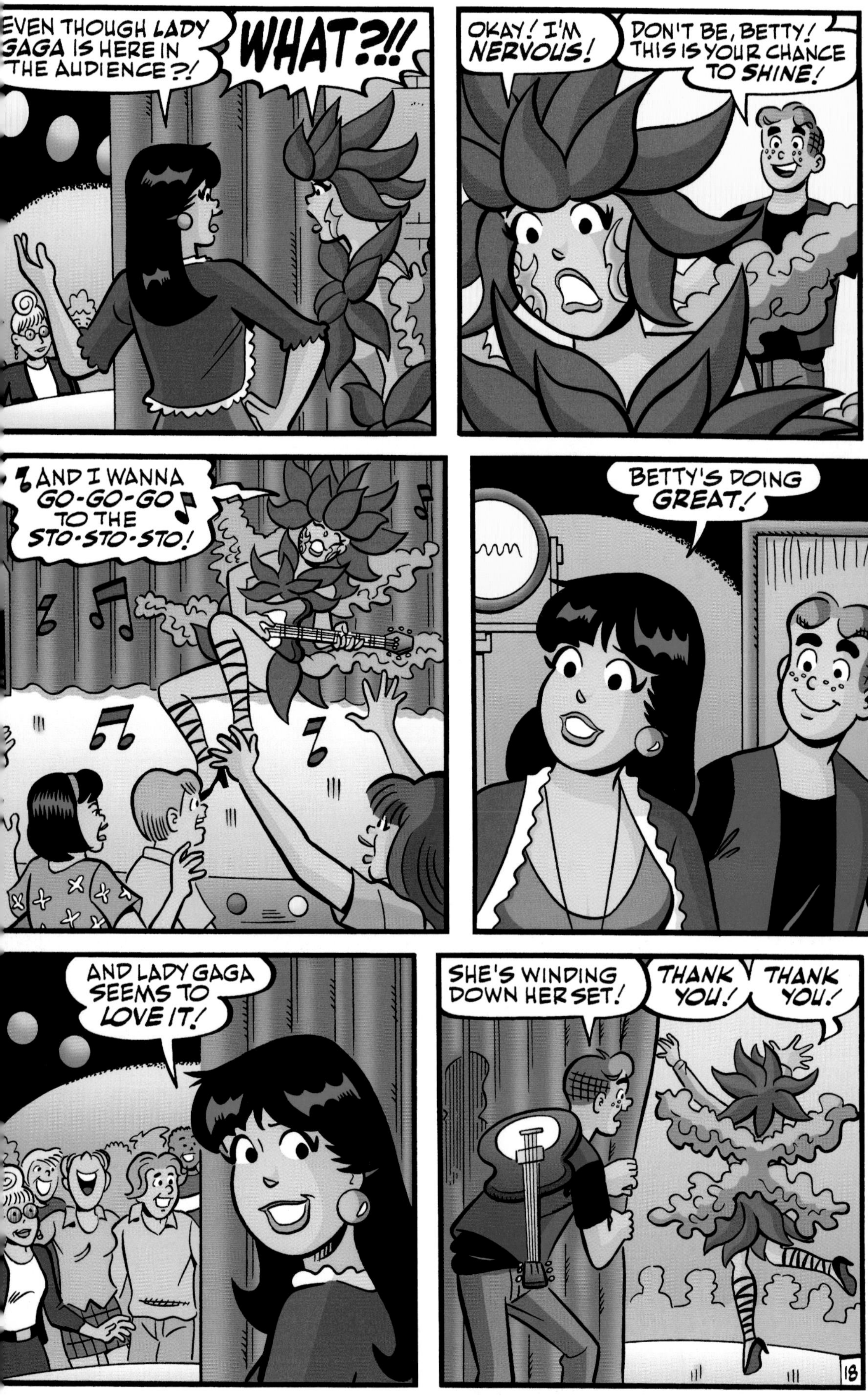
EVEN THOUGH LADY GAGA IS HERE IN THE AUDIENCE?!
WHAT?!!
OKAY! I'M NERVOUS!
DON'T BE, BETTY! THIS IS YOUR CHANCE TO SHINE!
AND I WANNA GO-GO-GO TO THE STO-STO-STO!
BETTY'S DOING GREAT!
AND LADY GAGA SEEMS TO LOVE IT!
SHE'S WINDING DOWN HER SET!
THANK YOU!
THANK YOU!

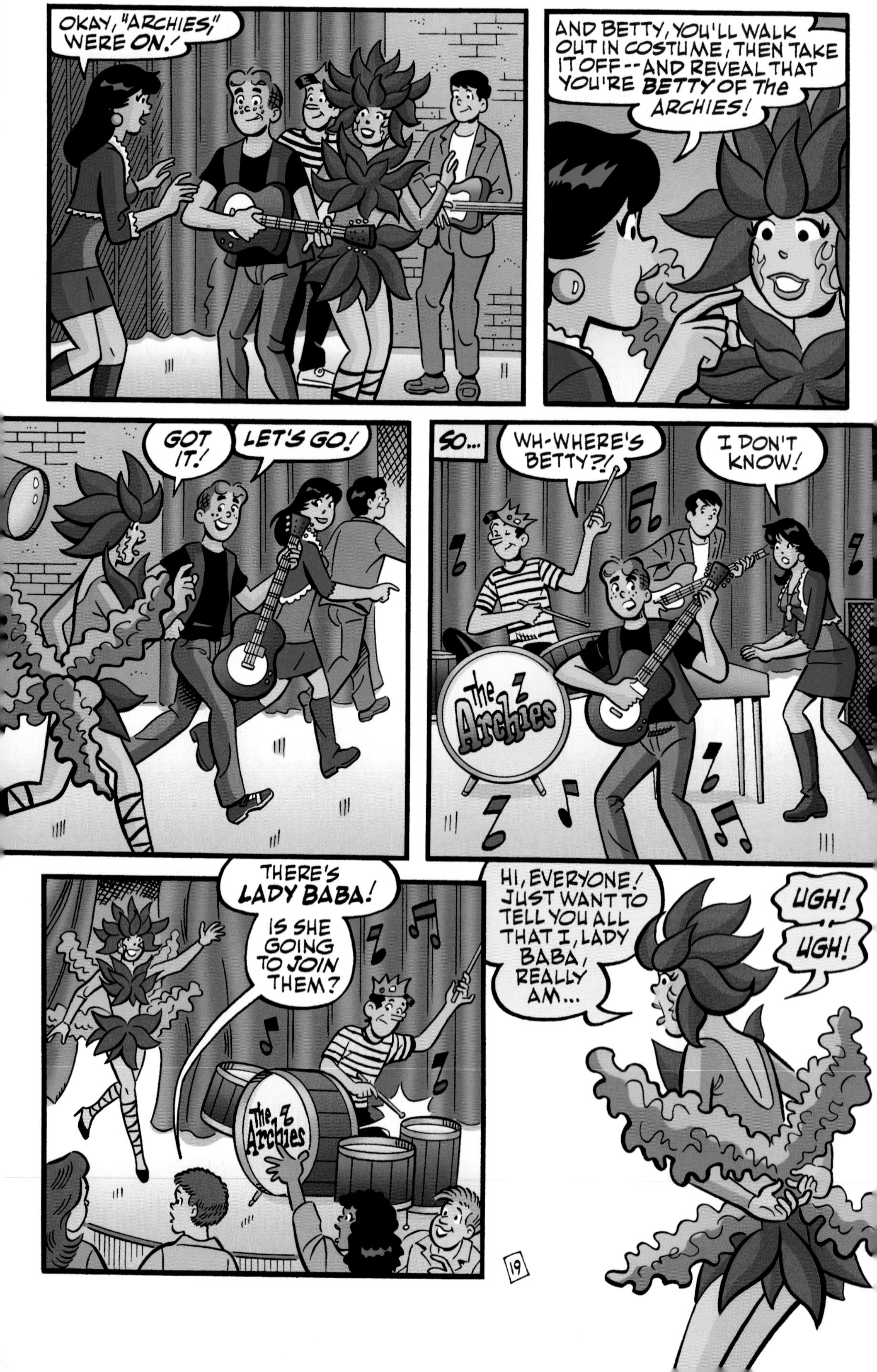

OKAY, "ARCHIES," WERE ON.!
AND BETTY, YOU'LL WALK OUT IN COSTUME, THEN TAKE IT OFF--AND REVEAL THAT YOU'RE BETTY OF THE ARCHIES!
GOT IT.!
LET'S GO!
SO...
WH-WHERE'S BETTY?!
I DON'T KNOW!
The Archies
THERE'S LADY BABA!
IS SHE GOING TO JOIN THEM?
The Archies
HI, EVERYONE! JUST WANT TO TELL YOU ALL THAT I, LADY BABA, REALLY AM...
UGH!
UGH!

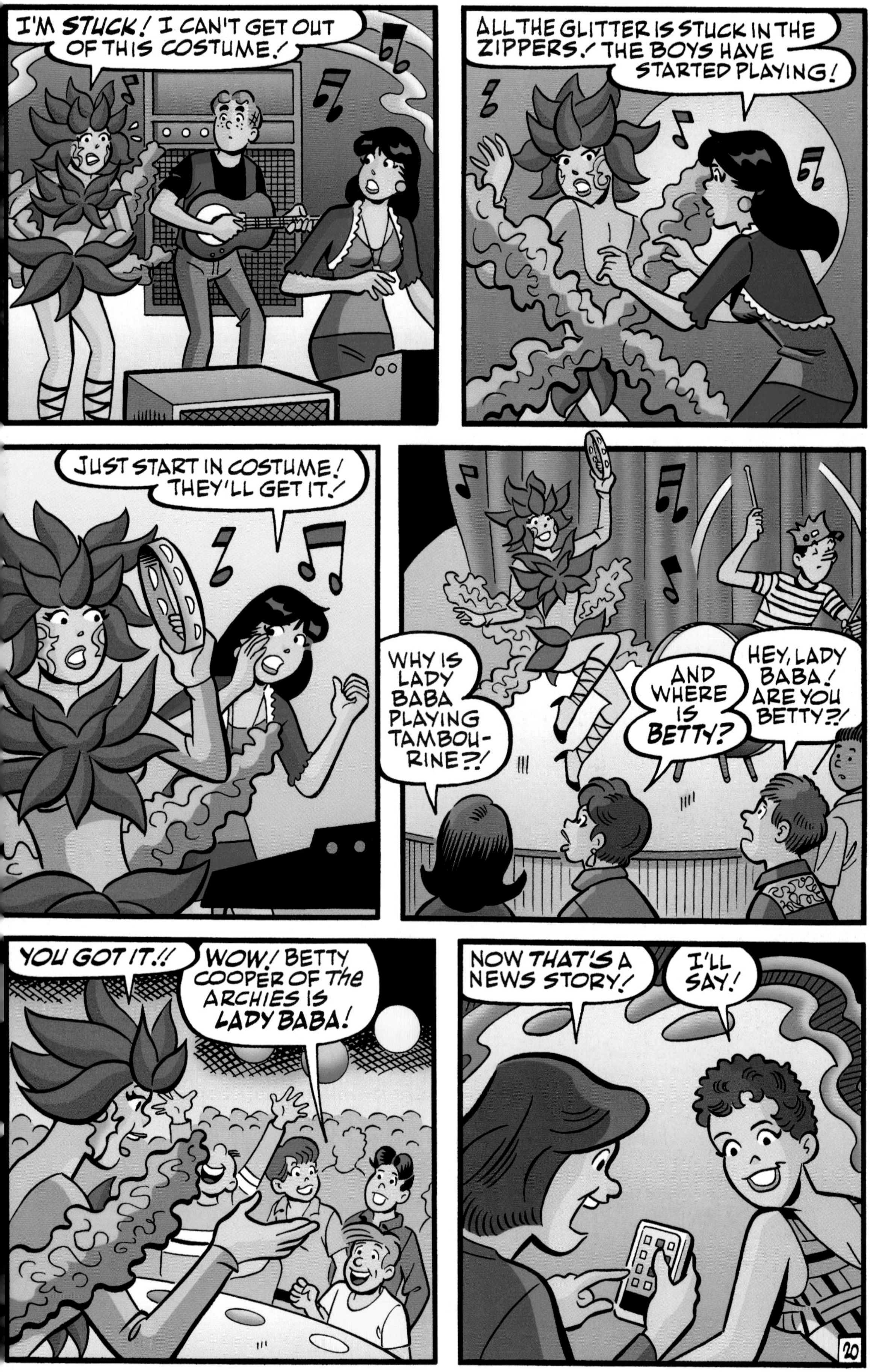
I'M STUCK! I CAN'T GET OUT OF THIS COSTUME!
ALL THE GLITTER IS STUCK IN THE ZIPPERS! THE BOYS HAVE STARTED PLAYING!
JUST START IN COSTUME! THEY'LL GET IT!
WHY IS LADY BABA PLAYING TAMBOU-RINE?!
AND WHERE IS BETTY?
HEY, LADY BABA! ARE YOU BETTY?!
YOU GOT IT!!
WOW! BETTY COOPER OF THE ARCHIES IS LADY BABA!
NOW THAT'S A NEWS STORY!
I'LL SAY!
20

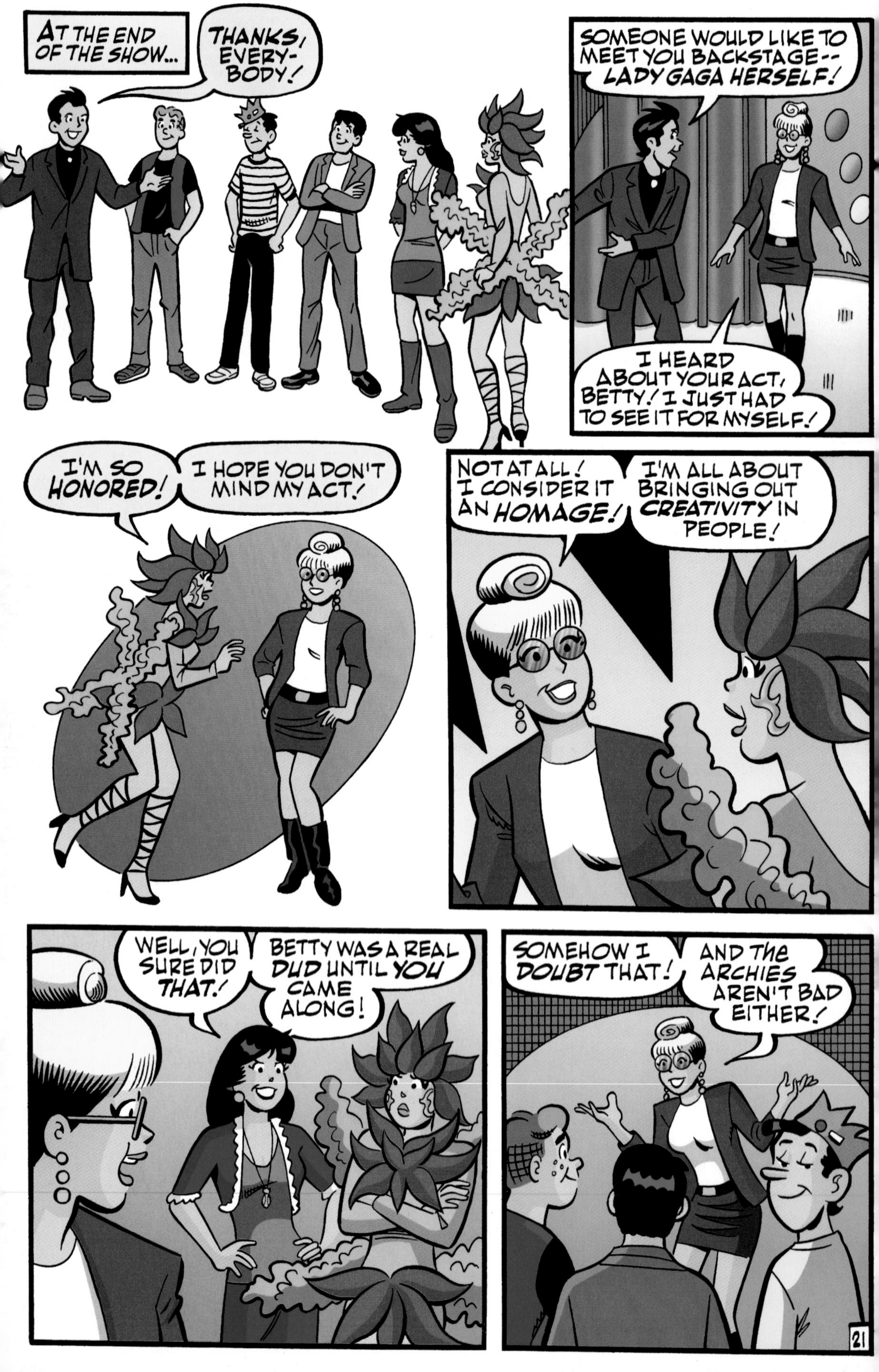
AT THE END OF THE SHOW...
THANKS, EVERYBODY!
SOMEONE WOULD LIKE TO MEET YOU BACKSTAGE-- LADY GAGA HERSELF!
I HEARD ABOUT YOUR ACT, BETTY! I JUST HAD TO SEE IT FOR MYSELF!
I'M SO HONORED!
I HOPE YOU DON'T MIND MY ACT!
NOT AT ALL! I CONSIDER IT AN HOMAGE!
I'M ALL ABOUT BRINGING OUT CREATIVITY IN PEOPLE!
WELL, YOU SURE DID THAT!
BETTY WAS A REAL DUD UNTIL YOU CAME ALONG!
SOMEHOW I DOUBT THAT!
AND THE ARCHIES AREN'T BAD EITHER!

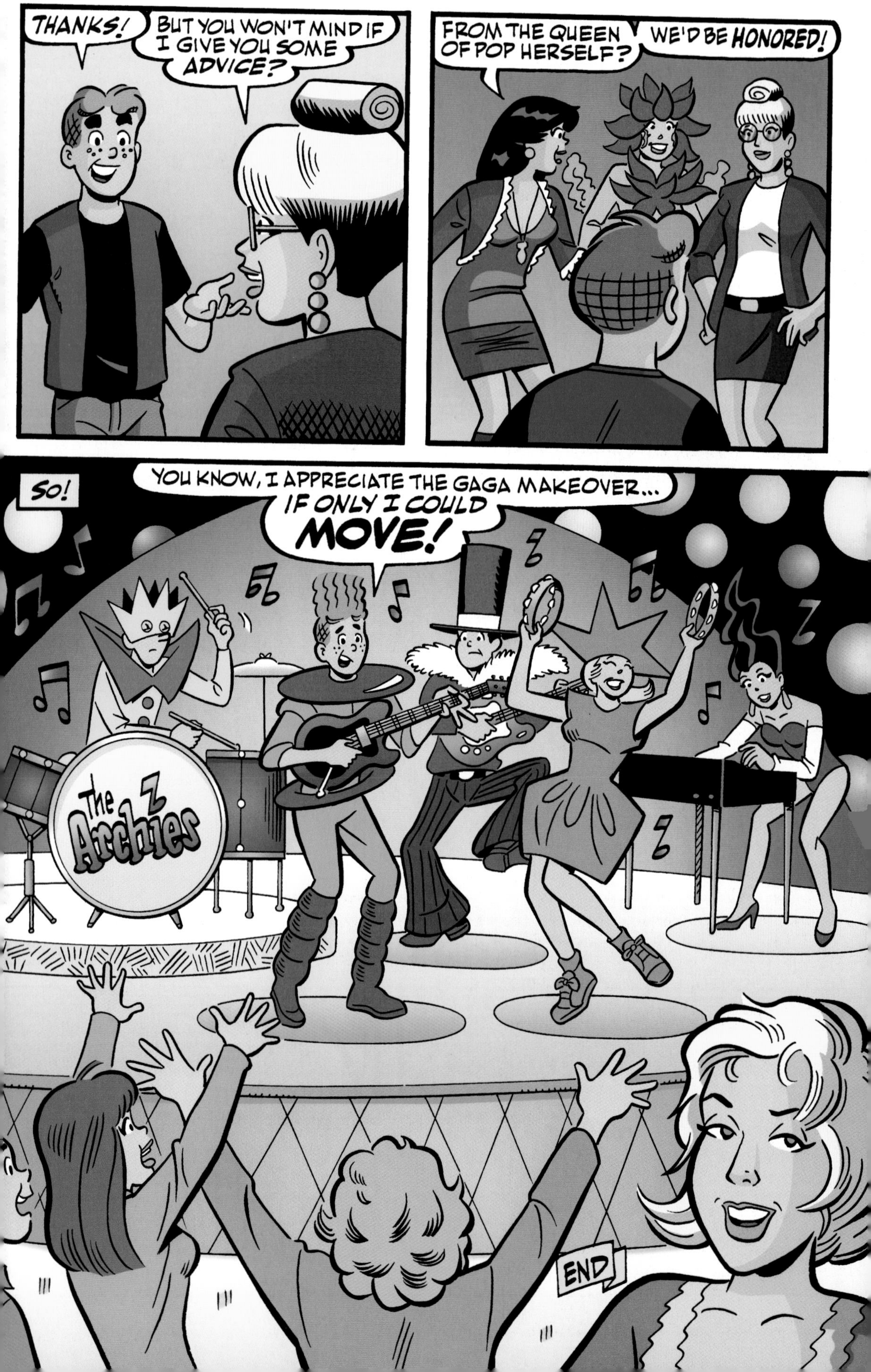
THANKS!
BUT YOU WON'T MIND IF I GIVE YOU SOME ADVICE?
FROM THE QUEEN OF POP HERSELF?
WE'D BE HONORED!
SO!
YOU KNOW, I APPRECIATE THE GAGA MAKEOVER... IF ONLY I COULD MOVE!
The Archies
END

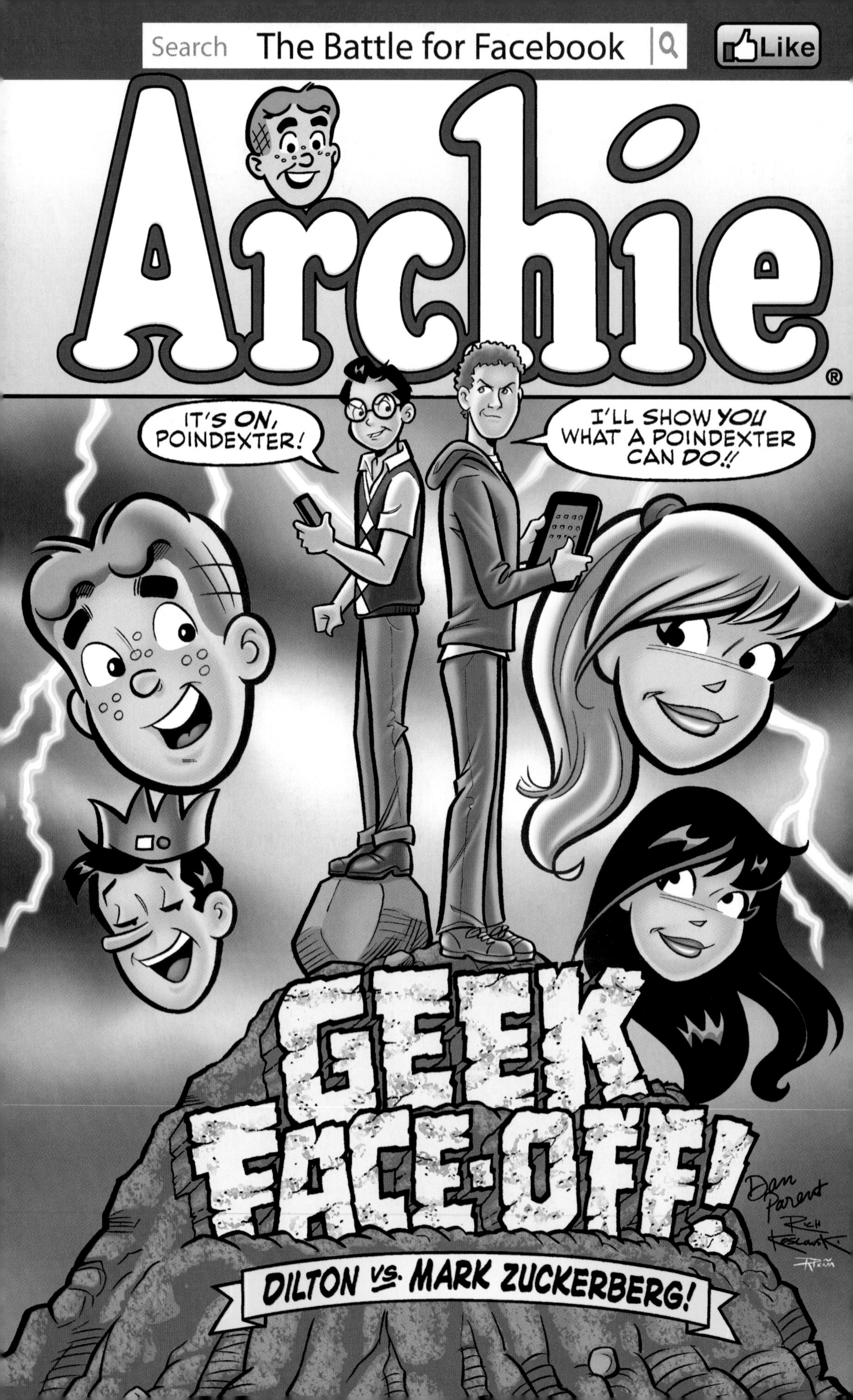
Search The Battle for Facebook
Like
Archie®
IT'S ON, POINDEXTER!
I'LL SHOW YOU WHAT A POINDEXTER CAN DO!!
GEEK FACE-OFF!
DILTON VS. MARK ZUCKERBERG!

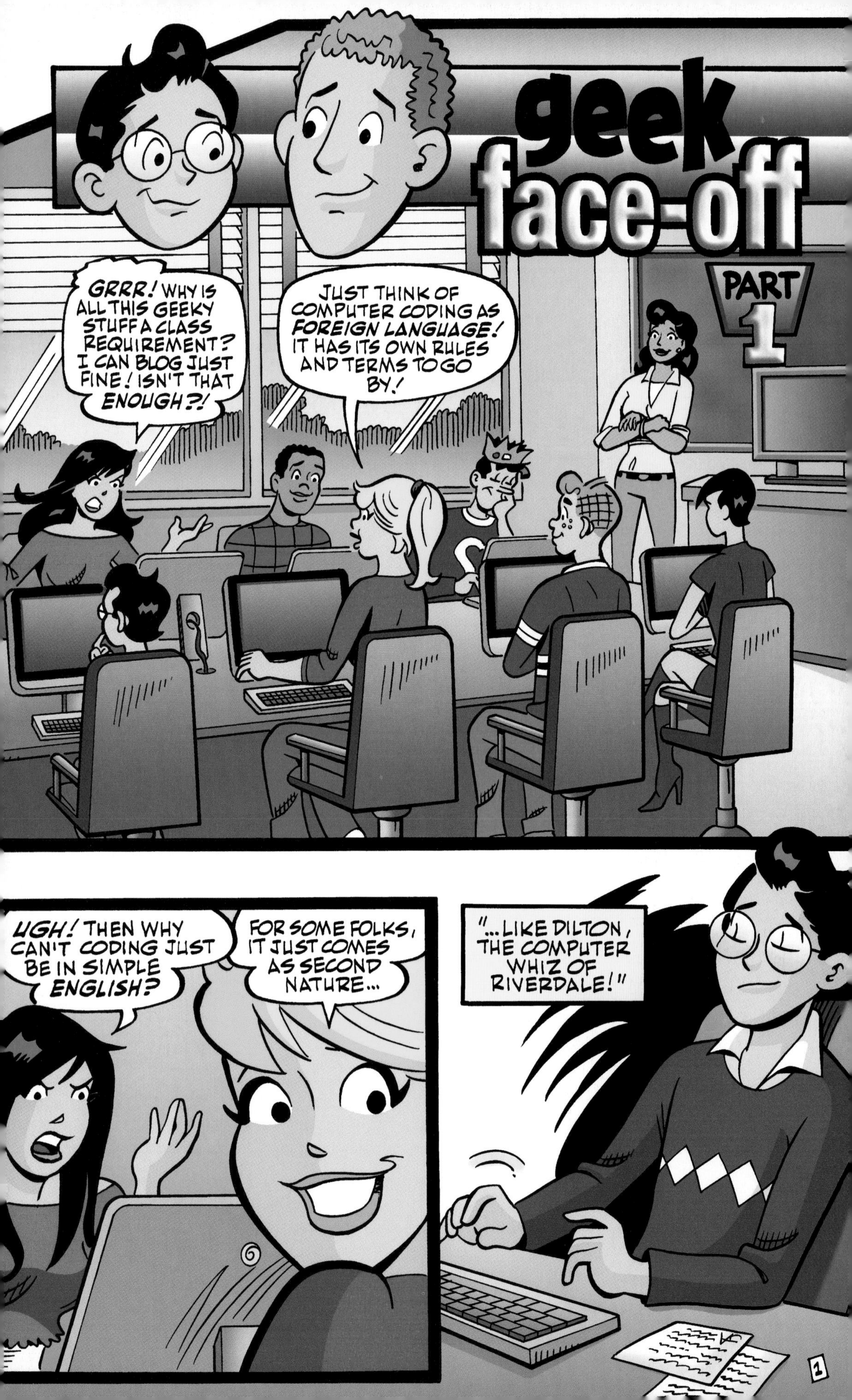
geek face-off
PART 1
GRRR! WHY IS ALL THIS GEEKY STUFF A CLASS REQUIREMENT? I CAN BLOG JUST FINE! ISN'T THAT ENOUGH?!
JUST THINK OF COMPUTER CODING AS FOREIGN LANGUAGE! IT HAS ITS OWN RULES AND TERMS TO GO BY!
UGH! THEN WHY CAN'T CODING JUST BE IN SIMPLE ENGLISH?
FOR SOME FOLKS, IT JUST COMES AS SECOND NATURE...
"...LIKE DILTON, THE COMPUTER WHIZ OF RIVERDALE!"

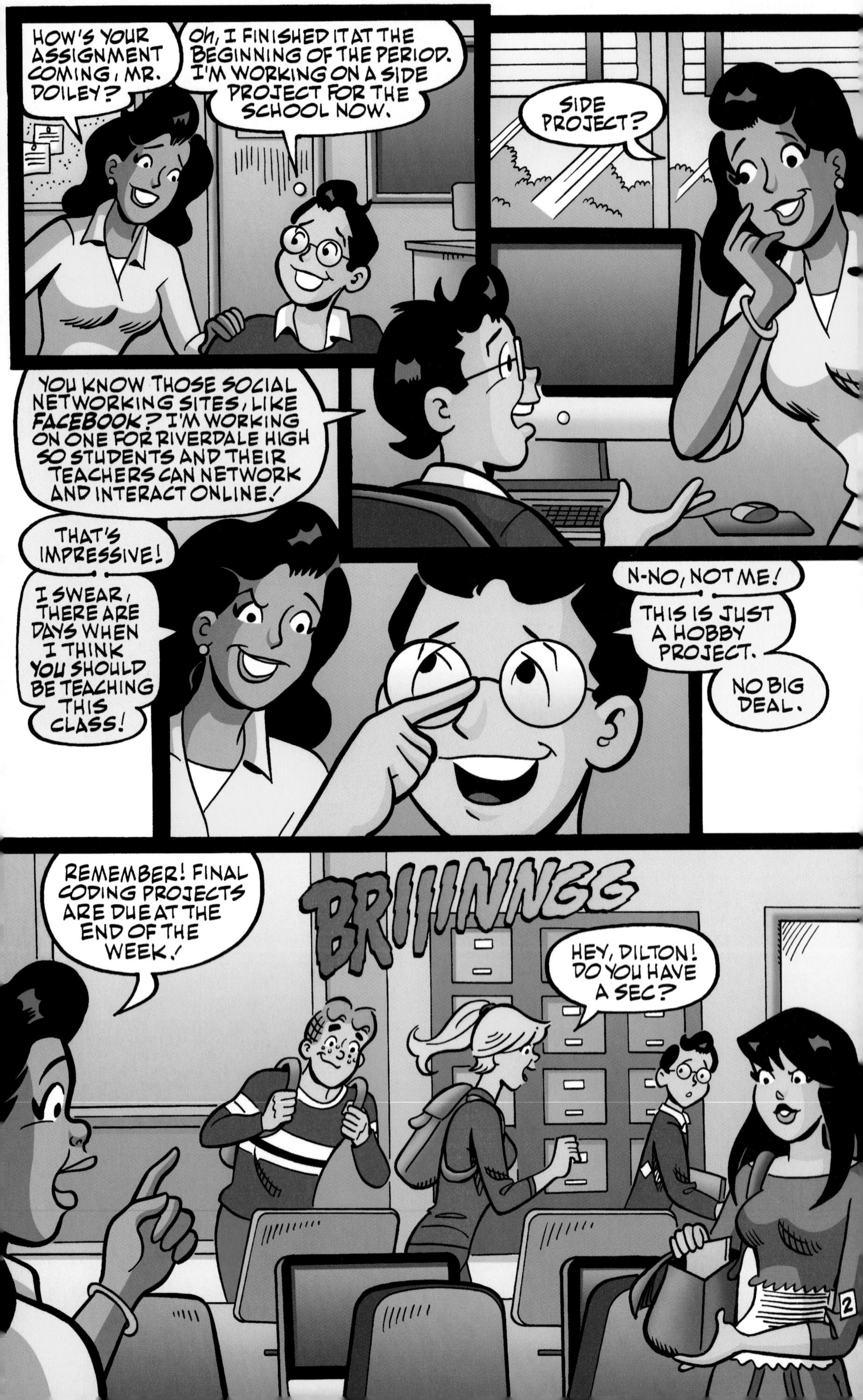

HOW'S YOUR ASSIGNMENT COMING, MR. DOILEY?
OH, I FINISHED IT AT THE BEGINNING OF THE PERIOD. I'M WORKING ON A SIDE PROJECT FOR THE SCHOOL NOW.
SIDE PROJECT?
YOU KNOW THOSE SOCIAL NETWORKING SITES, LIKE FACEBOOK? I'M WORKING ON ONE FOR RIVERDALE HIGH SO STUDENTS AND THEIR TEACHERS CAN NETWORK AND INTERACT ONLINE!
THAT'S IMPRESSIVE!
I SWEAR, THERE ARE DAYS WHEN I THINK YOU SHOULD BE TEACHING THIS CLASS!
N-NO, NOT ME!
THIS IS JUST A HOBBY PROJECT.
NO BIG DEAL.
REMEMBER! FINAL CODING PROJECTS ARE DUE AT THE END OF THE WEEK!
BRIIINNGG
HEY, DILTON! DO YOU HAVE A SEC?
2

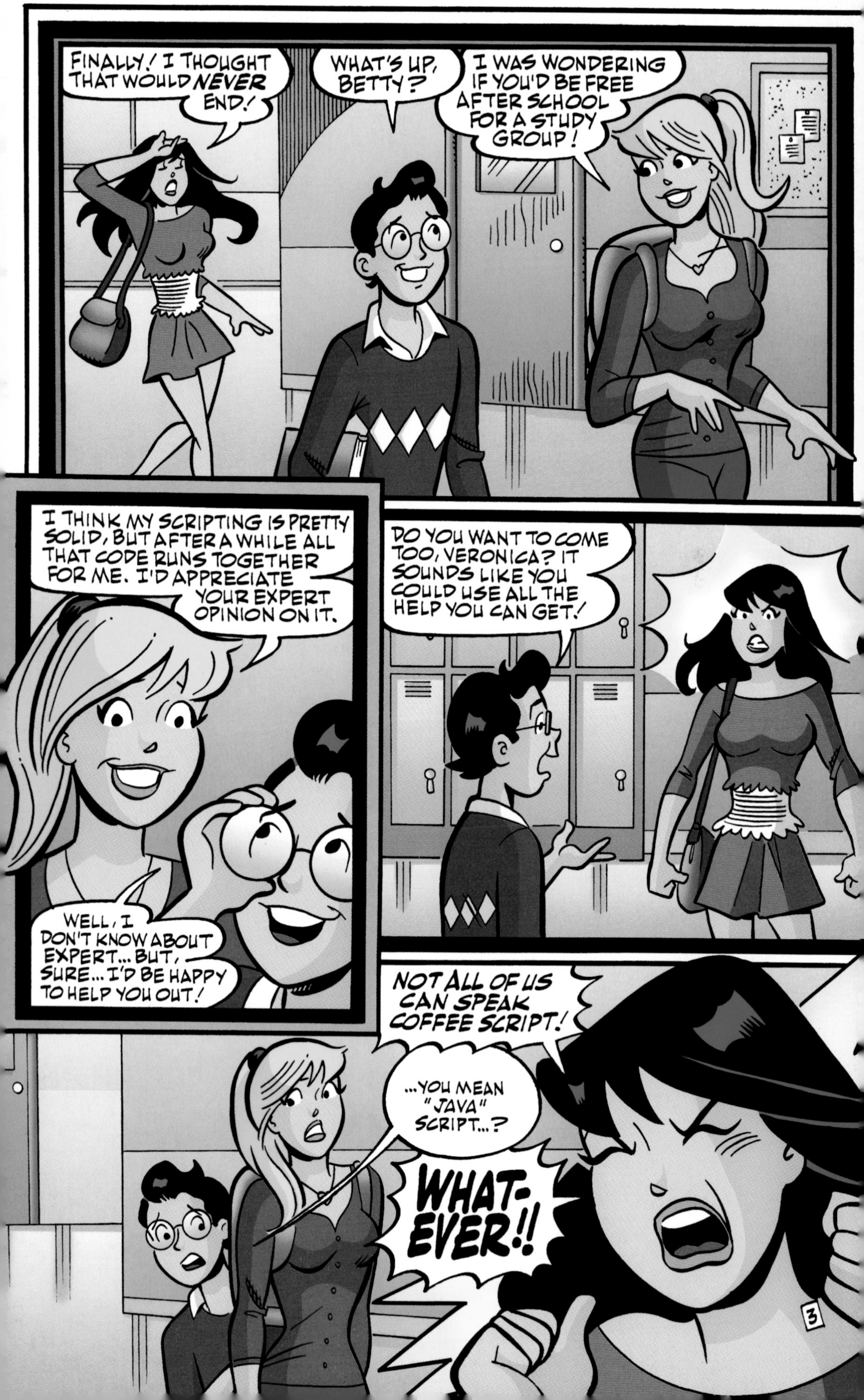

FINALLY! I THOUGHT THAT WOULD NEVER END!
WHAT'S UP, BETTY?
I WAS WONDERING IF YOU'D BE FREE AFTER SCHOOL FOR A STUDY GROUP!
I THINK MY SCRIPTING IS PRETTY SOLID, BUT AFTER A WHILE ALL THAT CODE RUNS TOGETHER FOR ME. I'D APPRECIATE YOUR EXPERT OPINION ON IT.
WELL, I DON'T KNOW ABOUT EXPERT... BUT, SURE... I'D BE HAPPY TO HELP YOU OUT!
DO YOU WANT TO COME TOO, VERONICA? IT SOUNDS LIKE YOU COULD USE ALL THE HELP YOU CAN GET!
NOT ALL OF US CAN SPEAK COFFEE SCRIPT!
...YOU MEAN "JAVA" SCRIPT...?
WHAT-EVER!!
3

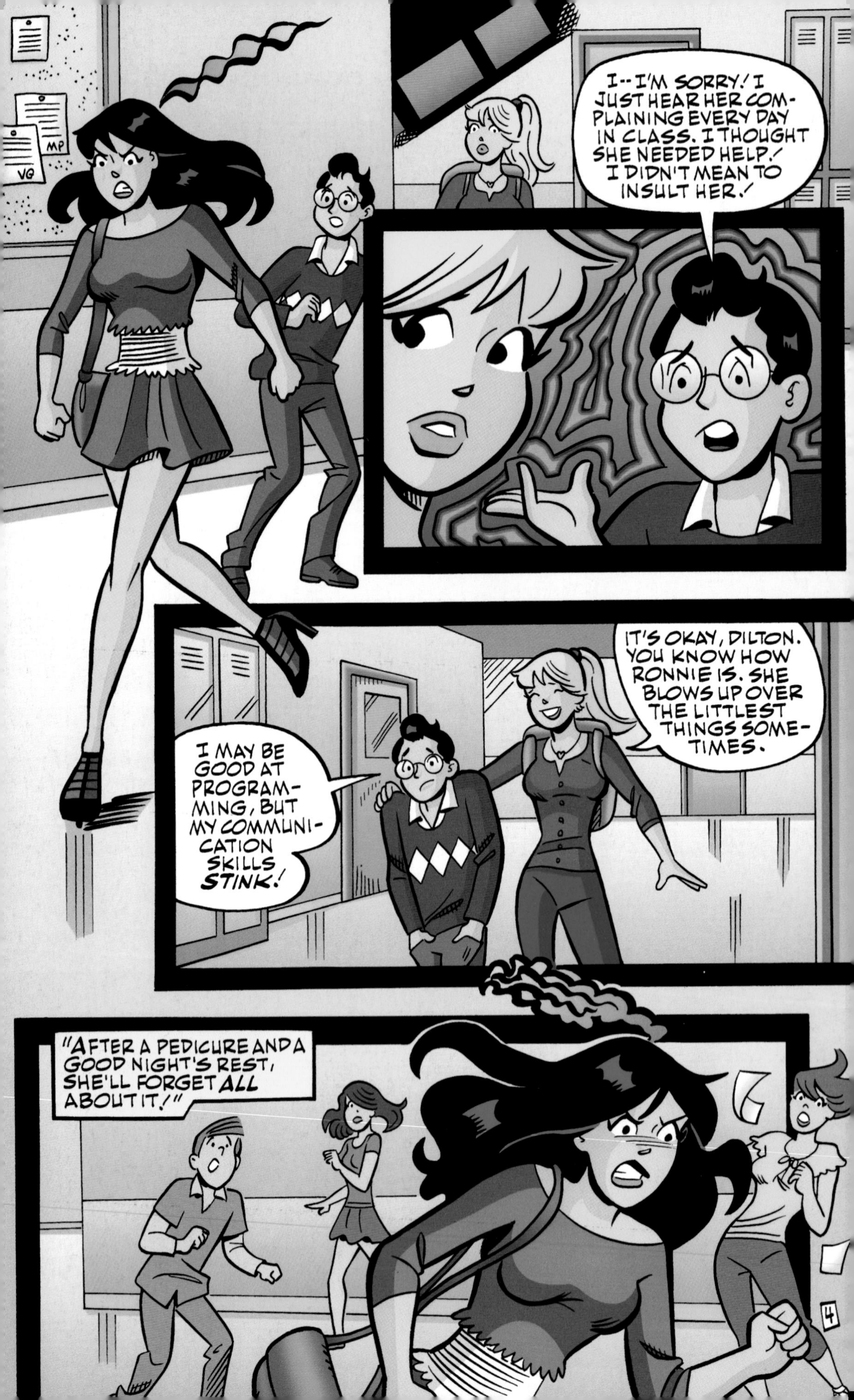
MP
VG
I-- I'M SORRY! I JUST HEAR HER COMPLAINING EVERY DAY IN CLASS. I THOUGHT SHE NEEDED HELP! I DIDN'T MEAN TO INSULT HER!
IT'S OKAY, DILTON. YOU KNOW HOW RONNIE IS. SHE BLOWS UP OVER THE LITTLEST THINGS SOMETIMES.
I MAY BE GOOD AT PROGRAMMING, BUT MY COMMUNICATION SKILLS STINK!
"AFTER A PEDICURE AND A GOOD NIGHT'S REST, SHE'LL FORGET ALL ABOUT IT!"
4

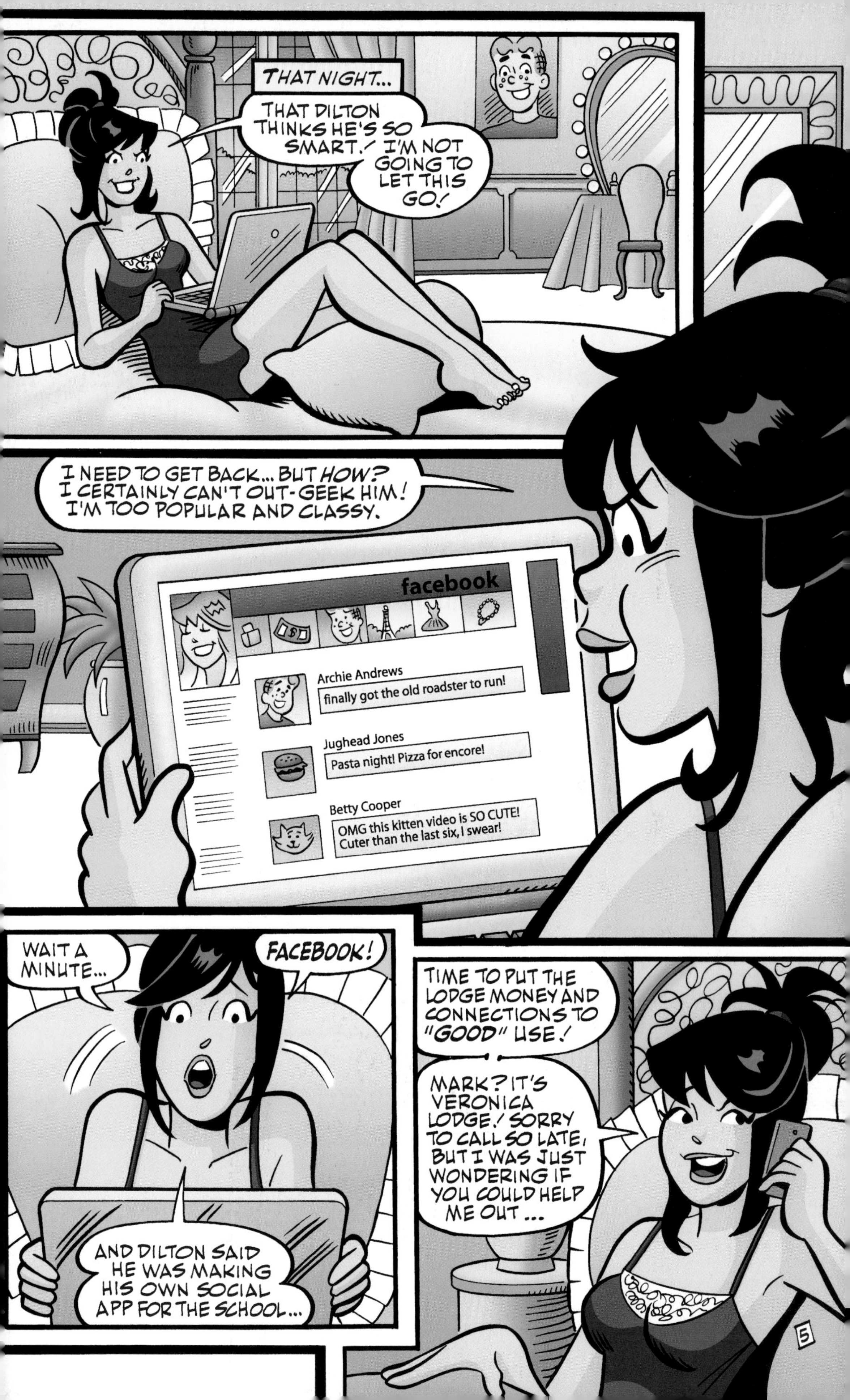

THAT NIGHT...
THAT DILTON THINKS HE'S SO SMART! I'M NOT GOING TO LET THIS GO!
I NEED TO GET BACK... BUT HOW? I CERTAINLY CAN'T OUT-GEEK HIM! I'M TOO POPULAR AND CLASSY.
facebook
Archie Andrews
finally got the old roadster to run!
Jughead Jones
Pasta night! Pizza for encore!
Betty Cooper
OMG this kitten video is SO CUTE! Cuter than the last six, I swear!
WAIT A MINUTE...
FACEBOOK!
AND DILTON SAID HE WAS MAKING HIS OWN SOCIAL APP FOR THE SCHOOL...
TIME TO PUT THE LODGE MONEY AND CONNECTIONS TO "GOOD" USE!
MARK? IT'S VERONICA LODGE! SORRY TO CALL SO LATE, BUT I WAS JUST WONDERING IF YOU COULD HELP ME OUT...

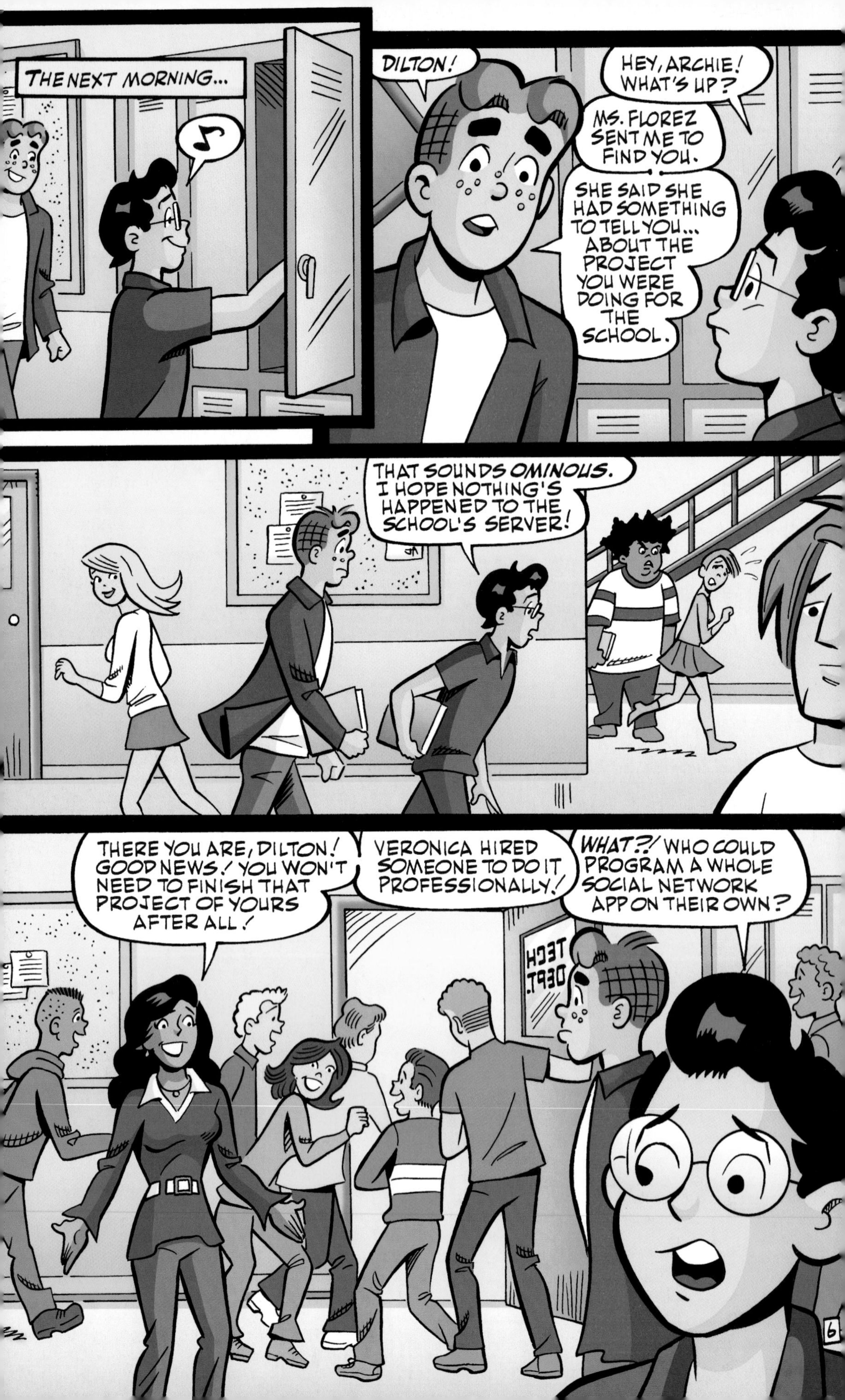
THE NEXT MORNING...
DILTON!
HEY, ARCHIE! WHAT'S UP?
MS. FLOREZ SENT ME TO FIND YOU.
SHE SAID SHE HAD SOMETHING TO TELL YOU... ABOUT THE PROJECT YOU WERE DOING FOR THE SCHOOL.
THAT SOUNDS OMINOUS. I HOPE NOTHING'S HAPPENED TO THE SCHOOL'S SERVER!
THERE YOU ARE, DILTON! GOOD NEWS! YOU WON'T NEED TO FINISH THAT PROJECT OF YOURS AFTER ALL!
VERONICA HIRED SOMEONE TO DO IT PROFESSIONALLY!
WHAT?! WHO COULD PROGRAM A WHOLE SOCIAL NETWORK APP ON THEIR OWN?
TECH DEPT.

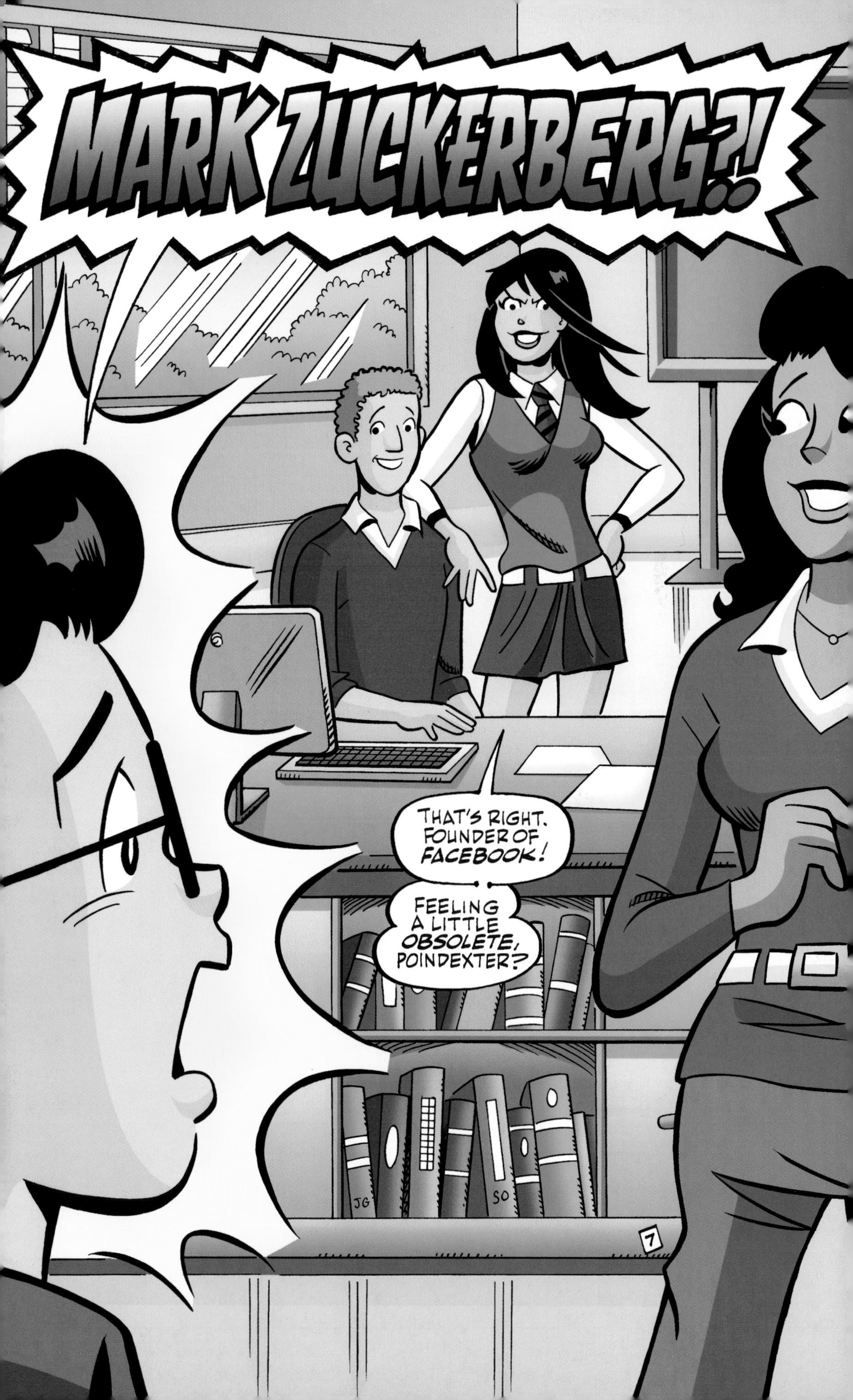
MARK ZUCKERBERG?!
THAT'S RIGHT. FOUNDER OF FACEBOOK!
FEELING A LITTLE OBSOLETE, POINDEXTER?
JG
SO
7

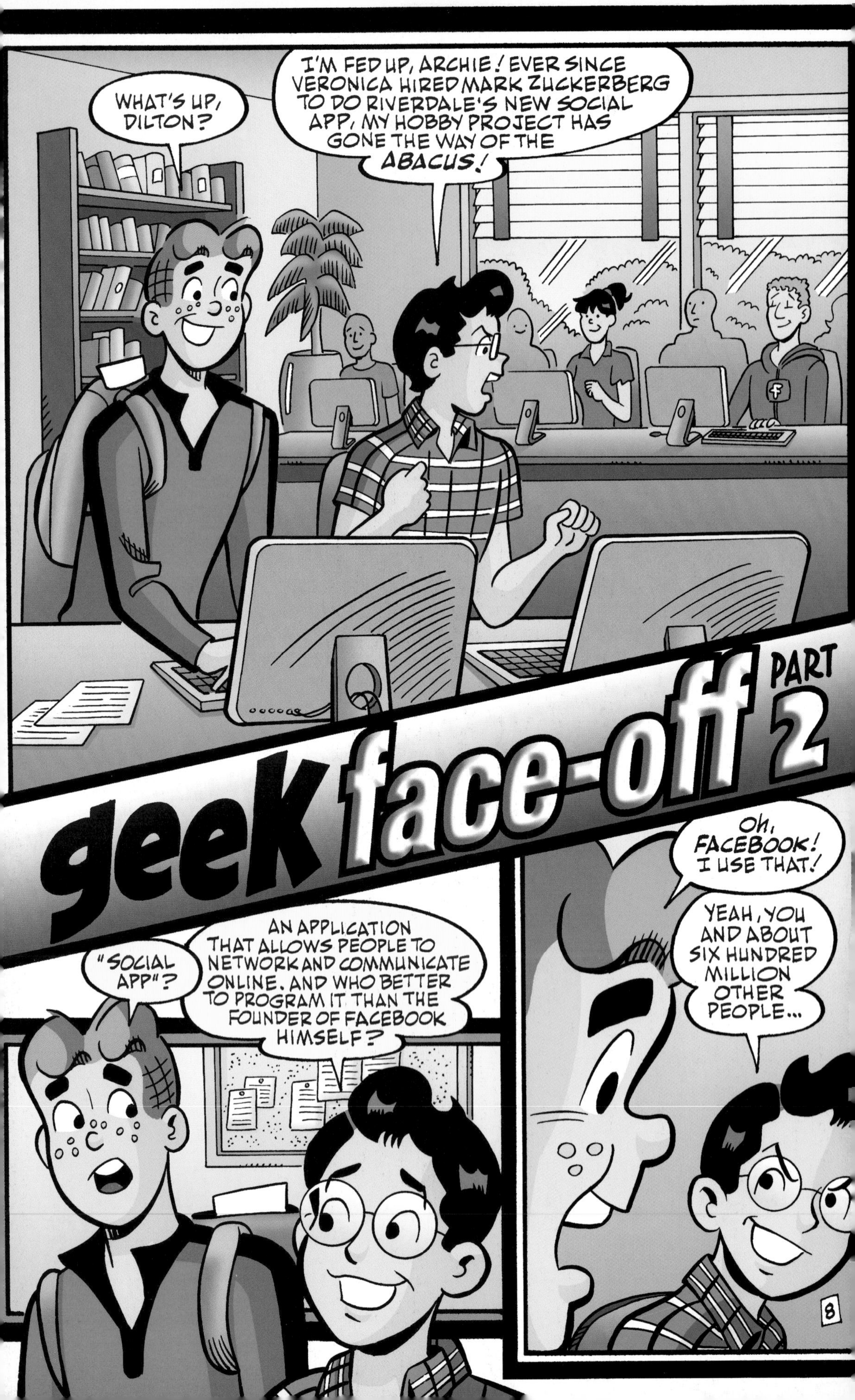
WHAT'S UP, DILTON?
I'M FED UP, ARCHIE! EVER SINCE VERONICA HIRED MARK ZUCKERBERG TO DO RIVERDALE'S NEW SOCIAL APP, MY HOBBY PROJECT HAS GONE THE WAY OF THE ABACUS!
geek face-off PART 2
"SOCIAL APP"?
AN APPLICATION THAT ALLOWS PEOPLE TO NETWORK AND COMMUNICATE ONLINE. AND WHO BETTER TO PROGRAM IT THAN THE FOUNDER OF FACEBOOK HIMSELF?
OH, FACEBOOK! I USE THAT!
YEAH, YOU AND ABOUT SIX HUNDRED MILLION OTHER PEOPLE...
8

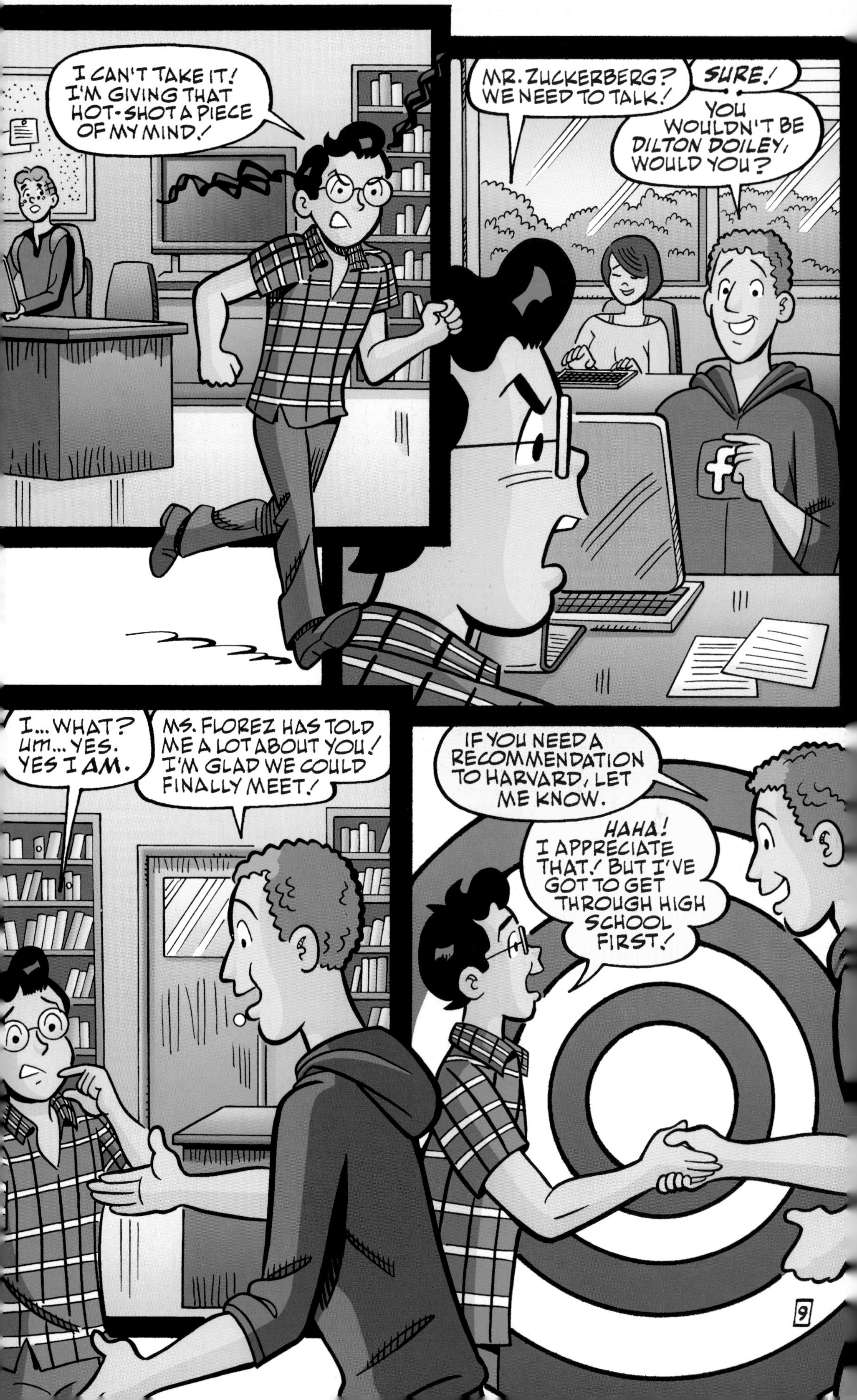
I CAN'T TAKE IT! I'M GIVING THAT HOT-SHOT A PIECE OF MY MIND!
MR. ZUCKERBERG? WE NEED TO TALK!
SURE!
YOU WOULDN'T BE DILTON DOILEY, WOULD YOU?
I... WHAT? UM... YES. YES I AM.
MS. FLOREZ HAS TOLD ME A LOT ABOUT YOU! I'M GLAD WE COULD FINALLY MEET!
IF YOU NEED A RECOMMENDATION TO HARVARD, LET ME KNOW.
HAHA! I APPRECIATE THAT! BUT I'VE GOT TO GET THROUGH HIGH SCHOOL FIRST!
9

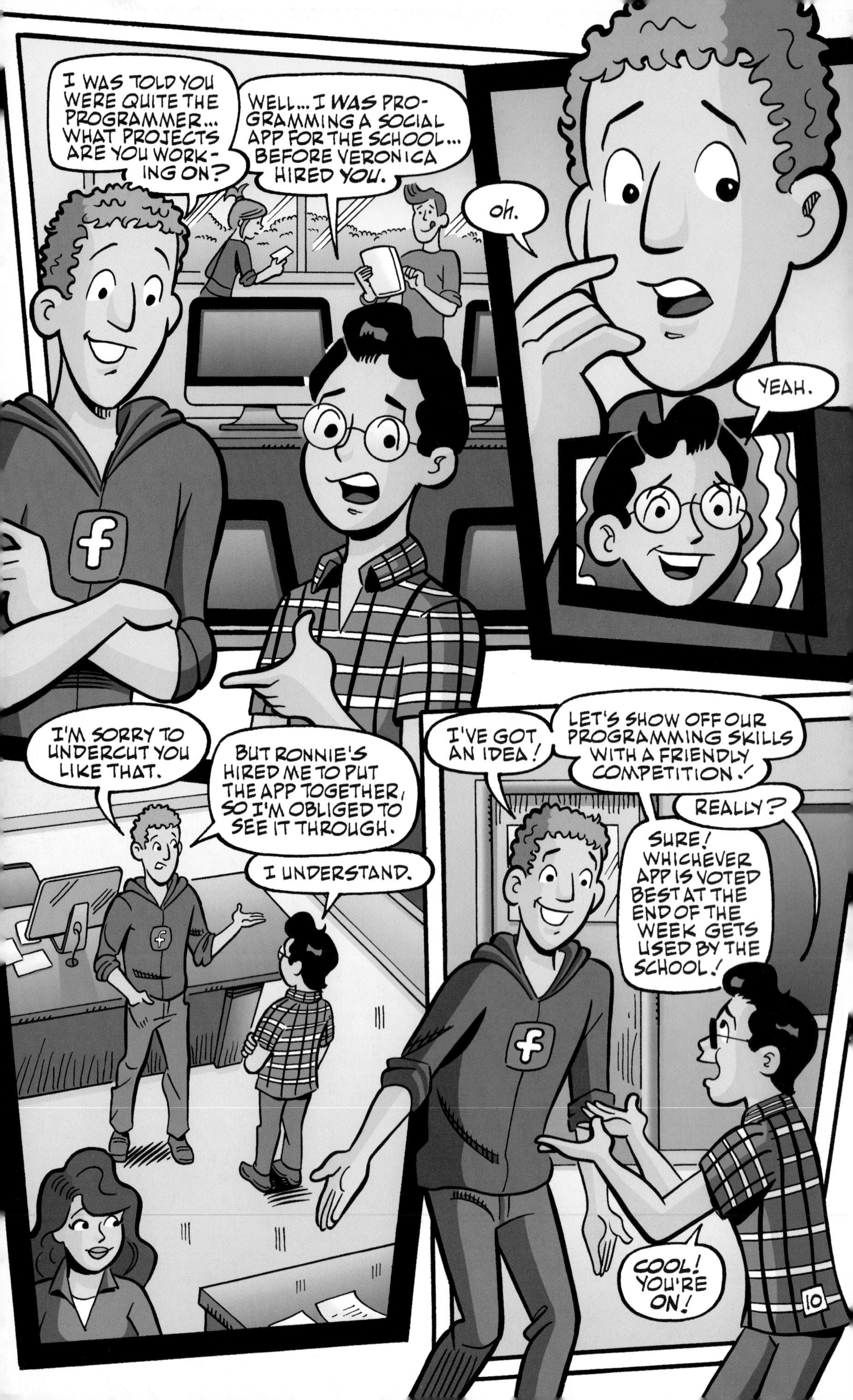
I WAS TOLD YOU WERE QUITE THE PROGRAMMER... WHAT PROJECTS ARE YOU WORKING ON?
WELL... I WAS PROGRAMMING A SOCIAL APP FOR THE SCHOOL... BEFORE VERONICA HIRED YOU.
oh.
YEAH.
I'M SORRY TO UNDERCUT YOU LIKE THAT.
BUT RONNIE'S HIRED ME TO PUT THE APP TOGETHER, SO I'M OBLIGED TO SEE IT THROUGH.
I UNDERSTAND.
I'VE GOT AN IDEA!
LET'S SHOW OFF OUR PROGRAMMING SKILLS WITH A FRIENDLY COMPETITION.!
REALLY?
SURE! WHICHEVER APP IS VOTED BEST AT THE END OF THE WEEK GETS USED BY THE SCHOOL.!
COOL! YOU'RE ON!
10

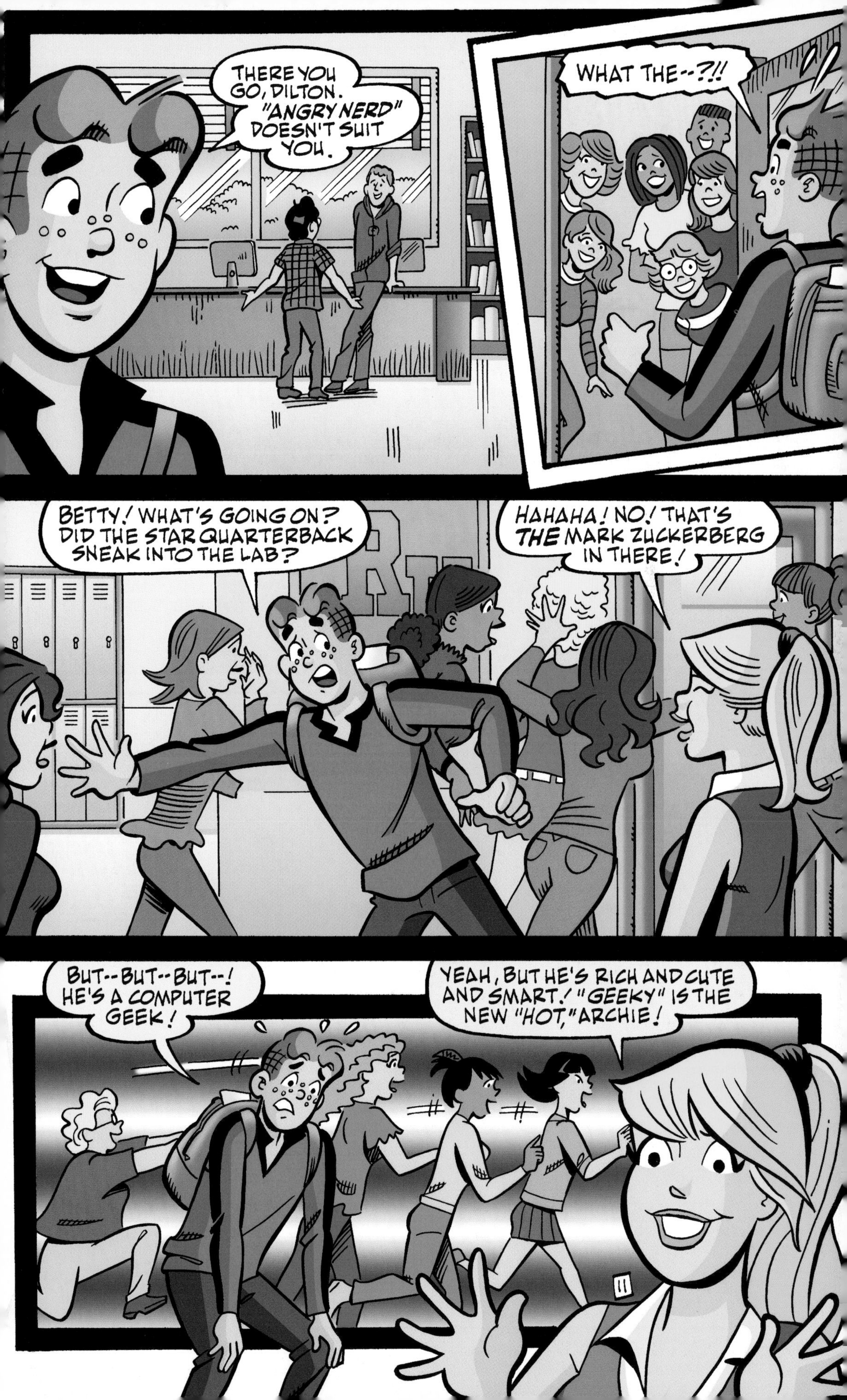

THERE YOU GO, DILTON. "ANGRY NERD" DOESN'T SUIT YOU.
WHAT THE--?!!
BETTY! WHAT'S GOING ON? DID THE STAR QUARTERBACK SNEAK INTO THE LAB?
HAHAHA! NO! THAT'S THE MARK ZUCKERBERG IN THERE!
BUT--BUT--BUT--! HE'S A COMPUTER GEEK!
YEAH, BUT HE'S RICH AND CUTE AND SMART! "GEEKY" IS THE NEW "HOT," ARCHIE!

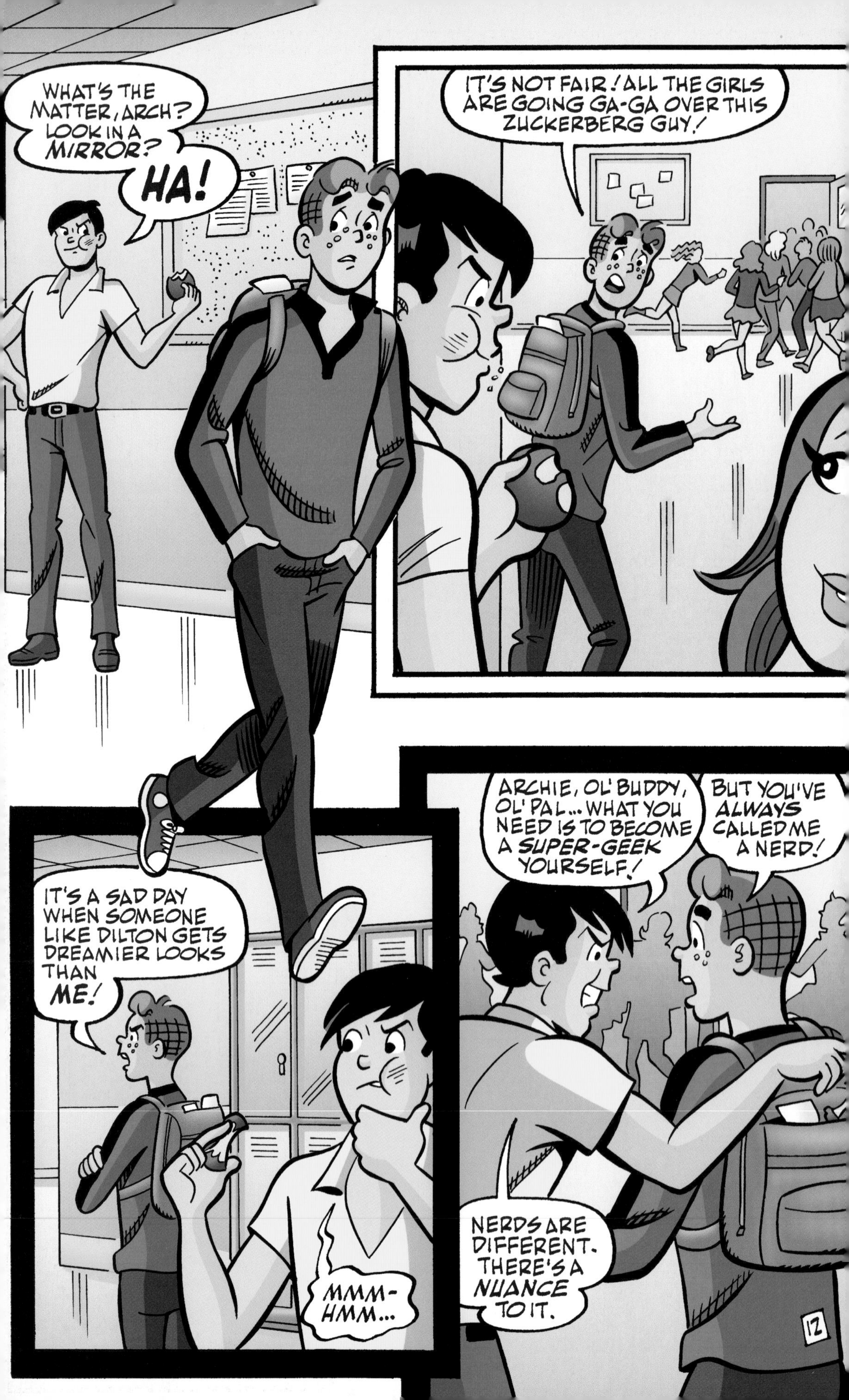
WHAT'S THE MATTER, ARCH? LOOK IN A MIRROR?
HA!
IT'S NOT FAIR! ALL THE GIRLS ARE GOING GA-GA OVER THIS ZUCKERBERG GUY!
IT'S A SAD DAY WHEN SOMEONE LIKE DILTON GETS DREAMIER LOOKS THAN ME!
MMM-HMM...
ARCHIE, OL' BUDDY, OL' PAL... WHAT YOU NEED IS TO BECOME A SUPER-GEEK YOURSELF!
BUT YOU'VE ALWAYS CALLED ME A NERD!
NERDS ARE DIFFERENT. THERE'S A NUANCE TO IT.
12

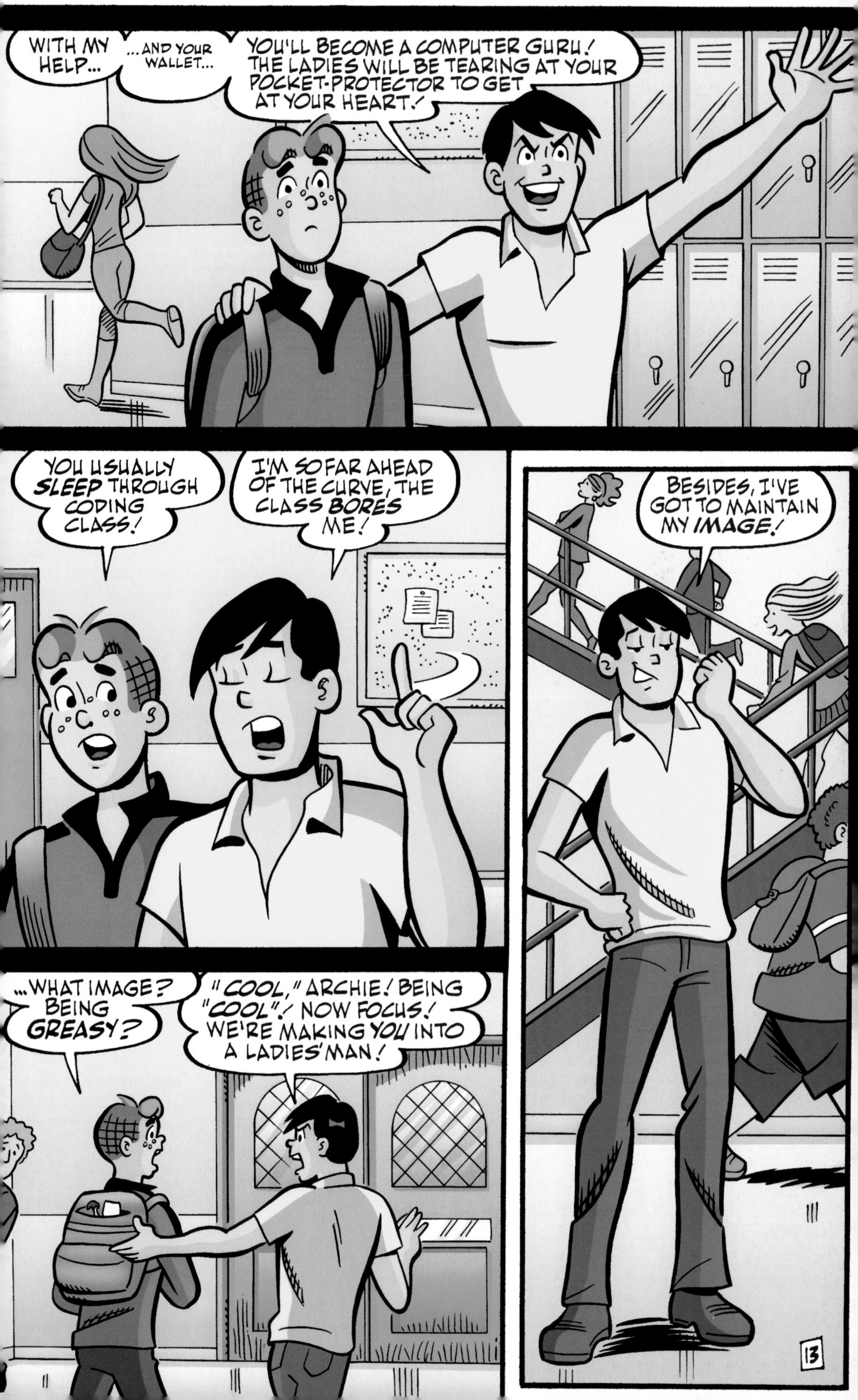
WITH MY HELP...
...AND YOUR WALLET...
YOU'LL BECOME A COMPUTER GURU! THE LADIES WILL BE TEARING AT YOUR POCKET-PROTECTOR TO GET AT YOUR HEART!
YOU USUALLY SLEEP THROUGH CODING CLASS!
I'M SO FAR AHEAD OF THE CURVE, THE CLASS BORES ME!
BESIDES, I'VE GOT TO MAINTAIN MY IMAGE!
...WHAT IMAGE? BEING GREASY?
"COOL," ARCHIE! BEING "COOL"! NOW FOCUS! WE'RE MAKING YOU INTO A LADIES' MAN!

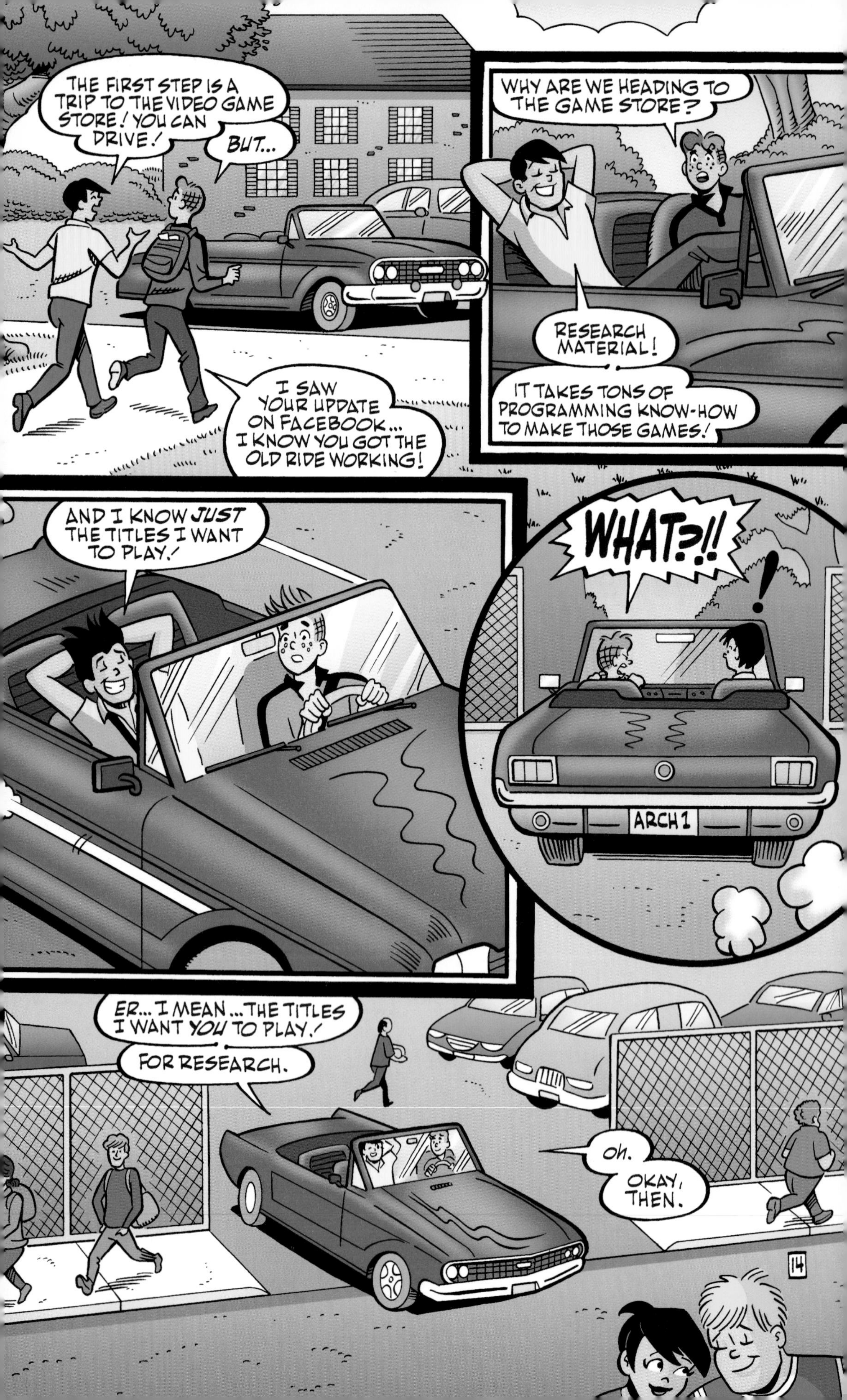
THE FIRST STEP IS A TRIP TO THE VIDEO GAME STORE! YOU CAN DRIVE!
BUT...
I SAW YOUR UPDATE ON FACEBOOK... I KNOW YOU GOT THE OLD RIDE WORKING!
WHY ARE WE HEADING TO THE GAME STORE?
RESEARCH MATERIAL!
IT TAKES TONS OF PROGRAMMING KNOW-HOW TO MAKE THOSE GAMES!
AND I KNOW JUST THE TITLES I WANT TO PLAY!
WHAT?!!
!
ARCH 1
ER... I MEAN ...THE TITLES I WANT YOU TO PLAY!
FOR RESEARCH.
oh.
OKAY, THEN.
14

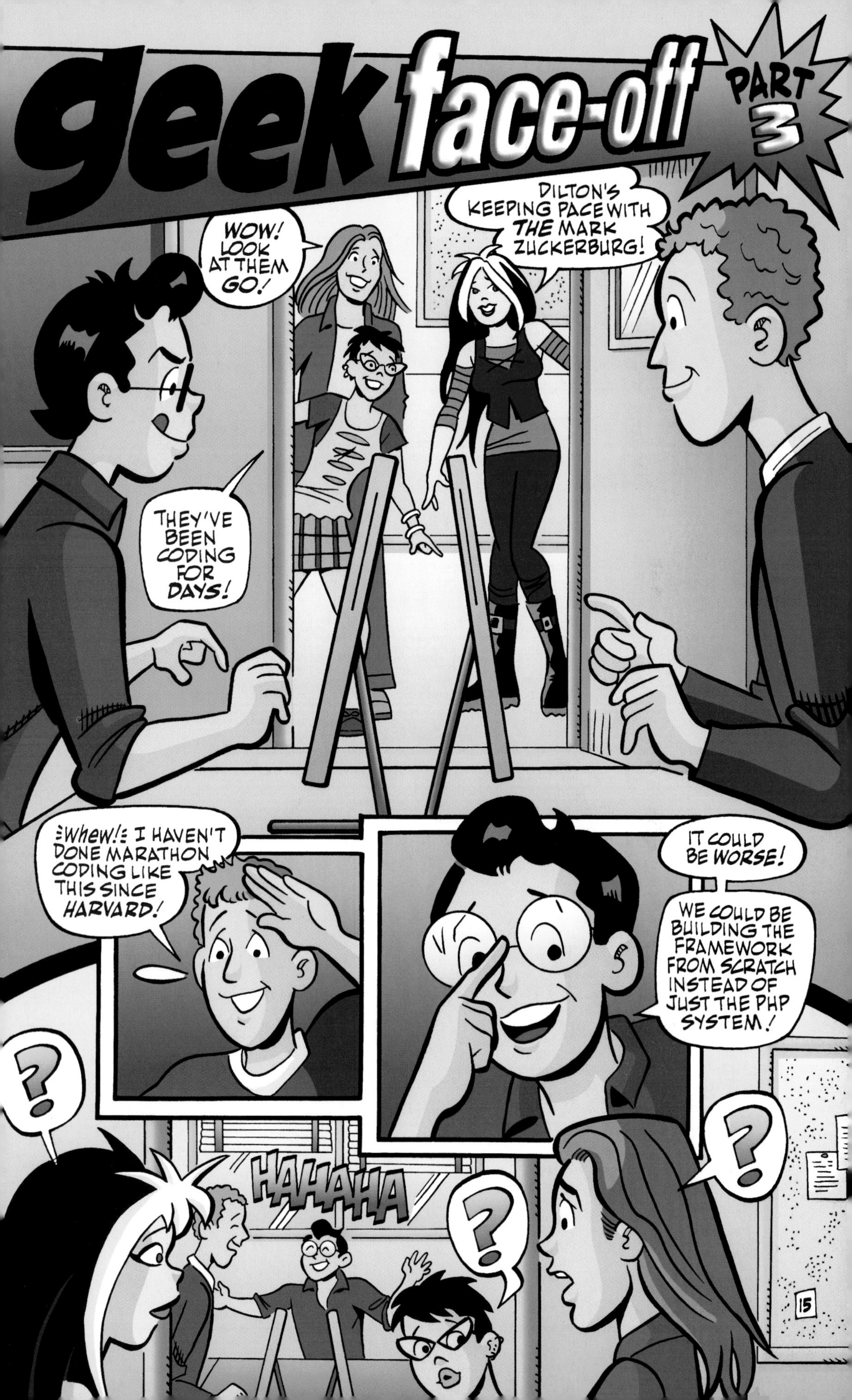
geek face-off
PART 3
WOW! LOOK AT THEM GO!
DILTON'S KEEPING PACE WITH THE MARK ZUCKERBURG!
THEY'VE BEEN CODING FOR DAYS!
whew! I HAVEN'T DONE MARATHON CODING LIKE THIS SINCE HARVARD!
IT COULD BE WORSE!
WE COULD BE BUILDING THE FRAMEWORK FROM SCRATCH INSTEAD OF JUST THE PHP SYSTEM!
HAHAHA
?
?
?
15

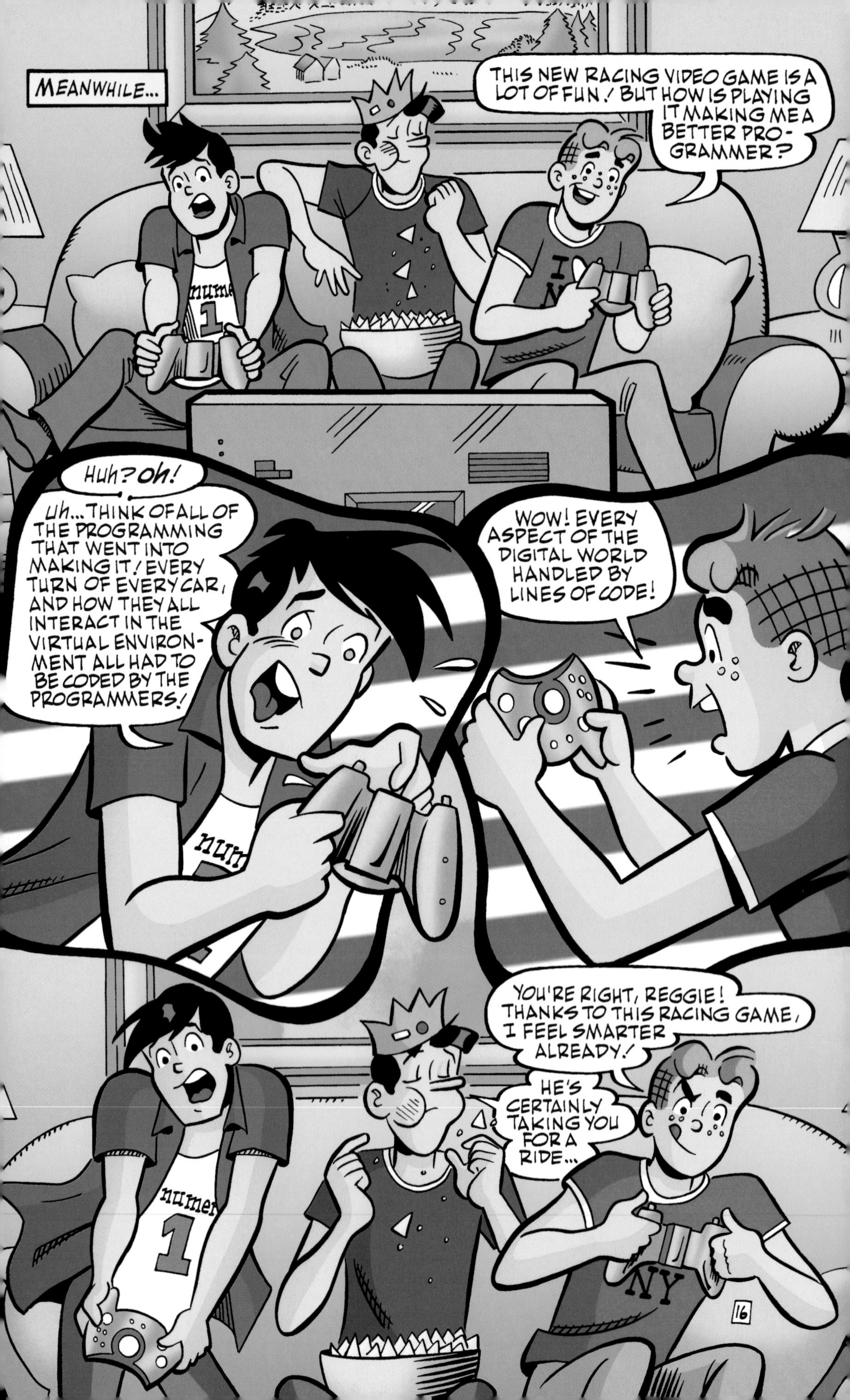
MEANWHILE...
THIS NEW RACING VIDEO GAME IS A LOT OF FUN! BUT HOW IS PLAYING IT MAKING ME A BETTER PRO-GRAMMER?
HUH? OH!
UH... THINK OF ALL OF THE PROGRAMMING THAT WENT INTO MAKING IT! EVERY TURN OF EVERY CAR, AND HOW THEY ALL INTERACT IN THE VIRTUAL ENVIRON-MENT ALL HAD TO BE CODED BY THE PROGRAMMERS!
WOW! EVERY ASPECT OF THE DIGITAL WORLD HANDLED BY LINES OF CODE!
YOU'RE RIGHT, REGGIE! THANKS TO THIS RACING GAME, I FEEL SMARTER ALREADY!
HE'S CERTAINLY TAKING YOU FOR A RIDE...
16

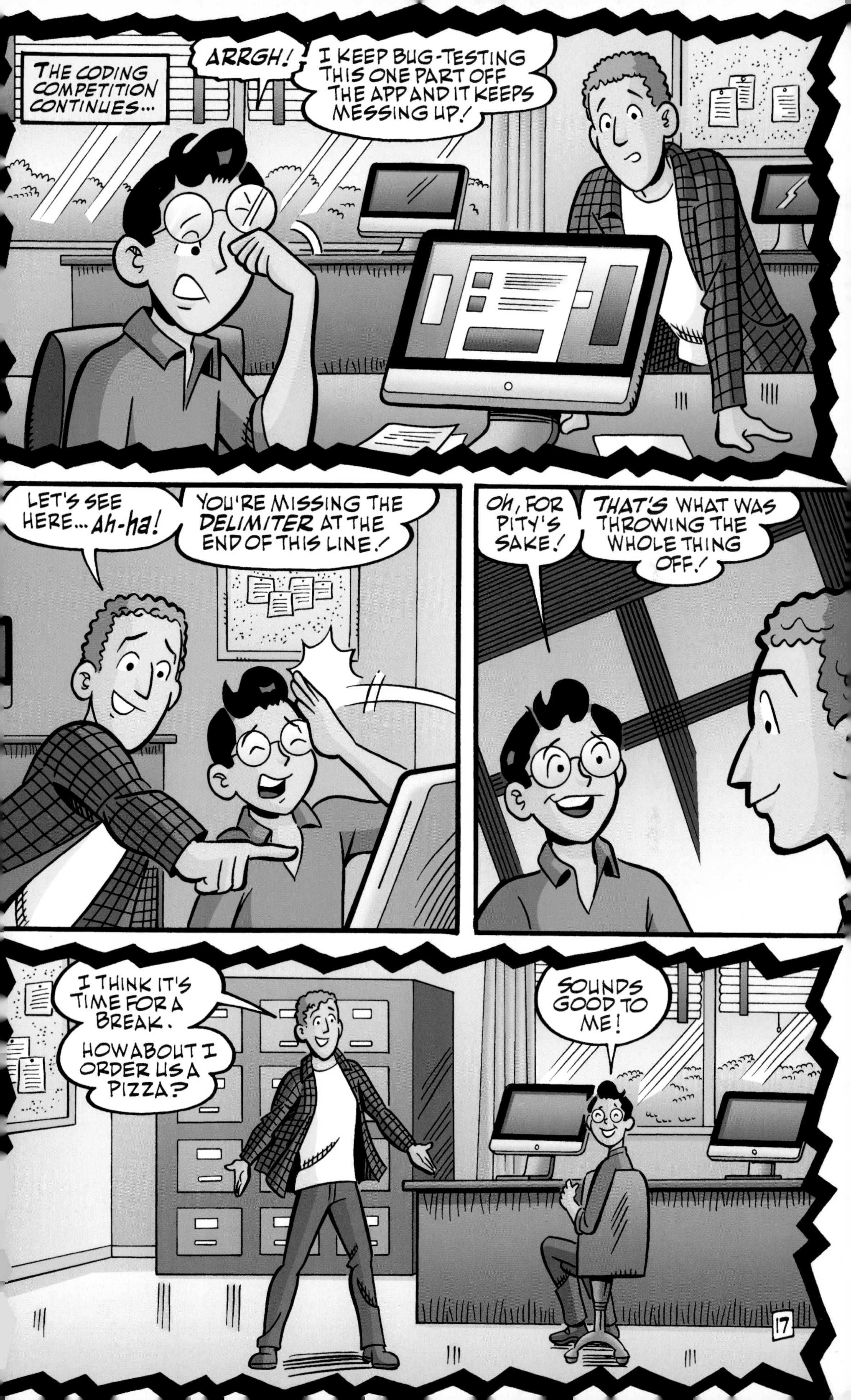
THE CODING COMPETITION CONTINUES...
ARRGH!
I KEEP BUG-TESTING THIS ONE PART OFF THE APP AND IT KEEPS MESSING UP!
LET'S SEE HERE... Ah-ha!
YOU'RE MISSING THE DELIMITER AT THE END OF THIS LINE!
Oh, FOR PITY'S SAKE!
THAT'S WHAT WAS THROWING THE WHOLE THING OFF!
I THINK IT'S TIME FOR A BREAK.
HOW ABOUT I ORDER US A PIZZA?
SOUNDS GOOD TO ME!
17

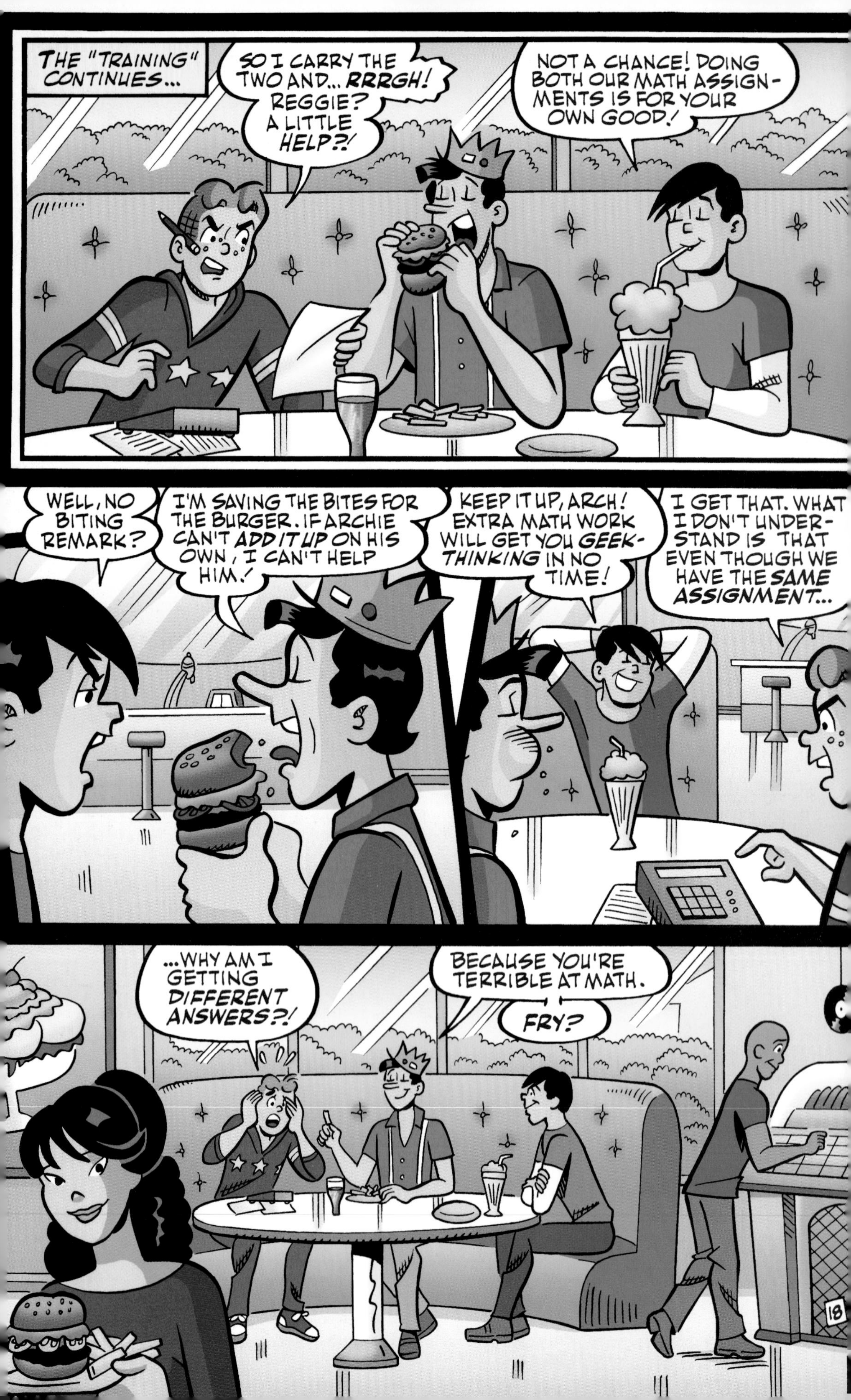
THE "TRAINING" CONTINUES...
SO I CARRY THE TWO AND... RRRGH! REGGIE? A LITTLE HELP?!
NOT A CHANCE! DOING BOTH OUR MATH ASSIGNMENTS IS FOR YOUR OWN GOOD!
WELL, NO BITING REMARK?
I'M SAVING THE BITES FOR THE BURGER. IF ARCHIE CAN'T ADD IT UP ON HIS OWN, I CAN'T HELP HIM!
KEEP IT UP, ARCH! EXTRA MATH WORK WILL GET YOU GEEK-THINKING IN NO TIME!
I GET THAT. WHAT I DON'T UNDERSTAND IS THAT EVEN THOUGH WE HAVE THE SAME ASSIGNMENT...
...WHY AM I GETTING DIFFERENT ANSWERS?!
BECAUSE YOU'RE TERRIBLE AT MATH.
FRY?
18

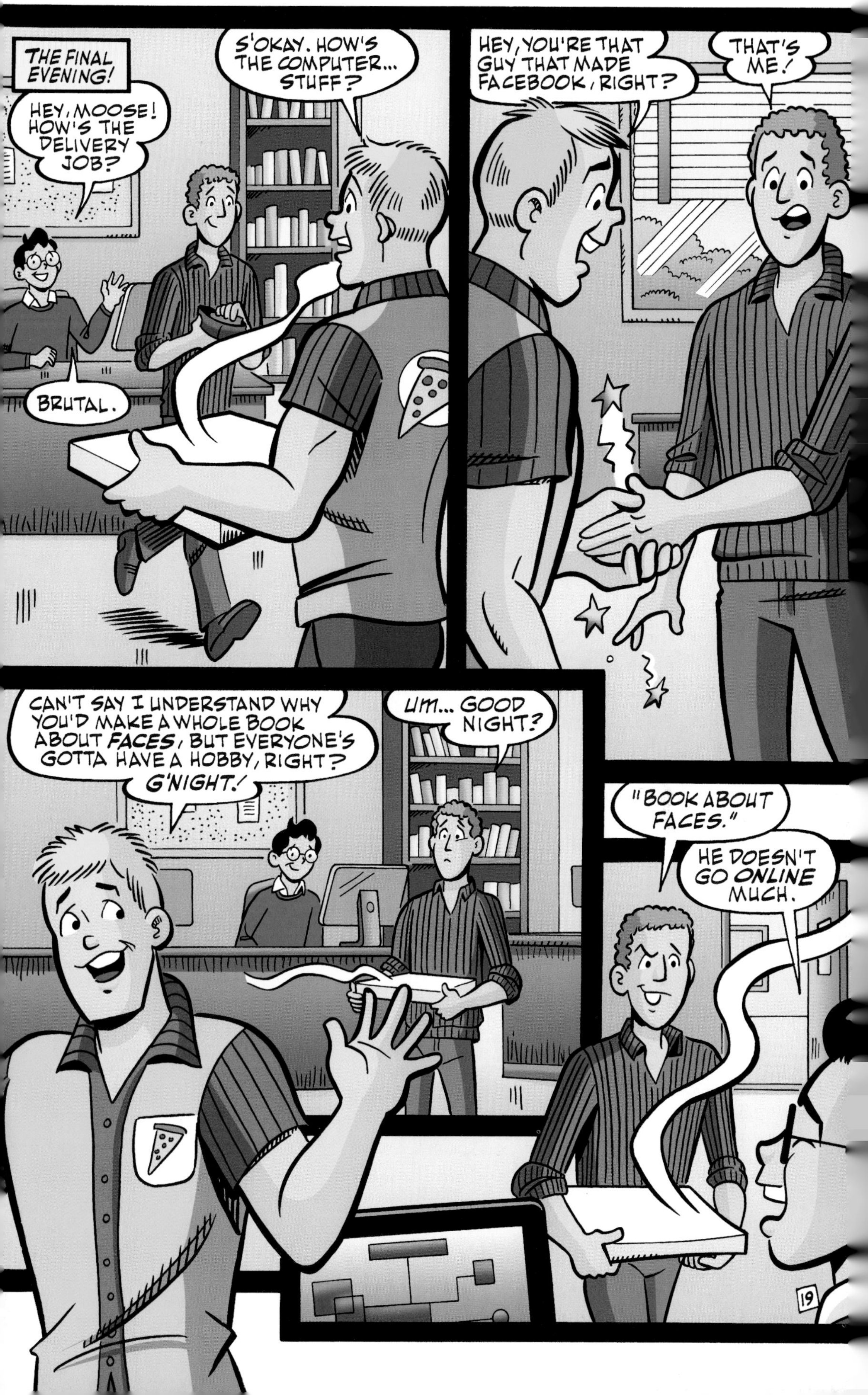
THE FINAL EVENING!
HEY, MOOSE! HOW'S THE DELIVERY JOB?
BRUTAL.
S'OKAY. HOW'S THE COMPUTER... STUFF?
HEY, YOU'RE THAT GUY THAT MADE FACEBOOK, RIGHT?
THAT'S ME!
CAN'T SAY I UNDERSTAND WHY YOU'D MAKE A WHOLE BOOK ABOUT FACES, BUT EVERYONE'S GOTTA HAVE A HOBBY, RIGHT? G'NIGHT!
UM... GOOD NIGHT?
"BOOK ABOUT FACES."
HE DOESN'T GO ONLINE MUCH.
19

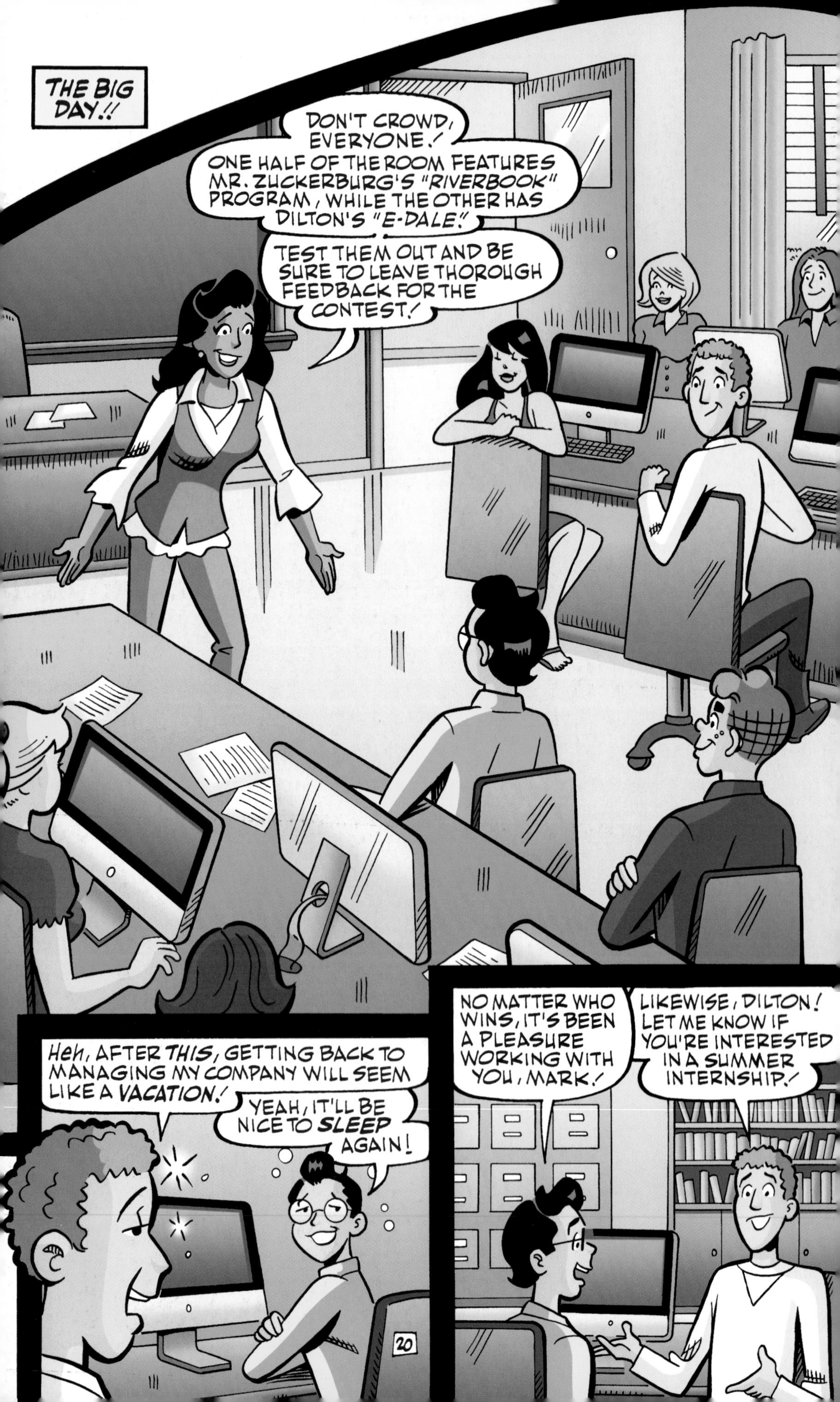
THE BIG DAY!!
DON'T CROWD, EVERYONE! ONE HALF OF THE ROOM FEATURES MR. ZUCKERBURG'S "RIVERBOOK" PROGRAM, WHILE THE OTHER HAS DILTON'S "E-DALE!"
TEST THEM OUT AND BE SURE TO LEAVE THOROUGH FEEDBACK FOR THE CONTEST!
Heh, AFTER THIS, GETTING BACK TO MANAGING MY COMPANY WILL SEEM LIKE A VACATION!
YEAH, IT'LL BE NICE TO SLEEP AGAIN!
NO MATTER WHO WINS, IT'S BEEN A PLEASURE WORKING WITH YOU, MARK!
LIKEWISE, DILTON! LET ME KNOW IF YOU'RE INTERESTED IN A SUMMER INTERNSHIP!
20

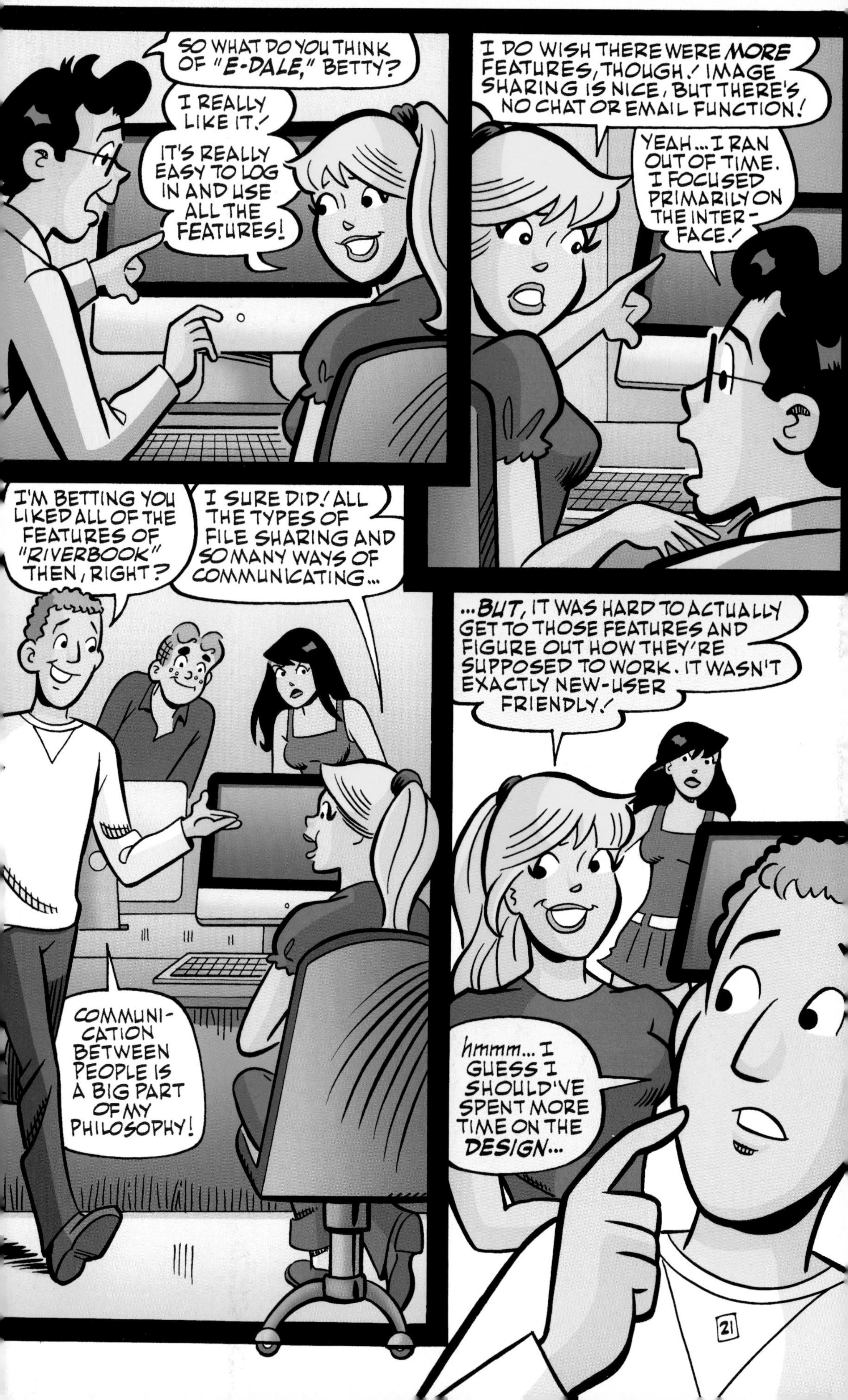
SO WHAT DO YOU THINK OF "E-DALE," BETTY?
I REALLY LIKE IT!
IT'S REALLY EASY TO LOG IN AND USE ALL THE FEATURES!
I DO WISH THERE WERE MORE FEATURES, THOUGH! IMAGE SHARING IS NICE, BUT THERE'S NO CHAT OR EMAIL FUNCTION!
YEAH... I RAN OUT OF TIME. I FOCUSED PRIMARILY ON THE INTER-FACE!
I'M BETTING YOU LIKED ALL OF THE FEATURES OF "RIVERBOOK" THEN, RIGHT?
I SURE DID! ALL THE TYPES OF FILE SHARING AND SO MANY WAYS OF COMMUNICATING...
COMMUNI-CATION BETWEEN PEOPLE IS A BIG PART OF MY PHILOSOPHY!
...BUT, IT WAS HARD TO ACTUALLY GET TO THOSE FEATURES AND FIGURE OUT HOW THEY'RE SUPPOSED TO WORK. IT WASN'T EXACTLY NEW-USER FRIENDLY!
hmmm... I GUESS I SHOULD'VE SPENT MORE TIME ON THE DESIGN...
21

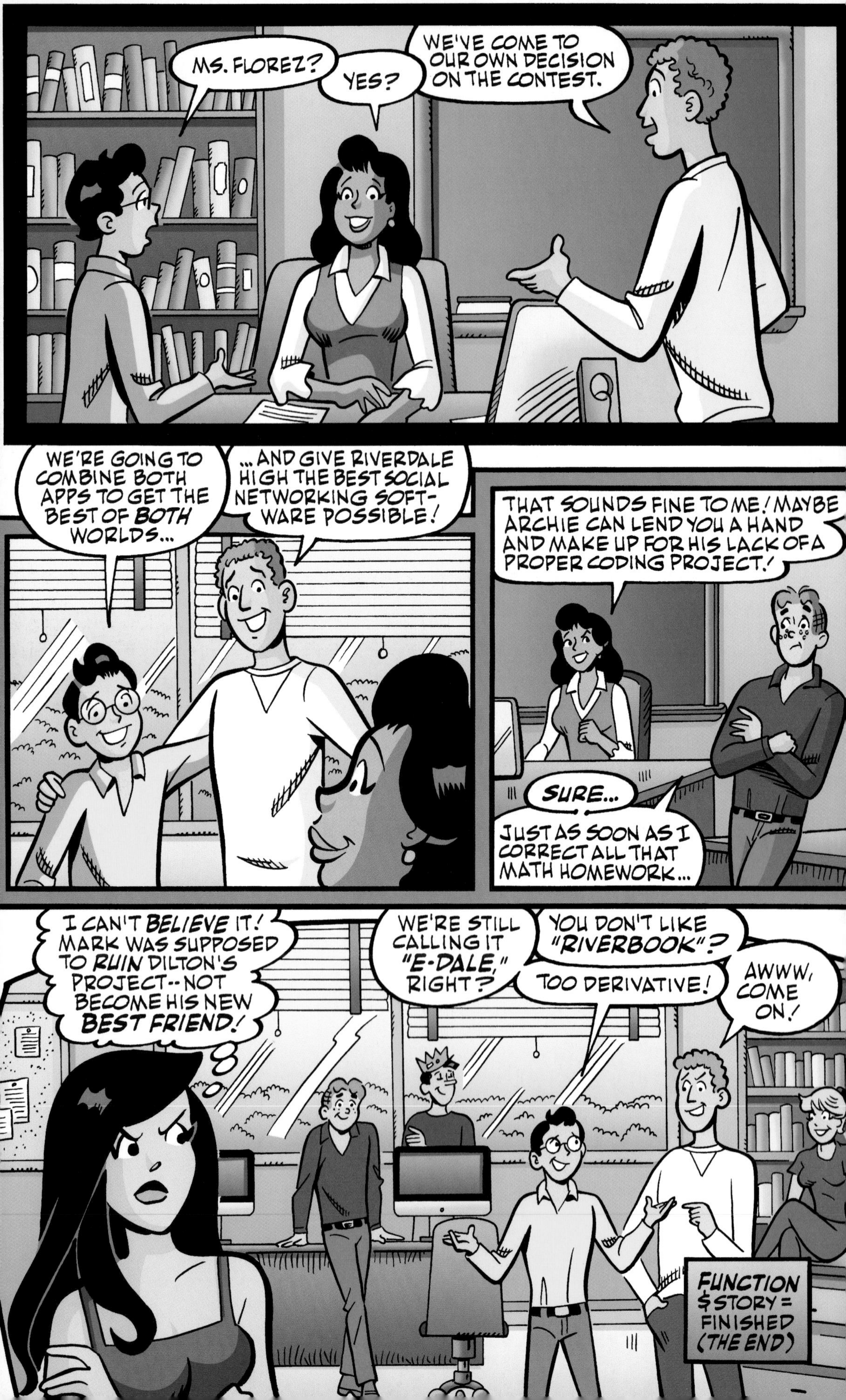
MS. FLOREZ?
YES?
WE'VE COME TO OUR OWN DECISION ON THE CONTEST.
WE'RE GOING TO COMBINE BOTH APPS TO GET THE BEST OF BOTH WORLDS...
...AND GIVE RIVERDALE HIGH THE BEST SOCIAL NETWORKING SOFT-WARE POSSIBLE!
THAT SOUNDS FINE TO ME! MAYBE ARCHIE CAN LEND YOU A HAND AND MAKE UP FOR HIS LACK OF A PROPER CODING PROJECT!
SURE...
JUST AS SOON AS I CORRECT ALL THAT MATH HOMEWORK...
I CAN'T BELIEVE IT! MARK WAS SUPPOSED TO RUIN DILTON'S PROJECT--NOT BECOME HIS NEW BEST FRIEND!
WE'RE STILL CALLING IT "E-DALE," RIGHT?
YOU DON'T LIKE "RIVERBOOK"?
TOO DERIVATIVE!
AWWW, COME ON!
FUNCTION $ STORY = FINISHED (THE END)

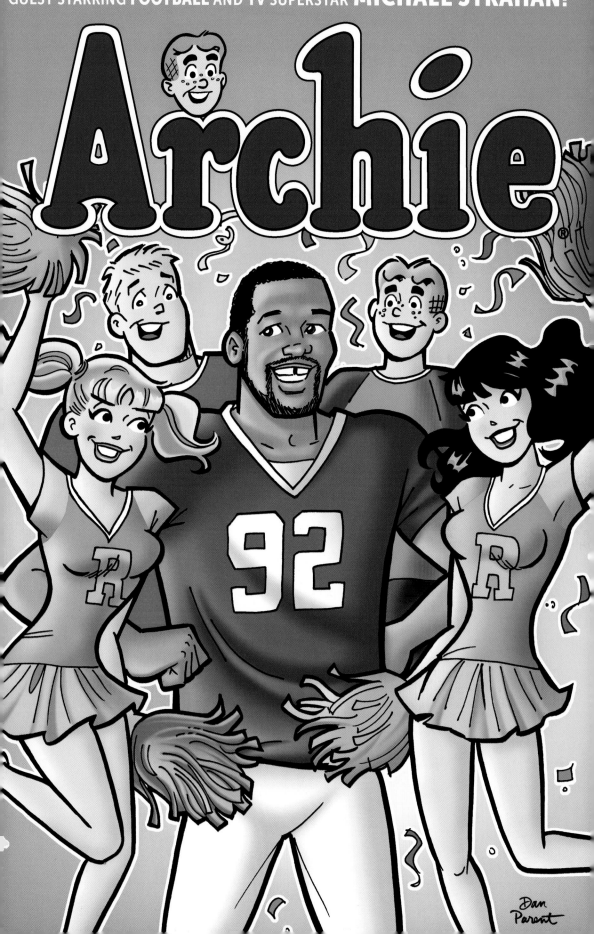

GUEST STARRING **FOOTBALL** AND **TV** SUPERSTAR **MICHAEL STRAHAN!**

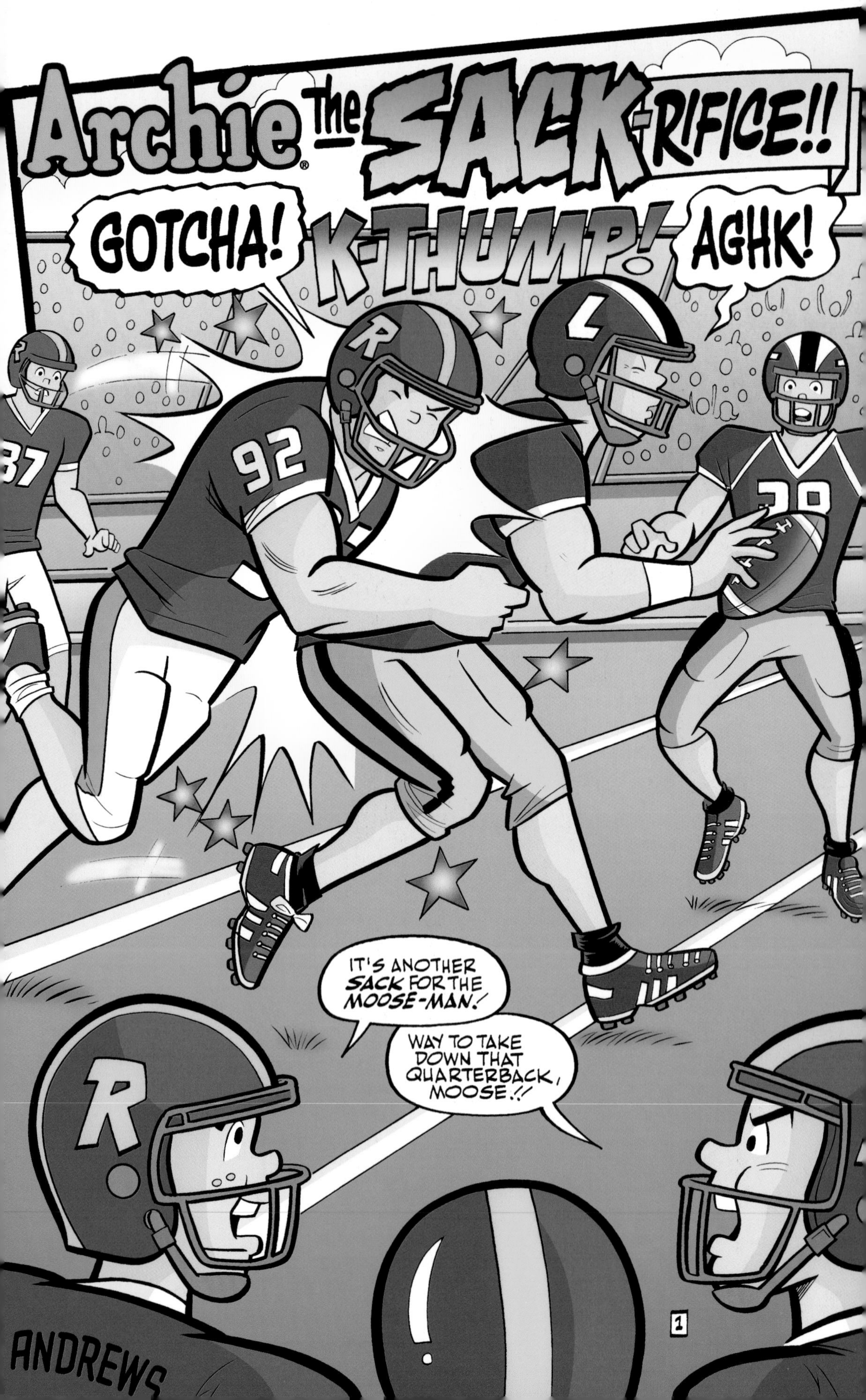
Archie
The SACK-RIFICE!!
GOTCHA!
K-THUMP!
AGHK!
IT'S ANOTHER SACK FOR THE MOOSE-MAN!
WAY TO TAKE DOWN THAT QUARTERBACK, MOOSE!!
1
ANDREWS

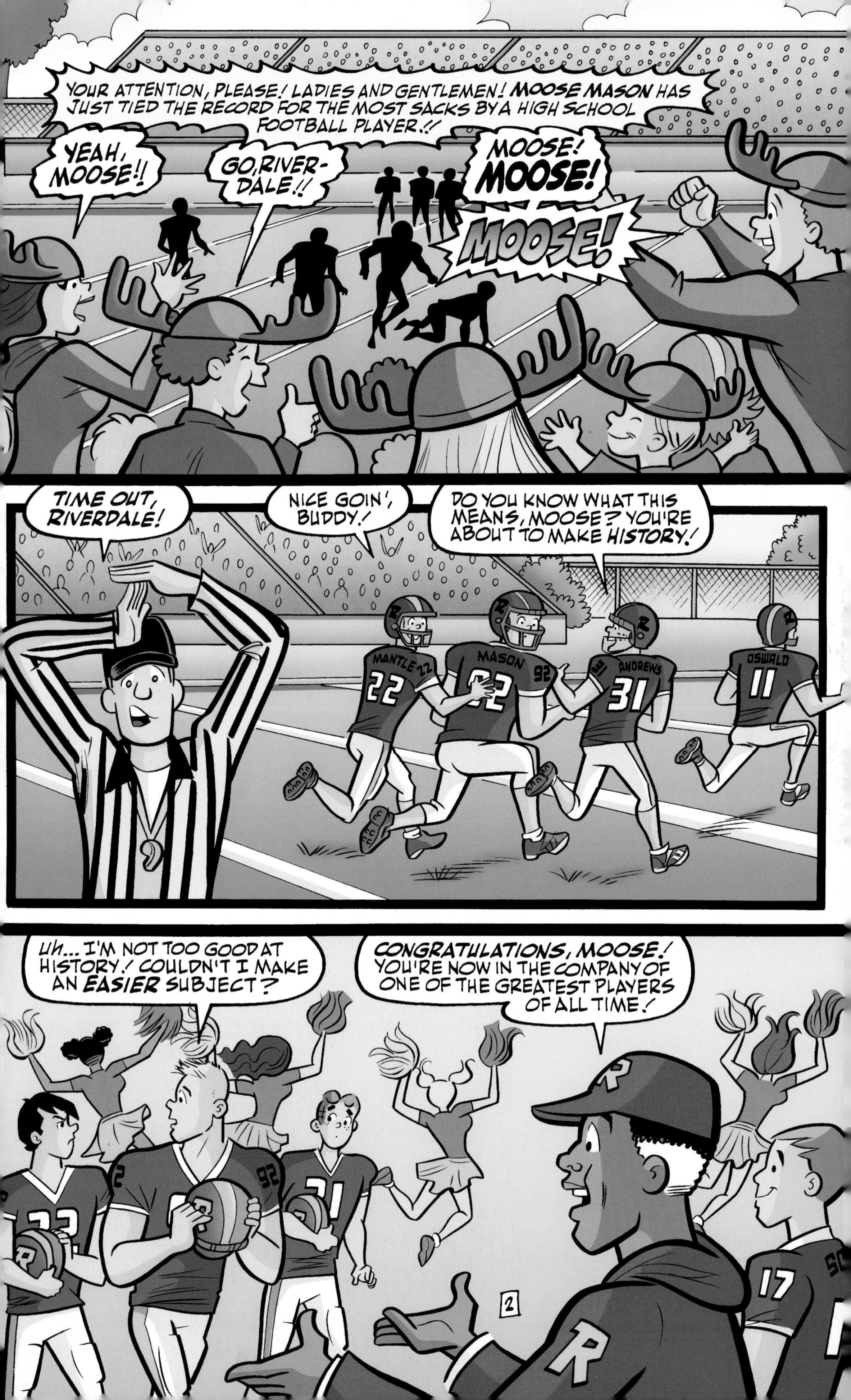
YOUR ATTENTION, PLEASE! LADIES AND GENTLEMEN! MOOSE MASON HAS JUST TIED THE RECORD FOR THE MOST SACKS BY A HIGH SCHOOL FOOTBALL PLAYER!!
YEAH, MOOSE!!
GO, RIVER-DALE!!
MOOSE! MOOSE!
MOOSE!
TIME OUT, RIVERDALE!
NICE GOIN', BUDDY!
DO YOU KNOW WHAT THIS MEANS, MOOSE? YOU'RE ABOUT TO MAKE HISTORY!
MANTLE 22
MASON
ANDREWS 31
OSWALD 11
UH... I'M NOT TOO GOOD AT HISTORY! COULDN'T I MAKE AN EASIER SUBJECT?
CONGRATULATIONS, MOOSE! YOU'RE NOW IN THE COMPANY OF ONE OF THE GREATEST PLAYERS OF ALL TIME!

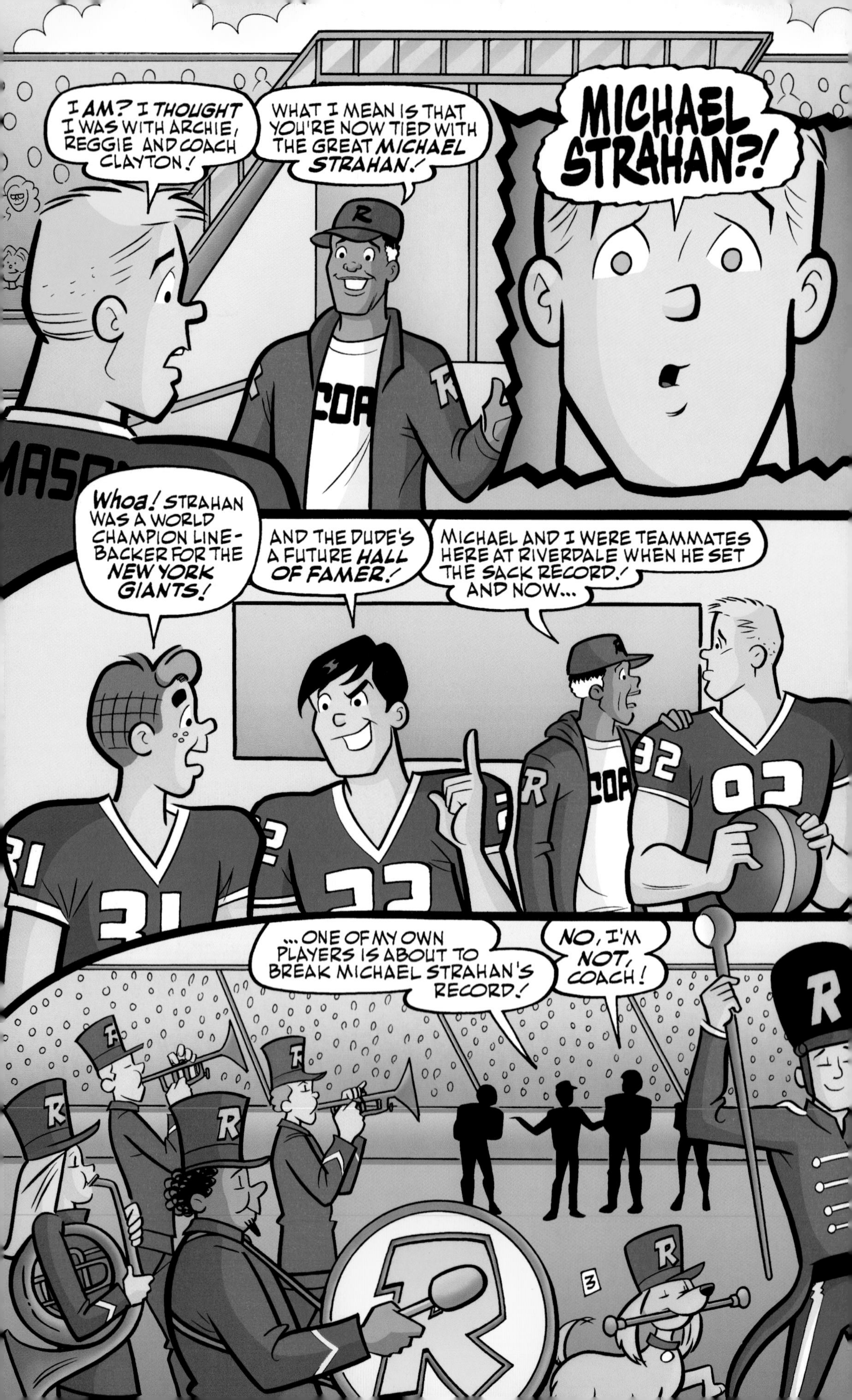
I AM? I THOUGHT I WAS WITH ARCHIE, REGGIE AND COACH CLAYTON!
WHAT I MEAN IS THAT YOU'RE NOW TIED WITH THE GREAT MICHAEL STRAHAN!
MICHAEL STRAHAN?!
Whoa! STRAHAN WAS A WORLD CHAMPION LINE-BACKER FOR THE NEW YORK GIANTS!
AND THE DUDE'S A FUTURE HALL OF FAMER!
MICHAEL AND I WERE TEAMMATES HERE AT RIVERDALE WHEN HE SET THE SACK RECORD! AND NOW...
...ONE OF MY OWN PLAYERS IS ABOUT TO BREAK MICHAEL STRAHAN'S RECORD!
NO, I'M NOT, COACH!
3

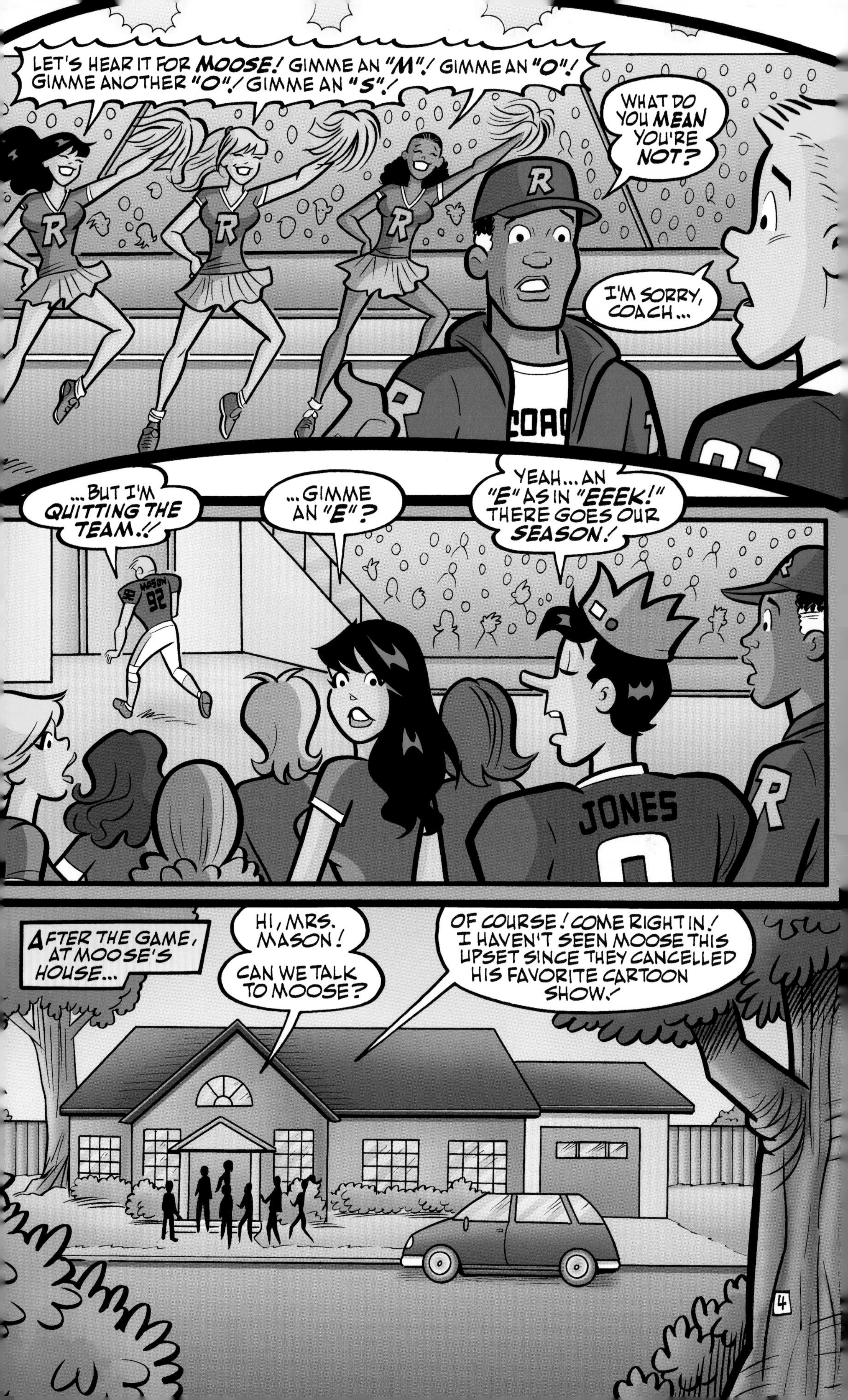
LET'S HEAR IT FOR MOOSE! GIMME AN "M"! GIMME AN "O"! GIMME ANOTHER "O"! GIMME AN "S"!
WHAT DO YOU MEAN YOU'RE NOT?
I'M SORRY, COACH...
COAC
...BUT I'M QUITTING THE TEAM.!!
...GIMME AN "E"?
YEAH...AN "E" AS IN "EEEK!" THERE GOES OUR SEASON!
MASON
92
JONES
AFTER THE GAME, AT MOOSE'S HOUSE...
HI, MRS. MASON!
CAN WE TALK TO MOOSE?
OF COURSE! COME RIGHT IN! I HAVEN'T SEEN MOOSE THIS UPSET SINCE THEY CANCELLED HIS FAVORITE CARTOON SHOW!
4

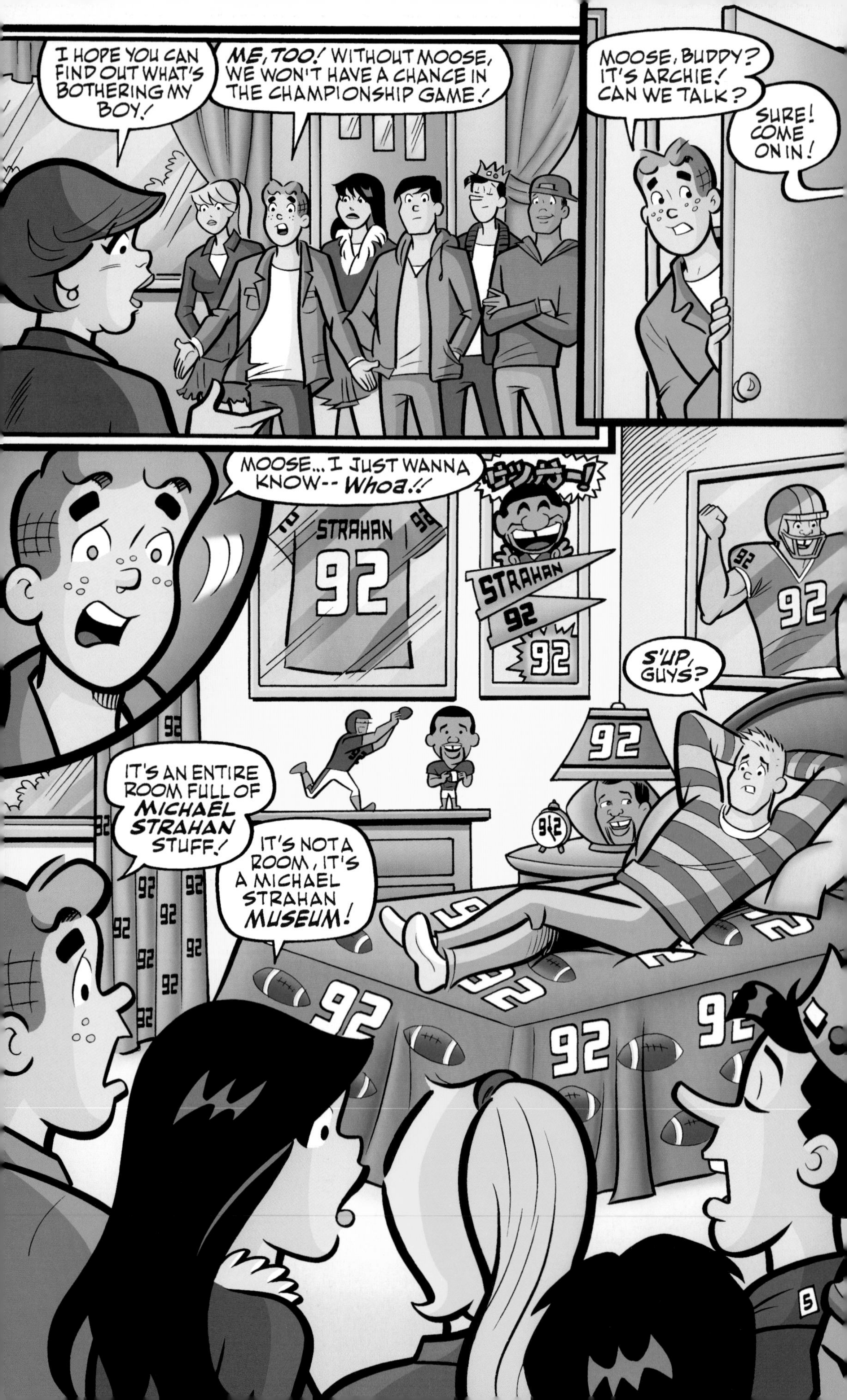
I HOPE YOU CAN FIND OUT WHAT'S BOTHERING MY BOY!
ME, TOO! WITHOUT MOOSE, WE WON'T HAVE A CHANCE IN THE CHAMPIONSHIP GAME!
MOOSE, BUDDY? IT'S ARCHIE! CAN WE TALK?
SURE! COME ON IN!
MOOSE... I JUST WANNA KNOW-- Whoa!!
STRAHAN
92
STRAHAN
92
92
S'UP, GUYS?
92
92
IT'S AN ENTIRE ROOM FULL OF MICHAEL STRAHAN STUFF!
IT'S NOT A ROOM, IT'S A MICHAEL STRAHAN MUSEUM!
5

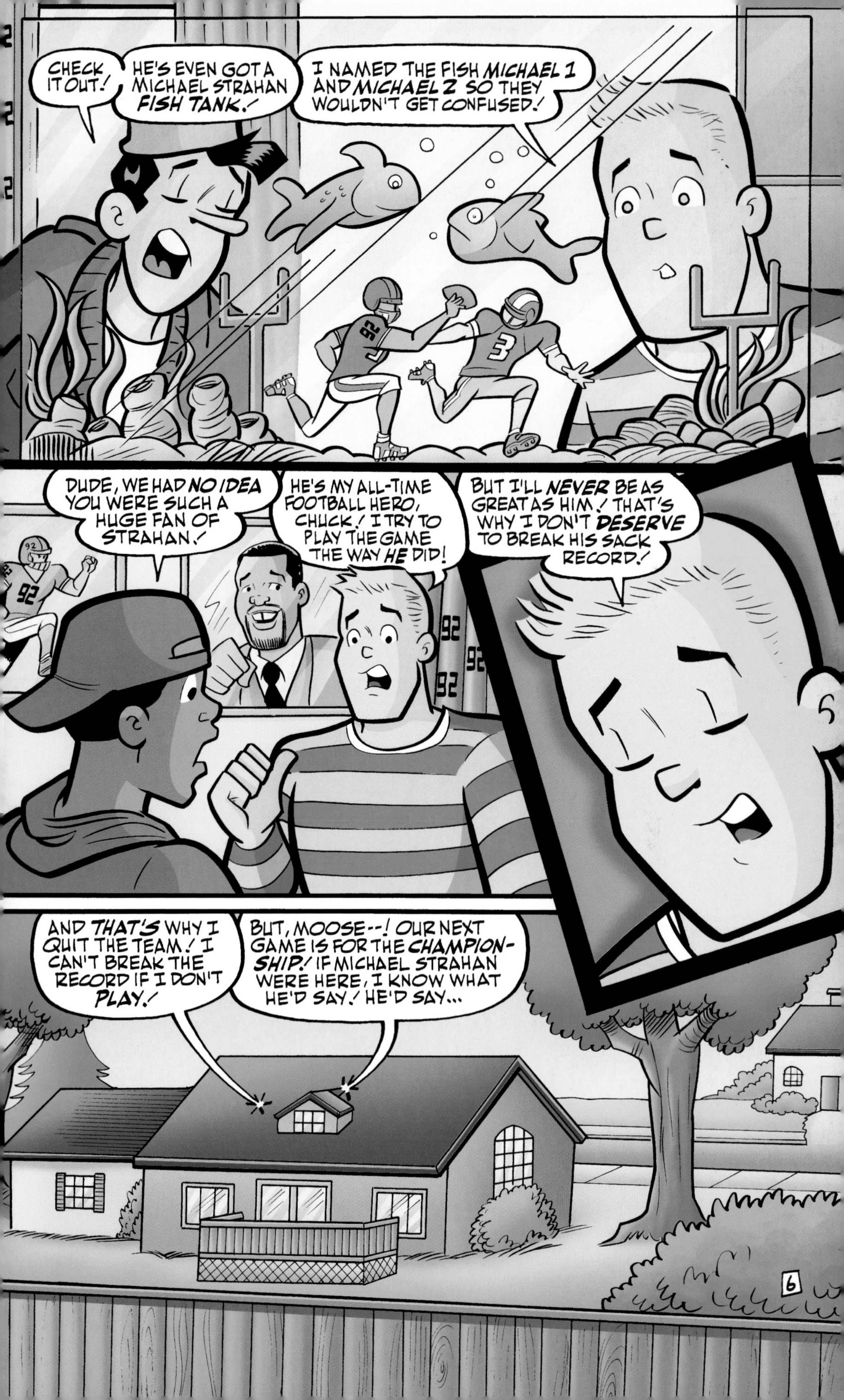
CHECK IT OUT!
HE'S EVEN GOT A MICHAEL STRAHAN FISH TANK!
I NAMED THE FISH MICHAEL 1 AND MICHAEL 2 SO THEY WOULDN'T GET CONFUSED!
DUDE, WE HAD NO IDEA YOU WERE SUCH A HUGE FAN OF STRAHAN!
HE'S MY ALL-TIME FOOTBALL HERO, CHUCK! I TRY TO PLAY THE GAME THE WAY HE DID!
BUT I'LL NEVER BE AS GREAT AS HIM! THAT'S WHY I DON'T DESERVE TO BREAK HIS SACK RECORD!
AND THAT'S WHY I QUIT THE TEAM! I CAN'T BREAK THE RECORD IF I DON'T PLAY!
BUT, MOOSE--! OUR NEXT GAME IS FOR THE CHAMPIONSHIP! IF MICHAEL STRAHAN WERE HERE, I KNOW WHAT HE'D SAY! HE'D SAY...

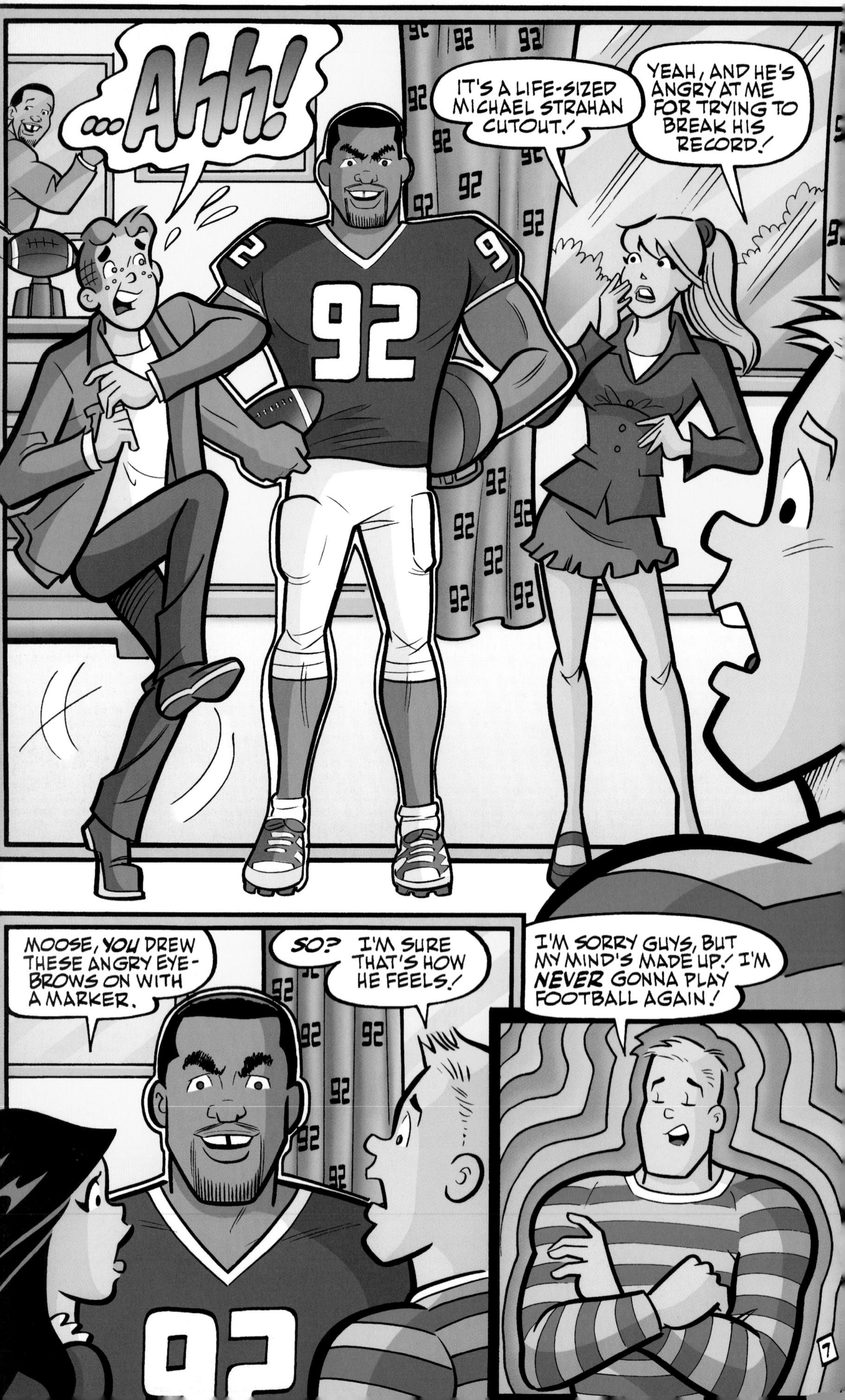
...Ahh!
IT'S A LIFE-SIZED MICHAEL STRAHAN CUTOUT!
YEAH, AND HE'S ANGRY AT ME FOR TRYING TO BREAK HIS RECORD!
MOOSE, YOU DREW THESE ANGRY EYE-BROWS ON WITH A MARKER.
SO? I'M SURE THAT'S HOW HE FEELS!
I'M SORRY GUYS, BUT MY MIND'S MADE UP! I'M NEVER GONNA PLAY FOOTBALL AGAIN!

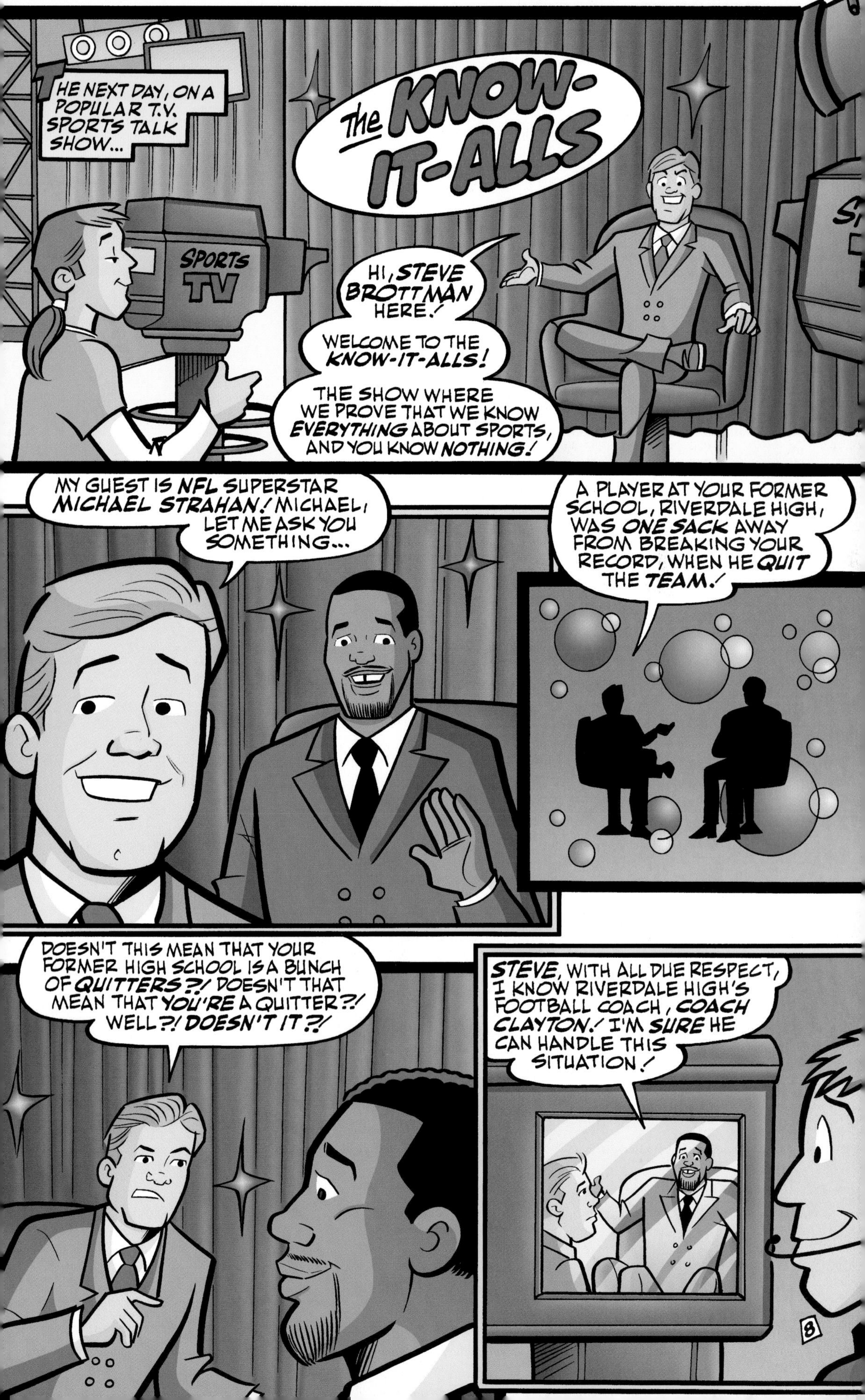
THE NEXT DAY, ON A POPULAR T.V. SPORTS TALK SHOW...
The KNOW-IT-ALLS
SPORTS TV
HI, STEVE BROTTMAN HERE!
WELCOME TO THE KNOW-IT-ALLS!
THE SHOW WHERE WE PROVE THAT WE KNOW EVERYTHING ABOUT SPORTS, AND YOU KNOW NOTHING!
MY GUEST IS NFL SUPERSTAR MICHAEL STRAHAN! MICHAEL, LET ME ASK YOU SOMETHING...
A PLAYER AT YOUR FORMER SCHOOL, RIVERDALE HIGH, WAS ONE SACK AWAY FROM BREAKING YOUR RECORD, WHEN HE QUIT THE TEAM!
DOESN'T THIS MEAN THAT YOUR FORMER HIGH SCHOOL IS A BUNCH OF QUITTERS?! DOESN'T THAT MEAN THAT YOU'RE A QUITTER?! WELL?! DOESN'T IT?!
STEVE, WITH ALL DUE RESPECT, I KNOW RIVERDALE HIGH'S FOOTBALL COACH, COACH CLAYTON! I'M SURE HE CAN HANDLE THIS SITUATION!
8

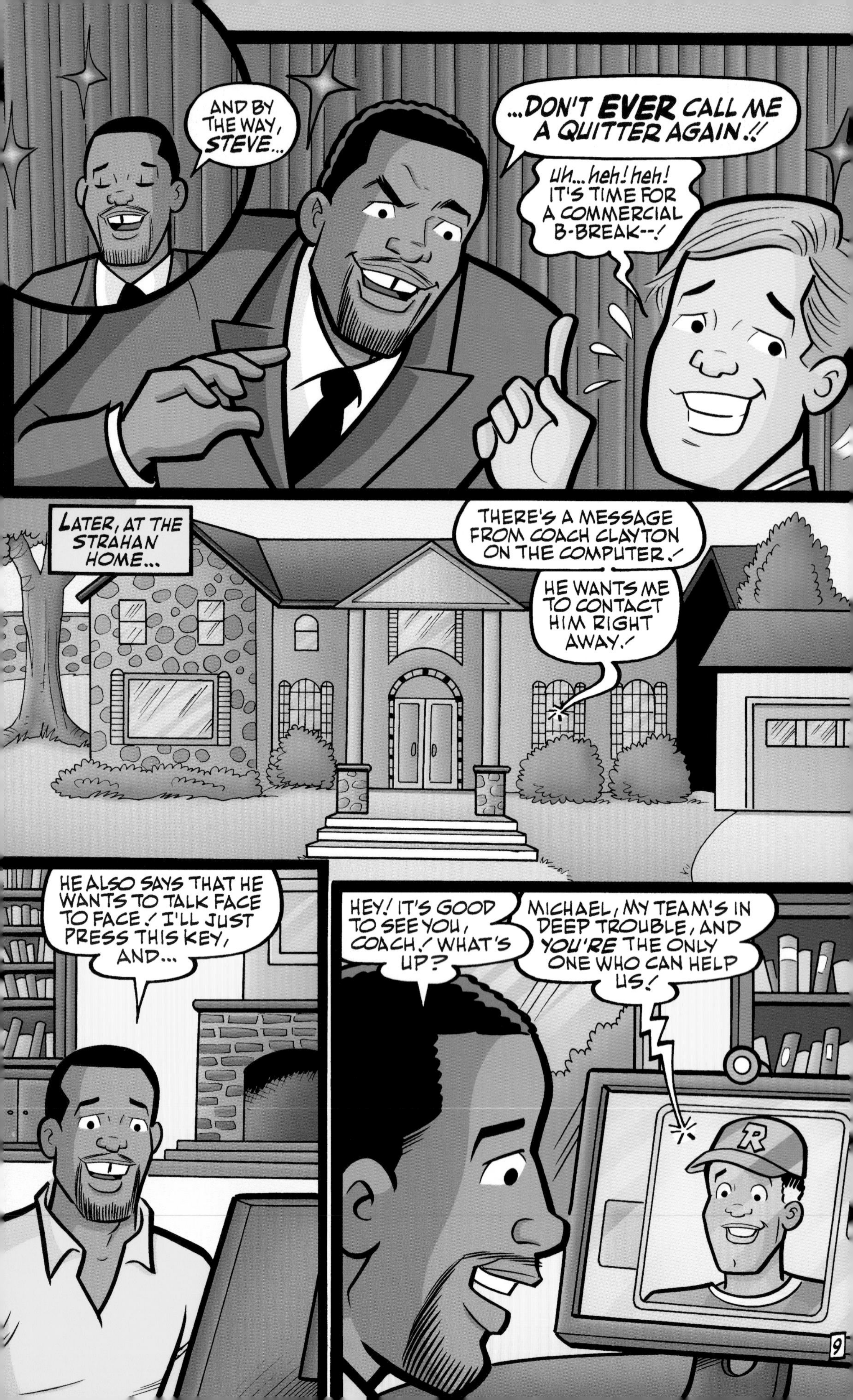
AND BY THE WAY, STEVE...
...DON'T EVER CALL ME A QUITTER AGAIN.!!
uh... heh! heh! IT'S TIME FOR A COMMERCIAL B-BREAK--!
LATER, AT THE STRAHAN HOME...
THERE'S A MESSAGE FROM COACH CLAYTON ON THE COMPUTER.!
HE WANTS ME TO CONTACT HIM RIGHT AWAY.!
HE ALSO SAYS THAT HE WANTS TO TALK FACE TO FACE.! I'LL JUST PRESS THIS KEY, AND...
HEY! IT'S GOOD TO SEE YOU, COACH.! WHAT'S UP?
MICHAEL, MY TEAM'S IN DEEP TROUBLE, AND YOU'RE THE ONLY ONE WHO CAN HELP US.!
R

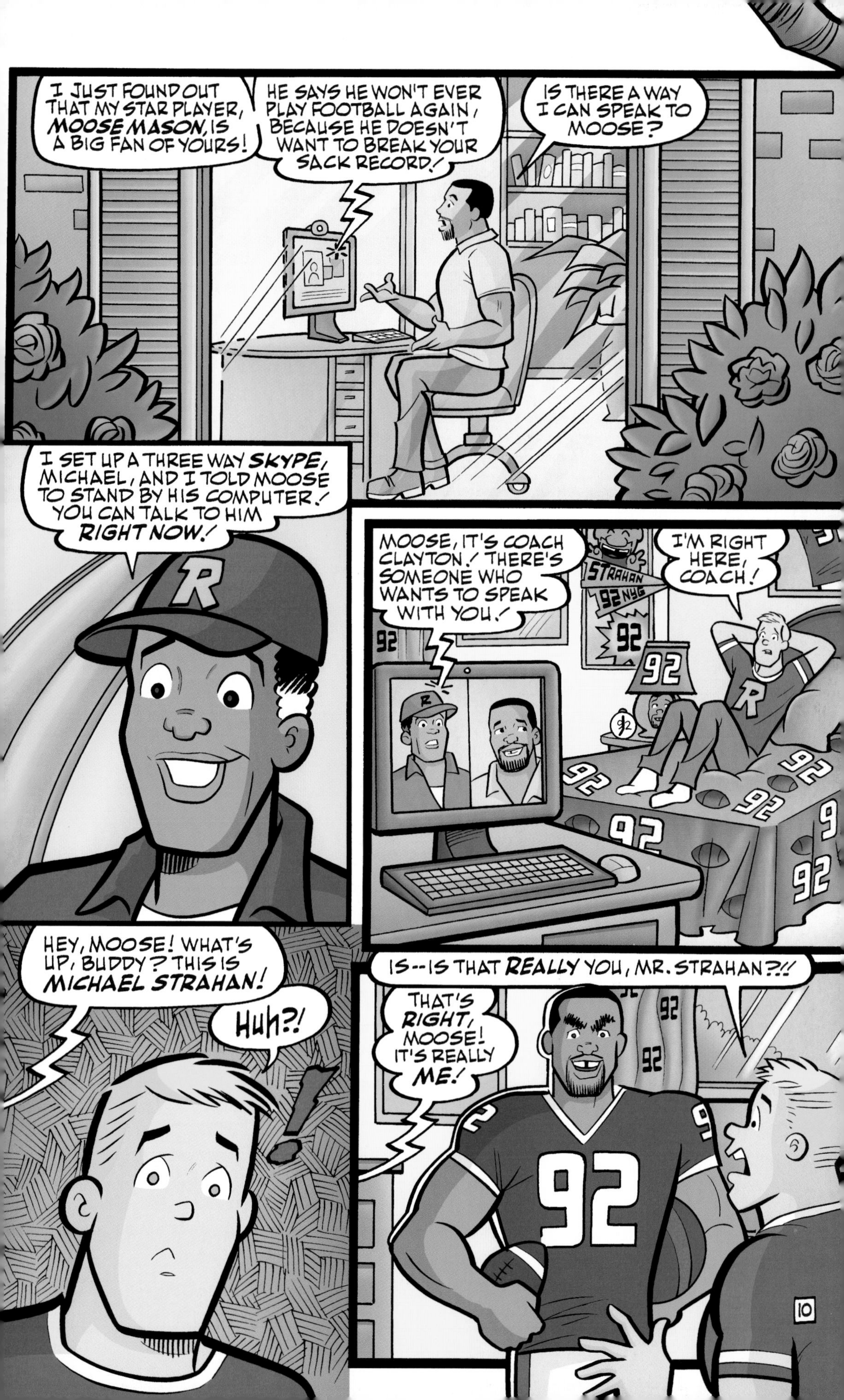
I JUST FOUND OUT THAT MY STAR PLAYER, MOOSE MASON, IS A BIG FAN OF YOURS!
HE SAYS HE WON'T EVER PLAY FOOTBALL AGAIN, BECAUSE HE DOESN'T WANT TO BREAK YOUR SACK RECORD!
IS THERE A WAY I CAN SPEAK TO MOOSE?
I SET UP A THREE WAY SKYPE, MICHAEL, AND I TOLD MOOSE TO STAND BY HIS COMPUTER! YOU CAN TALK TO HIM RIGHT NOW!
MOOSE, IT'S COACH CLAYTON! THERE'S SOMEONE WHO WANTS TO SPEAK WITH YOU!
I'M RIGHT HERE, COACH!
STRAHAN
92 NYG
HEY, MOOSE! WHAT'S UP, BUDDY? THIS IS MICHAEL STRAHAN!
Huh?!
IS--IS THAT REALLY YOU, MR. STRAHAN?!!
THAT'S RIGHT, MOOSE! IT'S REALLY ME!
10

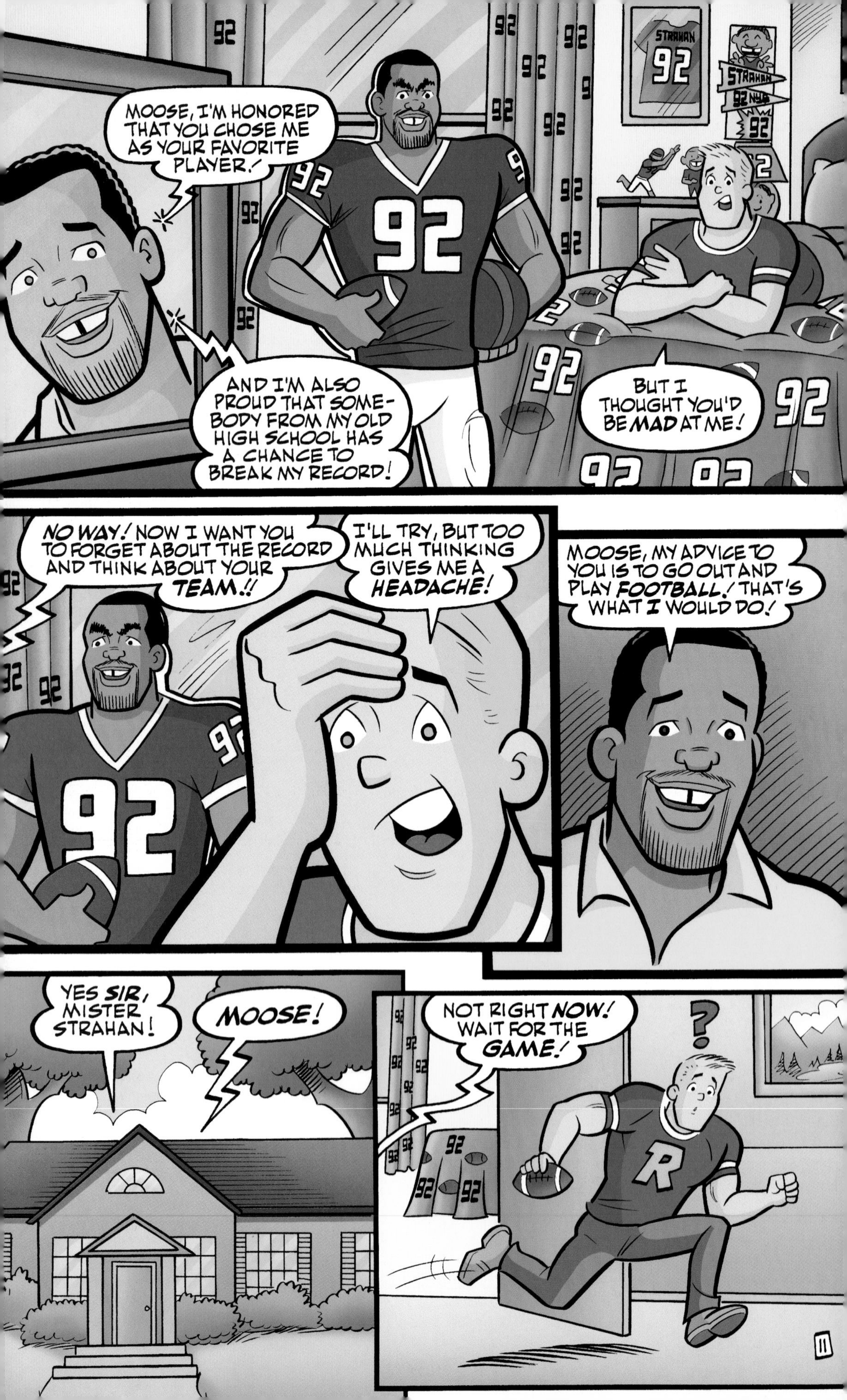
MOOSE, I'M HONORED THAT YOU CHOSE ME AS YOUR FAVORITE PLAYER!
AND I'M ALSO PROUD THAT SOMEBODY FROM MY OLD HIGH SCHOOL HAS A CHANCE TO BREAK MY RECORD!
BUT I THOUGHT YOU'D BE MAD AT ME!
NO WAY! NOW I WANT YOU TO FORGET ABOUT THE RECORD AND THINK ABOUT YOUR TEAM!!
I'LL TRY, BUT TOO MUCH THINKING GIVES ME A HEADACHE!
MOOSE, MY ADVICE TO YOU IS TO GO OUT AND PLAY FOOTBALL! THAT'S WHAT I WOULD DO!
YES SIR, MISTER STRAHAN!
MOOSE!
NOT RIGHT NOW! WAIT FOR THE GAME!
?

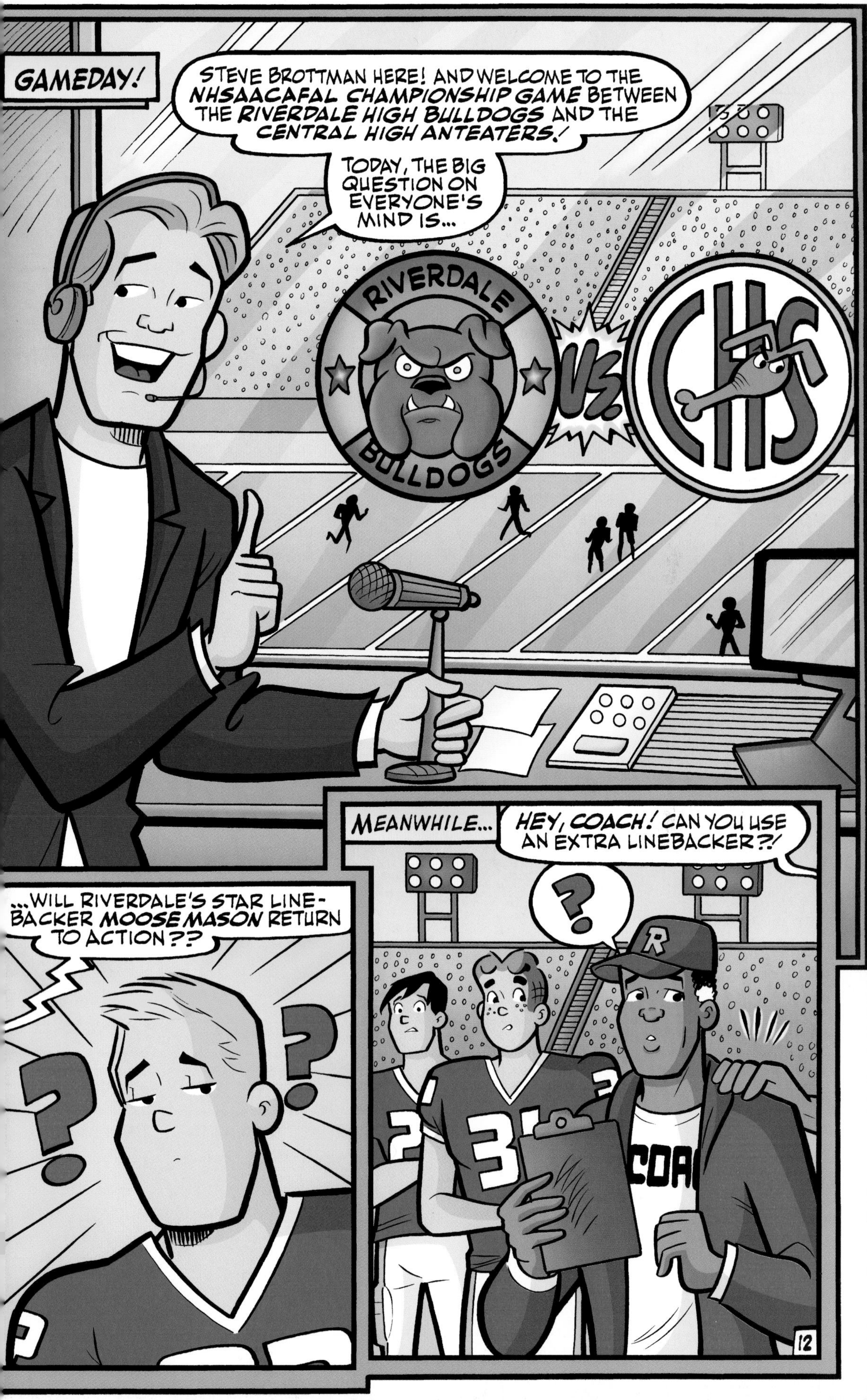
GAMEDAY!
STEVE BROTTMAN HERE! AND WELCOME TO THE NHSAACAFAL CHAMPIONSHIP GAME BETWEEN THE RIVERDALE HIGH BULLDOGS AND THE CENTRAL HIGH ANTEATERS!
TODAY, THE BIG QUESTION ON EVERYONE'S MIND IS...
RIVERDALE
BULLDOGS
VS.
CHS
...WILL RIVERDALE'S STAR LINE-BACKER MOOSE MASON RETURN TO ACTION??
MEANWHILE...
HEY, COACH! CAN YOU USE AN EXTRA LINEBACKER?!
?
COAC

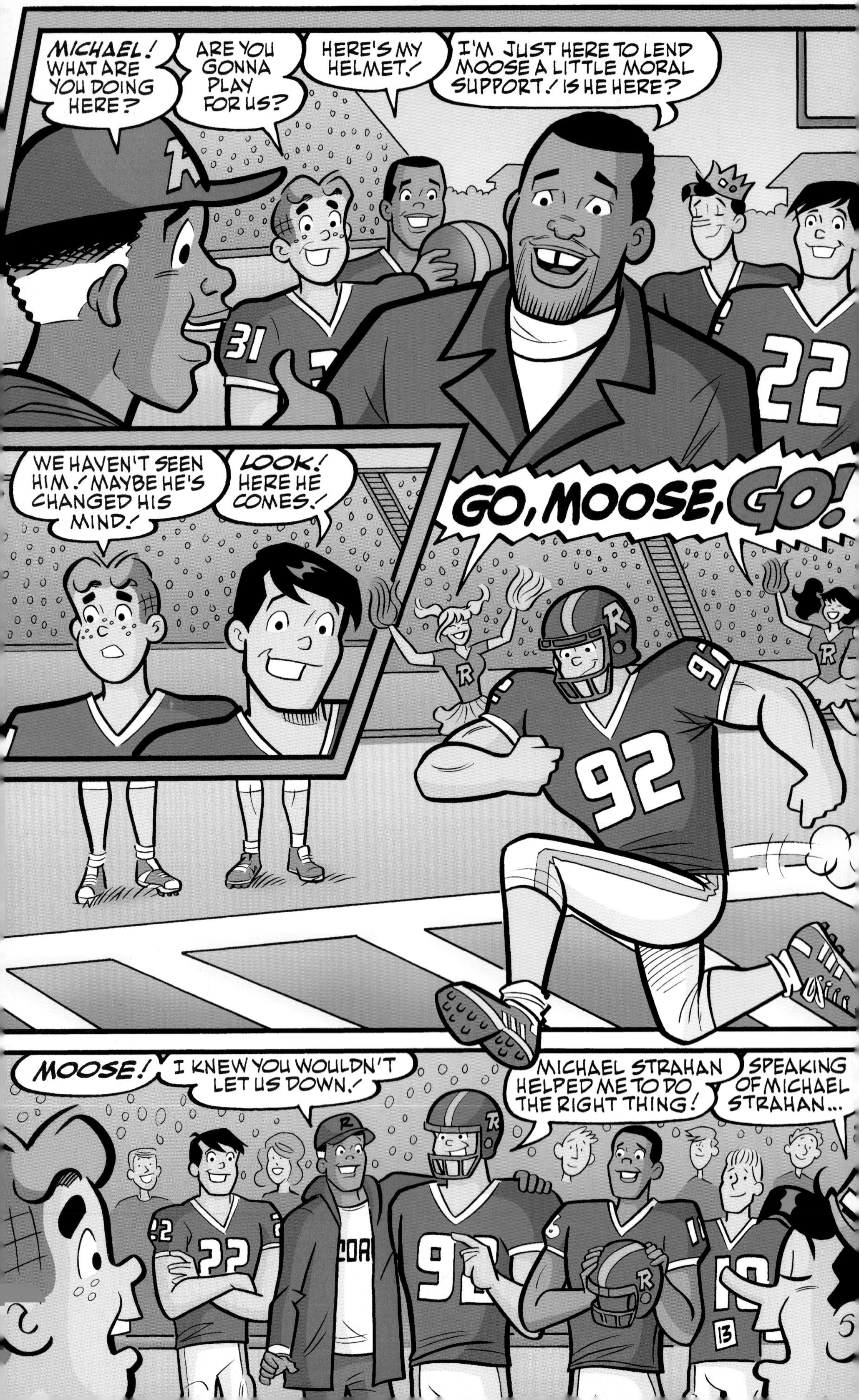
MICHAEL! WHAT ARE YOU DOING HERE?
ARE YOU GONNA PLAY FOR US?
HERE'S MY HELMET!
I'M JUST HERE TO LEND MOOSE A LITTLE MORAL SUPPORT! IS HE HERE?
WE HAVEN'T SEEN HIM! MAYBE HE'S CHANGED HIS MIND!
LOOK! HERE HE COMES!
GO, MOOSE, GO!
MOOSE!
I KNEW YOU WOULDN'T LET US DOWN!
MICHAEL STRAHAN HELPED ME TO DO THE RIGHT THING!
SPEAKING OF MICHAEL STRAHAN...

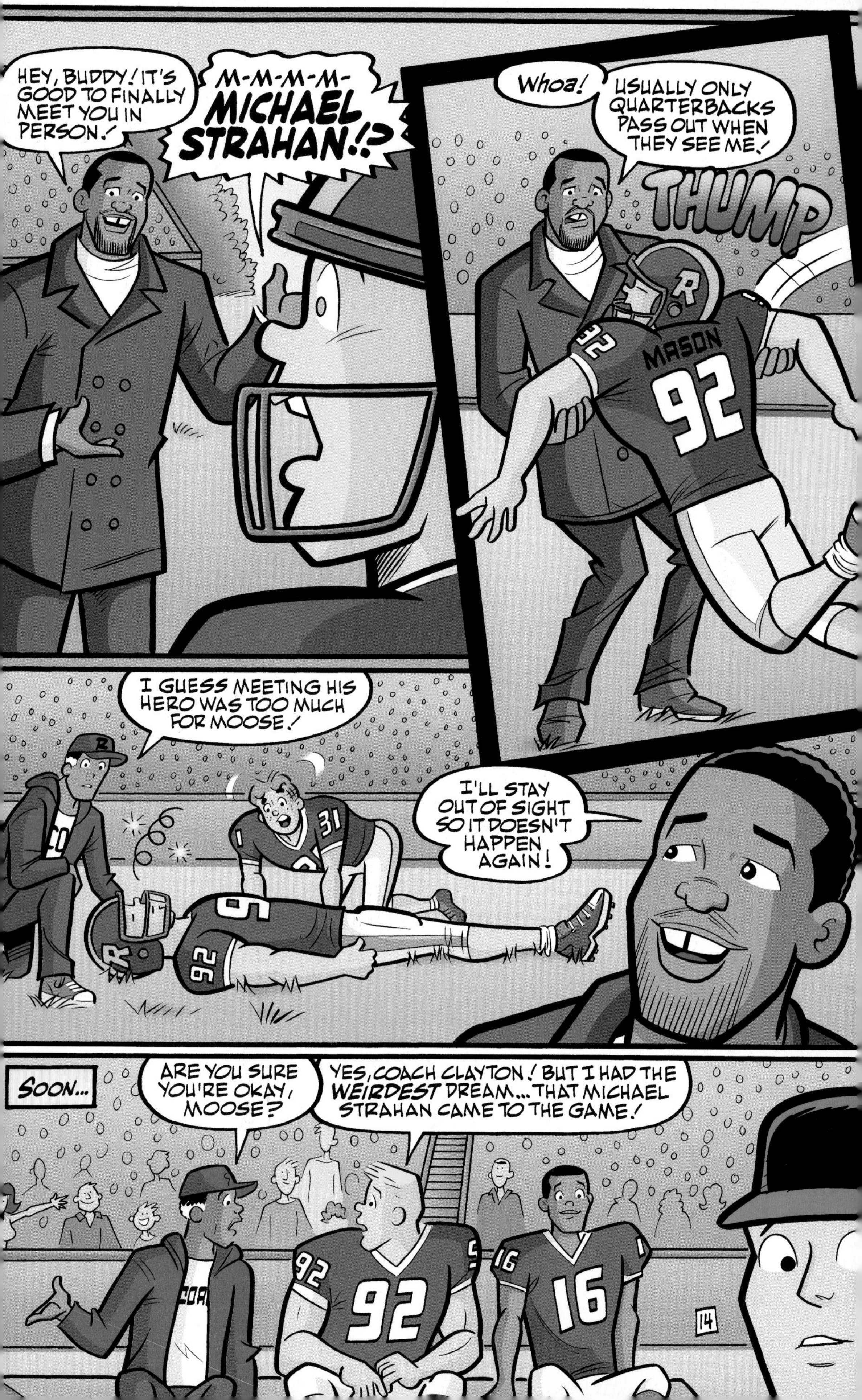
HEY, BUDDY! IT'S GOOD TO FINALLY MEET YOU IN PERSON!
M-M-M-M-MICHAEL STRAHAN!?
Whoa!
USUALLY ONLY QUARTERBACKS PASS OUT WHEN THEY SEE ME!
THUMP
MASON
92
I GUESS MEETING HIS HERO WAS TOO MUCH FOR MOOSE!
I'LL STAY OUT OF SIGHT SO IT DOESN'T HAPPEN AGAIN!
SOON...
ARE YOU SURE YOU'RE OKAY, MOOSE?
YES, COACH CLAYTON! BUT I HAD THE WEIRDEST DREAM... THAT MICHAEL STRAHAN CAME TO THE GAME!

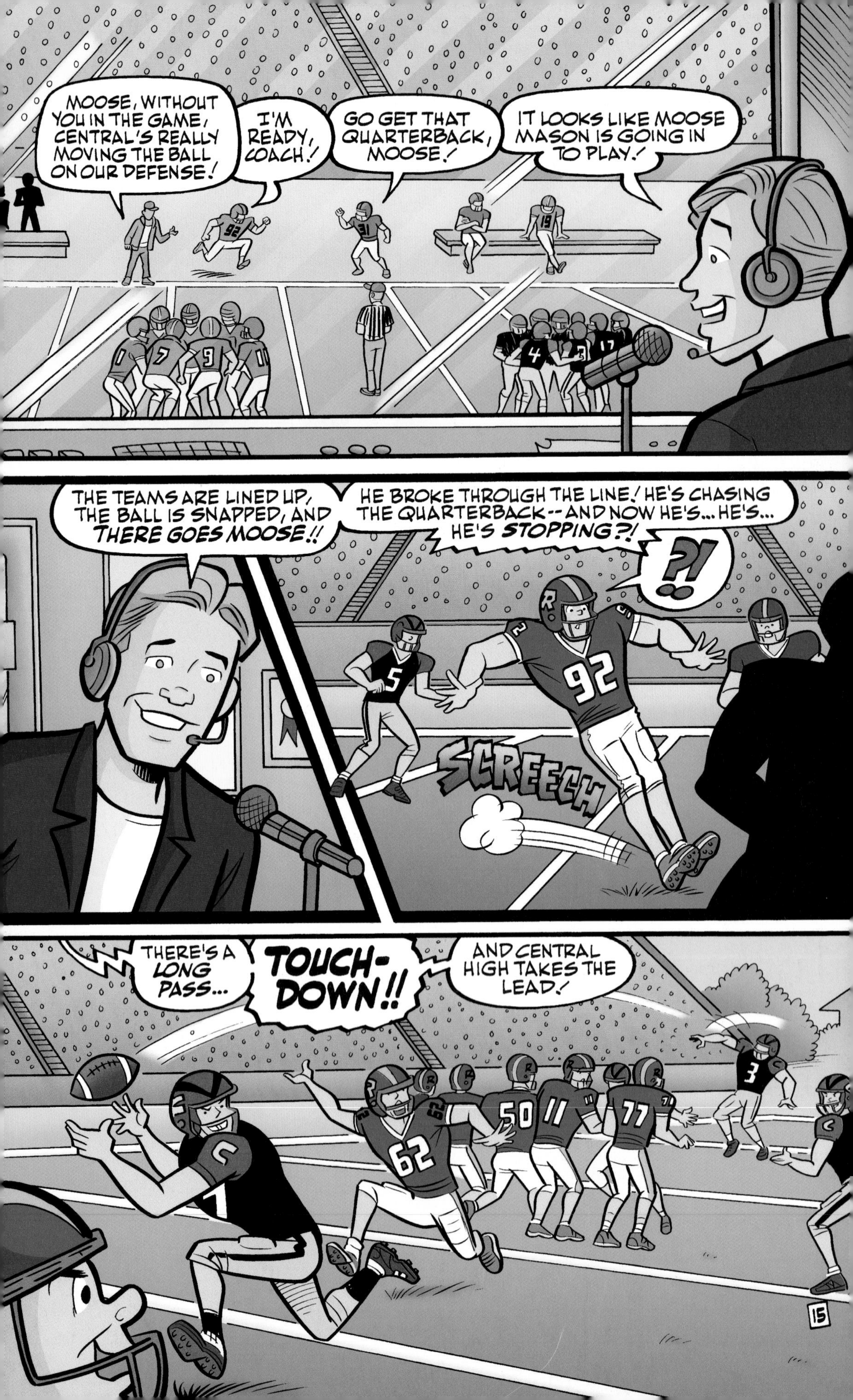
MOOSE, WITHOUT YOU IN THE GAME, CENTRAL'S REALLY MOVING THE BALL ON OUR DEFENSE!
I'M READY, COACH!
GO GET THAT QUARTERBACK, MOOSE!
IT LOOKS LIKE MOOSE MASON IS GOING IN TO PLAY!
THE TEAMS ARE LINED UP, THE BALL IS SNAPPED, AND THERE GOES MOOSE!!
HE BROKE THROUGH THE LINE! HE'S CHASING THE QUARTERBACK--AND NOW HE'S... HE'S... HE'S STOPPING?!
?!
SCREECH
THERE'S A LONG PASS...
TOUCH-DOWN!!
AND CENTRAL HIGH TAKES THE LEAD!

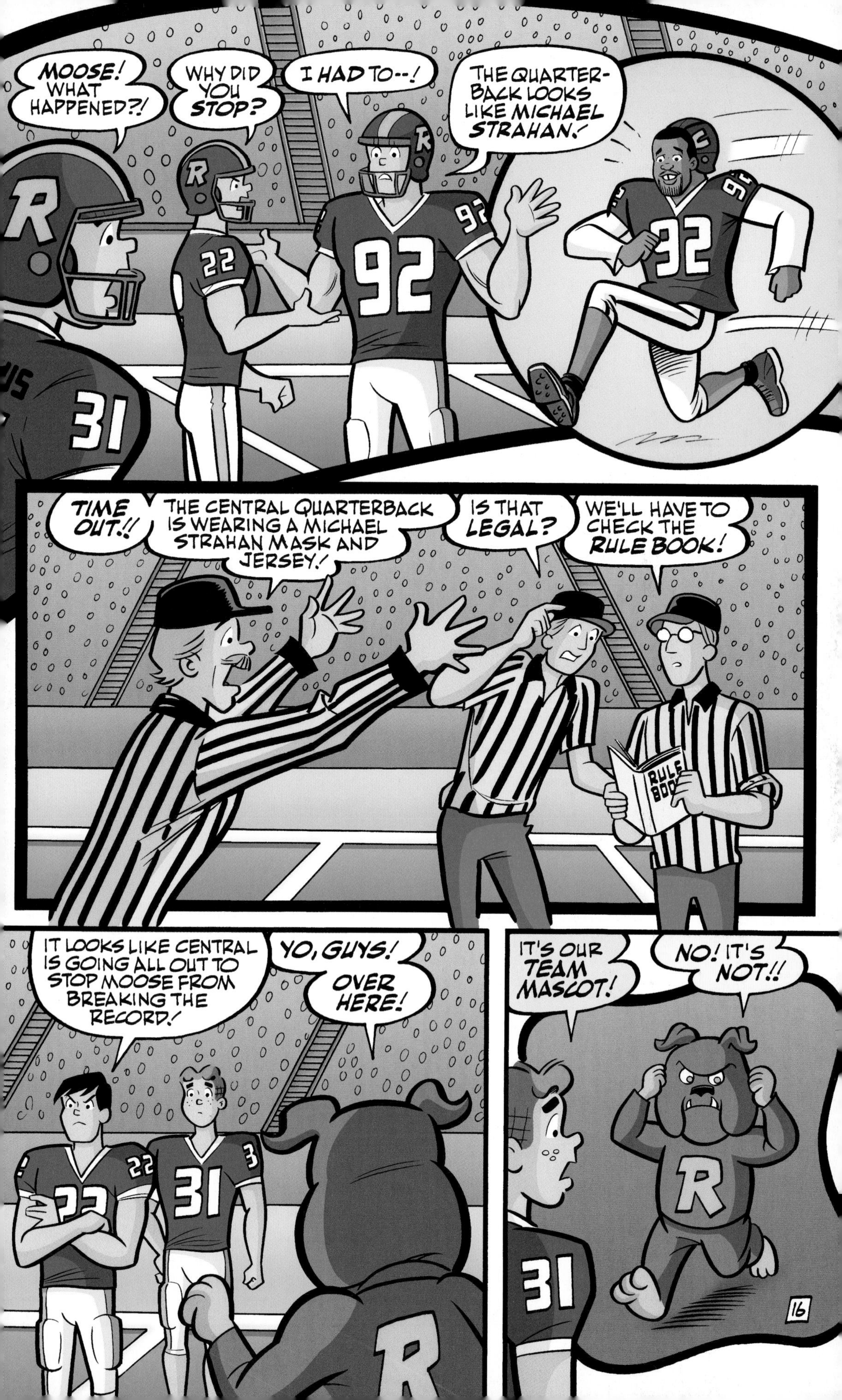

MOOSE! WHAT HAPPENED?!
WHY DID YOU STOP?
I HAD TO--!
THE QUARTER-BACK LOOKS LIKE MICHAEL STRAHAN!
TIME OUT!!
THE CENTRAL QUARTERBACK IS WEARING A MICHAEL STRAHAN MASK AND JERSEY!
IS THAT LEGAL?
WE'LL HAVE TO CHECK THE RULE BOOK!
RULE BOOK
IT LOOKS LIKE CENTRAL IS GOING ALL OUT TO STOP MOOSE FROM BREAKING THE RECORD!
YO, GUYS!
OVER HERE!
IT'S OUR TEAM MASCOT!
NO! IT'S NOT!!

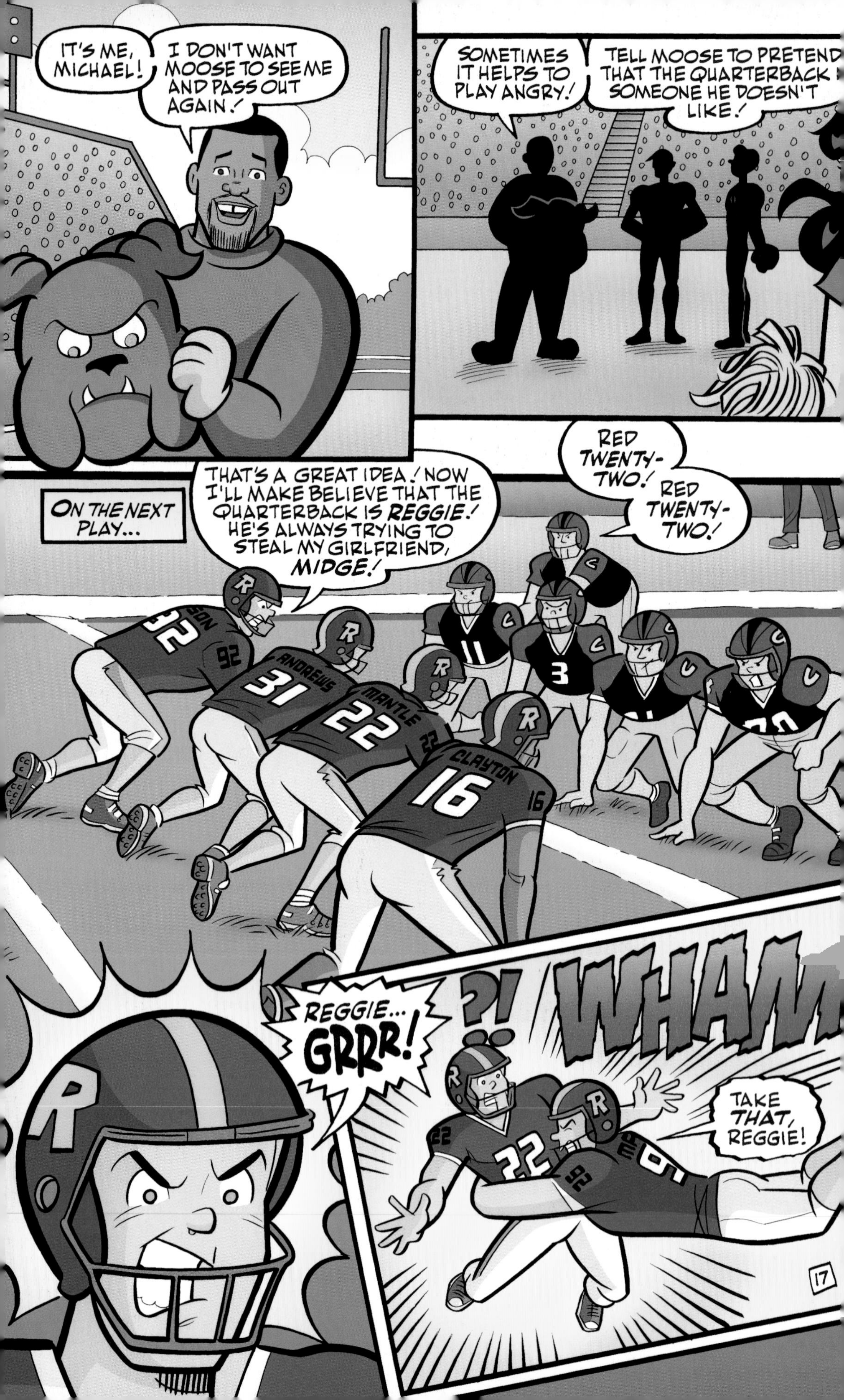
IT'S ME, MICHAEL!
I DON'T WANT MOOSE TO SEE ME AND PASS OUT AGAIN!
SOMETIMES IT HELPS TO PLAY ANGRY!
TELL MOOSE TO PRETEND THAT THE QUARTERBACK IS SOMEONE HE DOESN'T LIKE!
ON THE NEXT PLAY...
THAT'S A GREAT IDEA! NOW I'LL MAKE BELIEVE THAT THE QUARTERBACK IS REGGIE! HE'S ALWAYS TRYING TO STEAL MY GIRLFRIEND, MIDGE!
RED TWENTY-TWO!
RED TWENTY-TWO!
REGGIE... GRRR!
?!
WHAM
TAKE THAT, REGGIE!

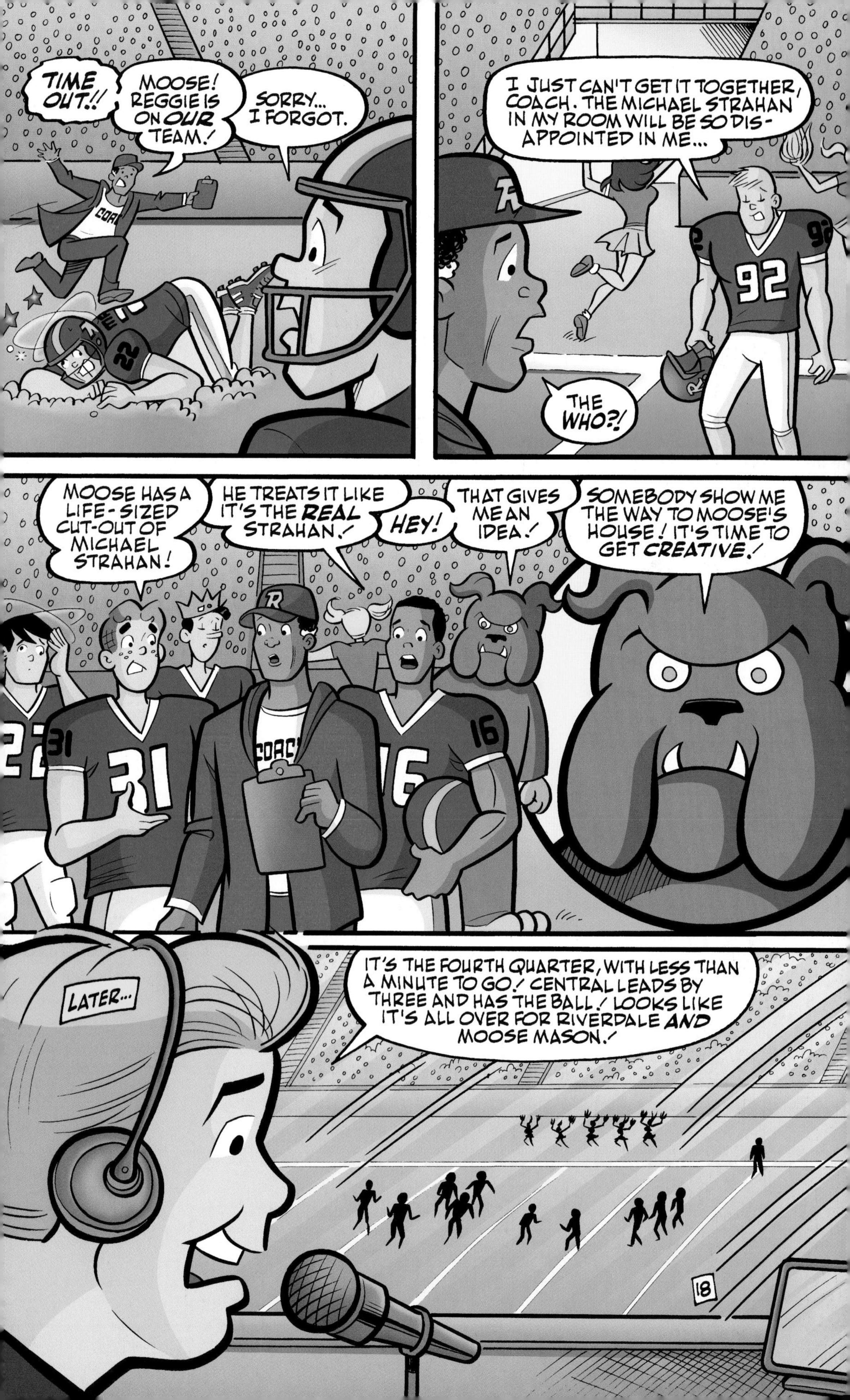
TIME OUT!!
MOOSE! REGGIE IS ON OUR TEAM!
SORRY... I FORGOT.
I JUST CAN'T GET IT TOGETHER, COACH. THE MICHAEL STRAHAN IN MY ROOM WILL BE SO DIS-APPOINTED IN ME...
THE WHO?!
MOOSE HAS A LIFE-SIZED CUT-OUT OF MICHAEL STRAHAN!
HE TREATS IT LIKE IT'S THE REAL STRAHAN!
HEY!
THAT GIVES ME AN IDEA!
SOMEBODY SHOW ME THE WAY TO MOOSE'S HOUSE! IT'S TIME TO GET CREATIVE!
LATER...
IT'S THE FOURTH QUARTER, WITH LESS THAN A MINUTE TO GO! CENTRAL LEADS BY THREE AND HAS THE BALL! LOOKS LIKE IT'S ALL OVER FOR RIVERDALE AND MOOSE MASON!
18

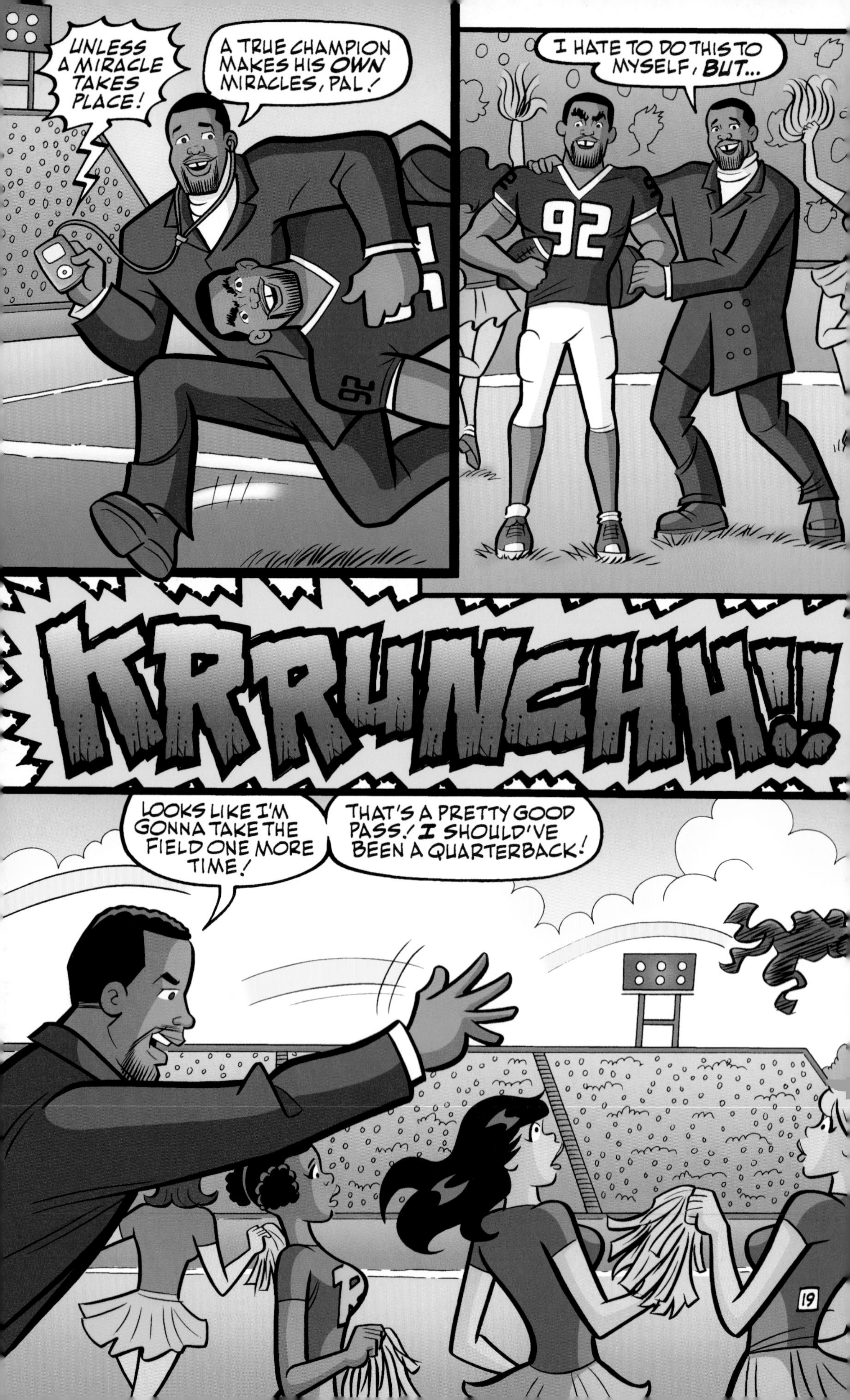

UNLESS A MIRACLE TAKES PLACE!
A TRUE CHAMPION MAKES HIS OWN MIRACLES, PAL!
I HATE TO DO THIS TO MYSELF, BUT...
92
KRRUNCHH!!
LOOKS LIKE I'M GONNA TAKE THE FIELD ONE MORE TIME!
THAT'S A PRETTY GOOD PASS! I SHOULD'VE BEEN A QUARTERBACK!

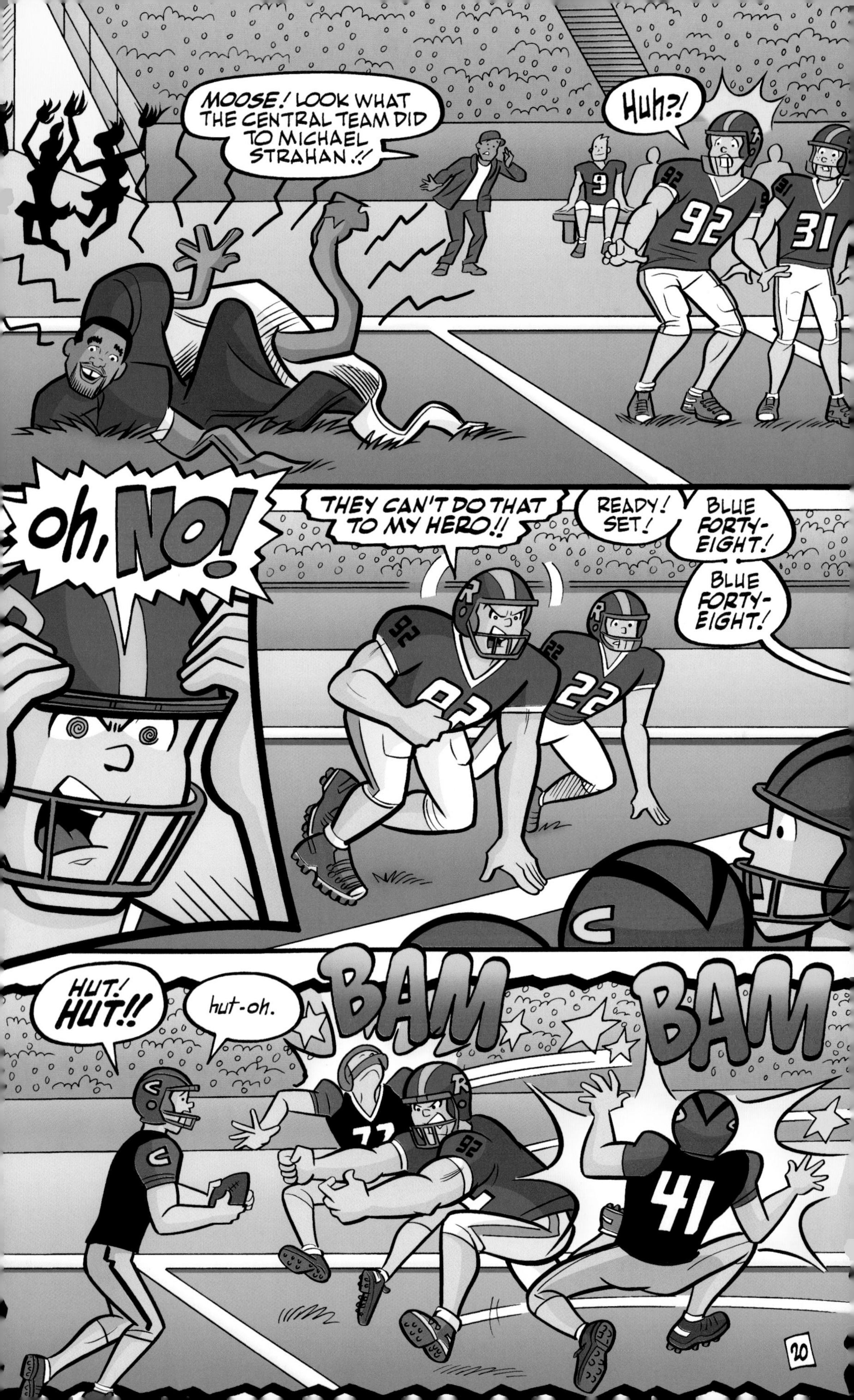
MOOSE! LOOK WHAT THE CENTRAL TEAM DID TO MICHAEL STRAHAN.!!
Huh?!
oh, NO!
THEY CAN'T DO THAT TO MY HERO!!
READY! SET!
BLUE FORTY-EIGHT!
BLUE FORTY-EIGHT!
HUT! HUT!!
hut-oh.
BAM
BAM

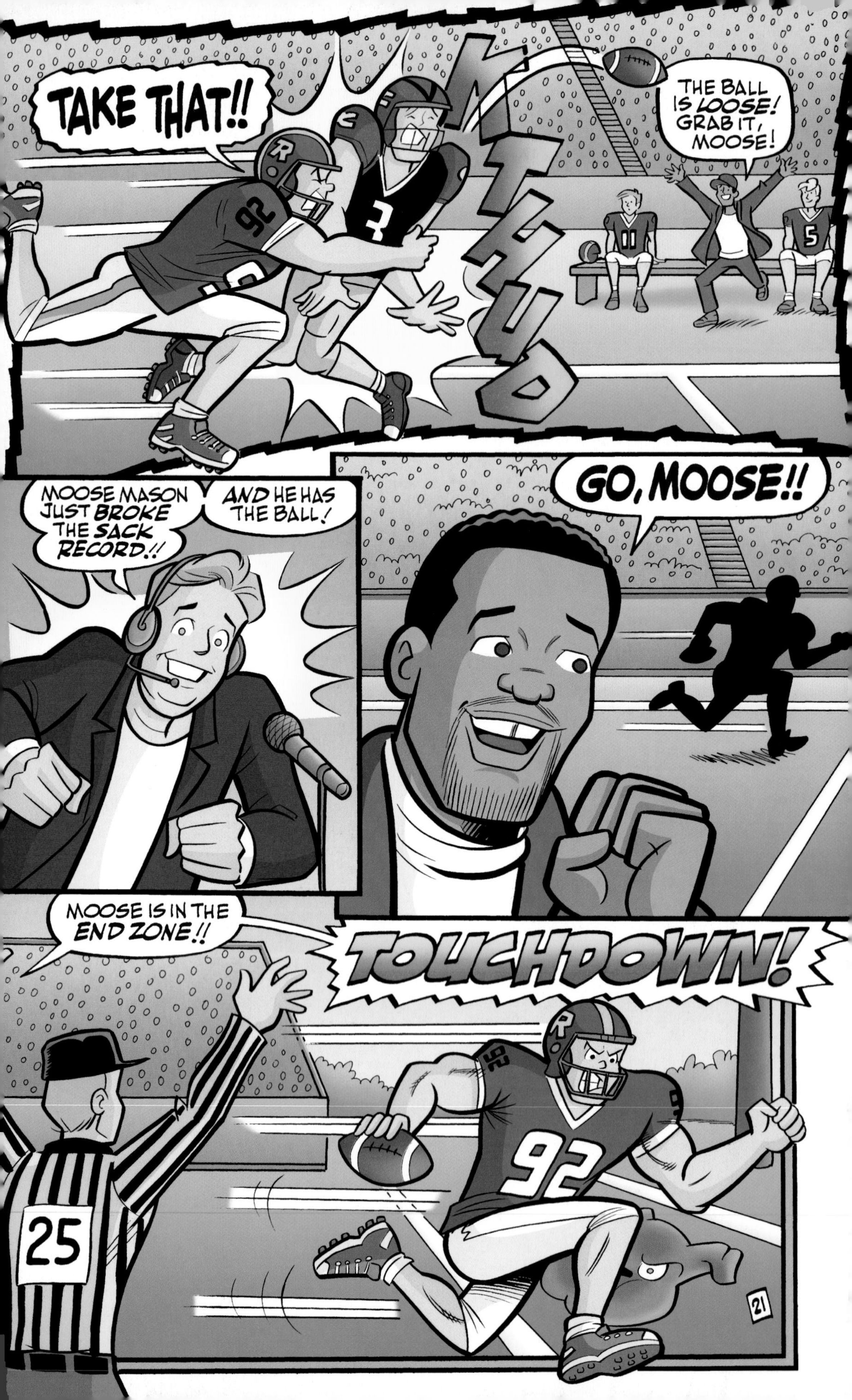
TAKE THAT!!
THUD
THE BALL IS LOOSE! GRAB IT, MOOSE!
MOOSE MASON JUST BROKE THE SACK RECORD!!
AND HE HAS THE BALL!
GO, MOOSE!!
MOOSE IS IN THE END ZONE!!
TOUCHDOWN!

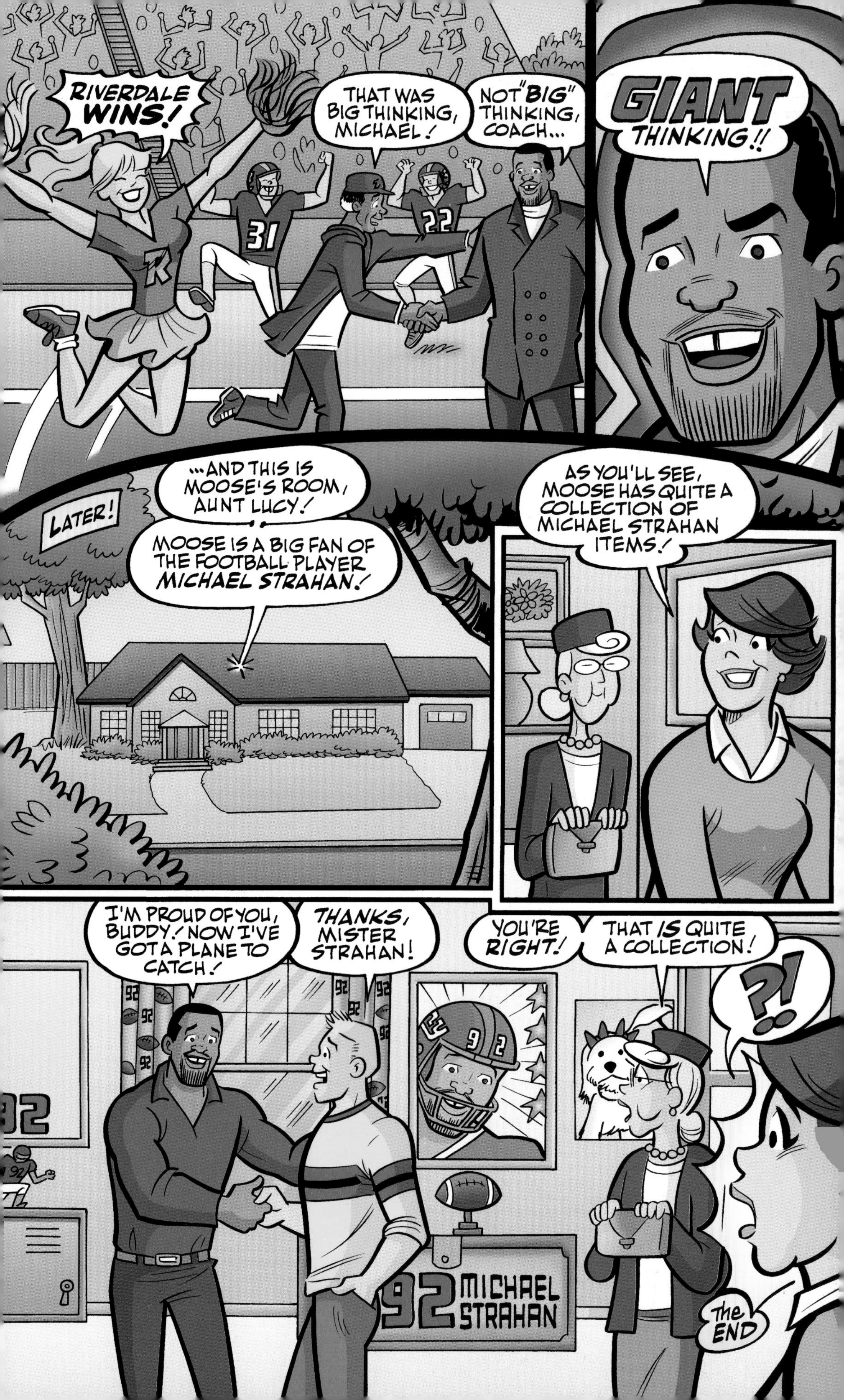
RIVERDALE WINS!
THAT WAS BIG THINKING, MICHAEL!
NOT "BIG" THINKING, COACH...
GIANT THINKING!!
LATER!
...AND THIS IS MOOSE'S ROOM, AUNT LUCY!
MOOSE IS A BIG FAN OF THE FOOTBALL PLAYER MICHAEL STRAHAN!
AS YOU'LL SEE, MOOSE HAS QUITE A COLLECTION OF MICHAEL STRAHAN ITEMS!
I'M PROUD OF YOU, BUDDY! NOW I'VE GOT A PLANE TO CATCH!
THANKS, MISTER STRAHAN!
YOU'RE RIGHT!
THAT IS QUITE A COLLECTION!
?!
92 MICHAEL STRAHAN
The END

Archie
CROSSOVER COLLECTION

Oh, MY!

As a preteen and a teenager, I read Archie Comics and really thought that Riverdale's community and Archie's circle of friends was something perfectly Americana. But I never imagined at that time that I would be a part of that Americana. I applaud a forward-thinking comic like *Kevin Keller*.

Comics play an important role in contributing to a healthy, sociable community and Kevin is a great role model for the youth of America. Riverdale reflects the diversity of America and embraces that diversity as a positive, which is why everyone wants to live there. I am honored to be a part of Archie's history and I think Dan Parent did a tremendous job—a very flattering likeness!

George Takei

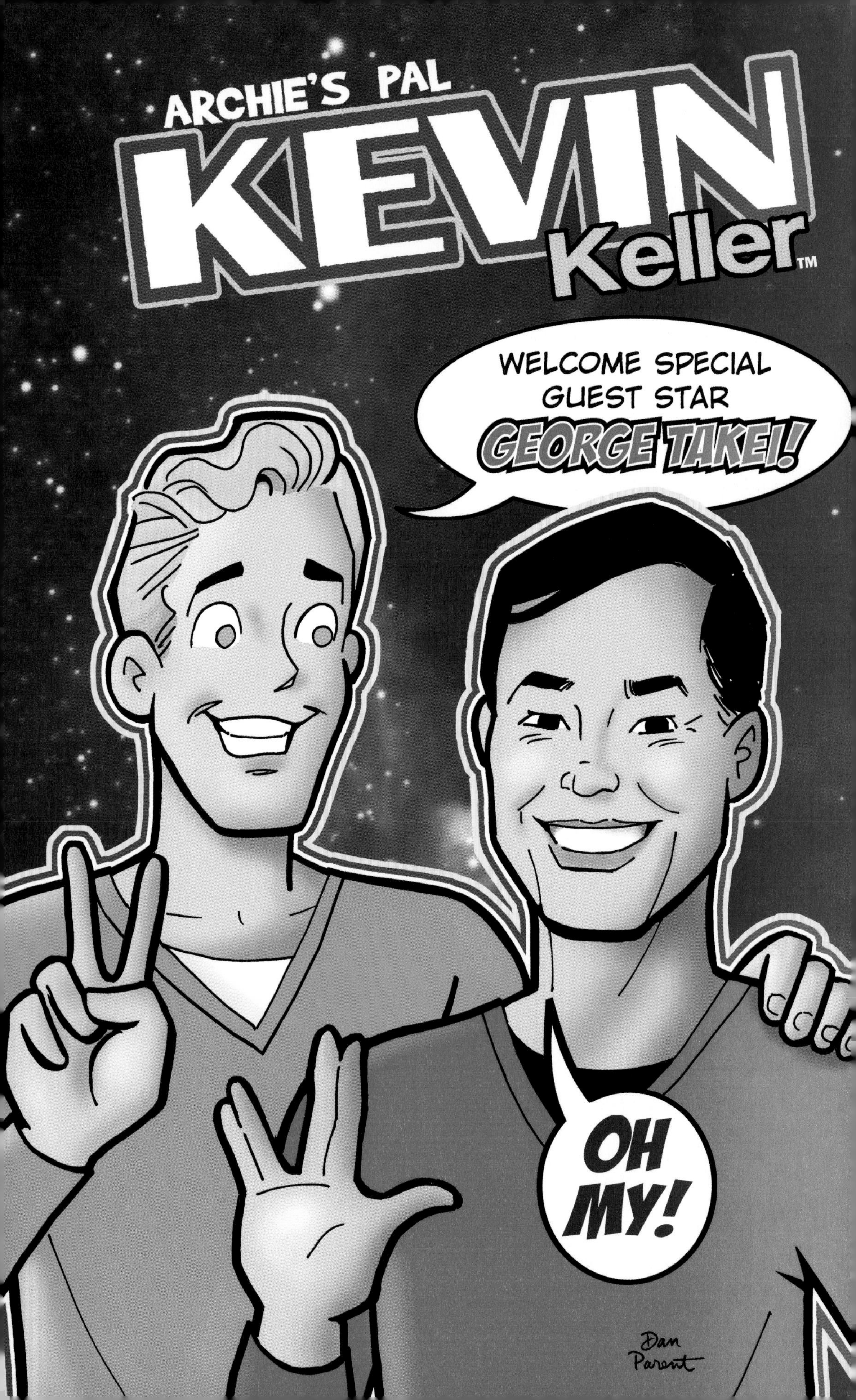
ARCHIE'S PAL
KEVIN Keller™
WELCOME SPECIAL GUEST STAR GEORGE TAKEI!
OH MY!
Dan Parent

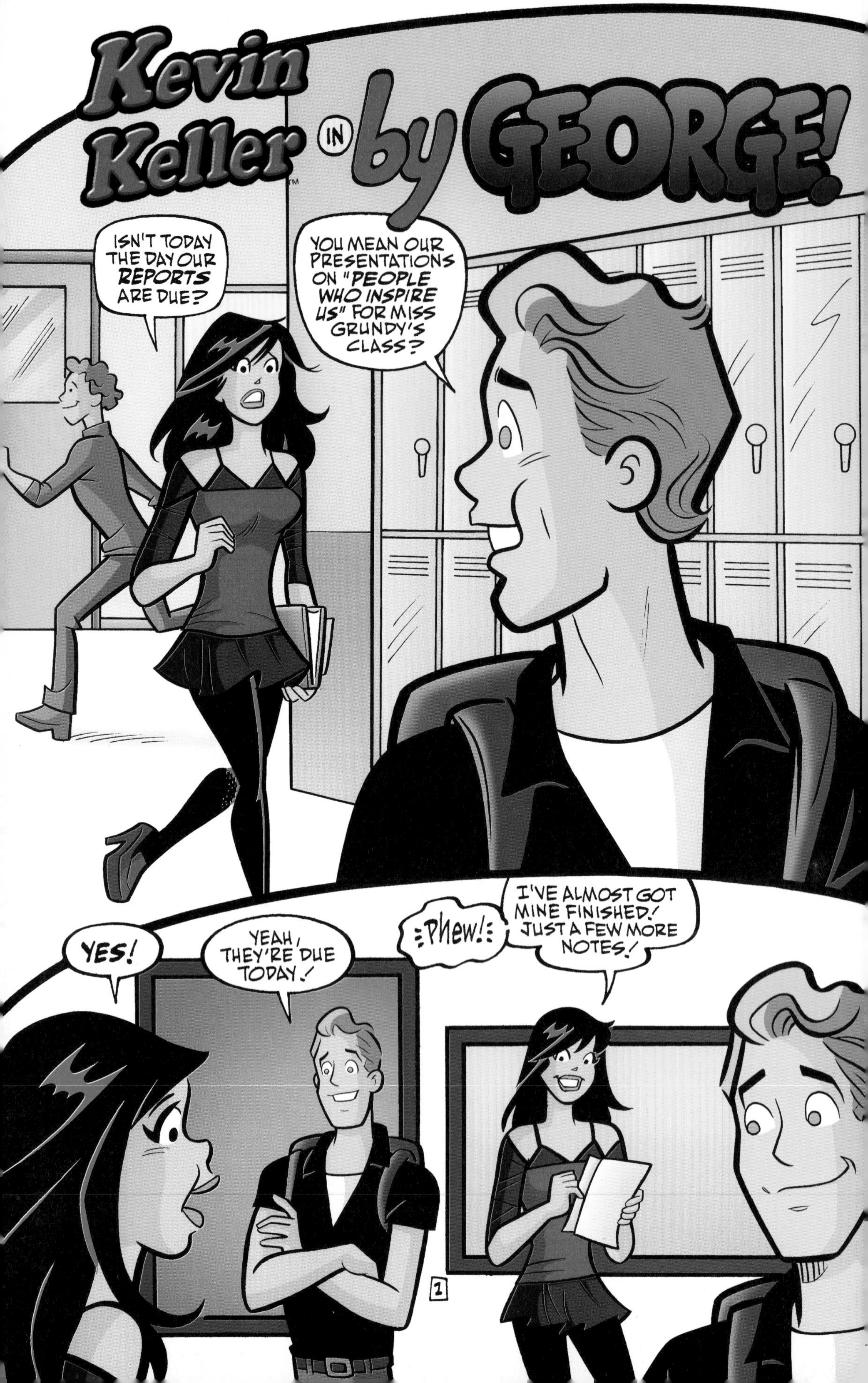
Kevin Keller™ IN by GEORGE!
ISN'T TODAY THE DAY OUR REPORTS ARE DUE?
YOU MEAN OUR PRESENTATIONS ON "PEOPLE WHO INSPIRE US" FOR MISS GRUNDY'S CLASS?
YES!
YEAH, THEY'RE DUE TODAY!
PHEW!
I'VE ALMOST GOT MINE FINISHED! JUST A FEW MORE NOTES!
1

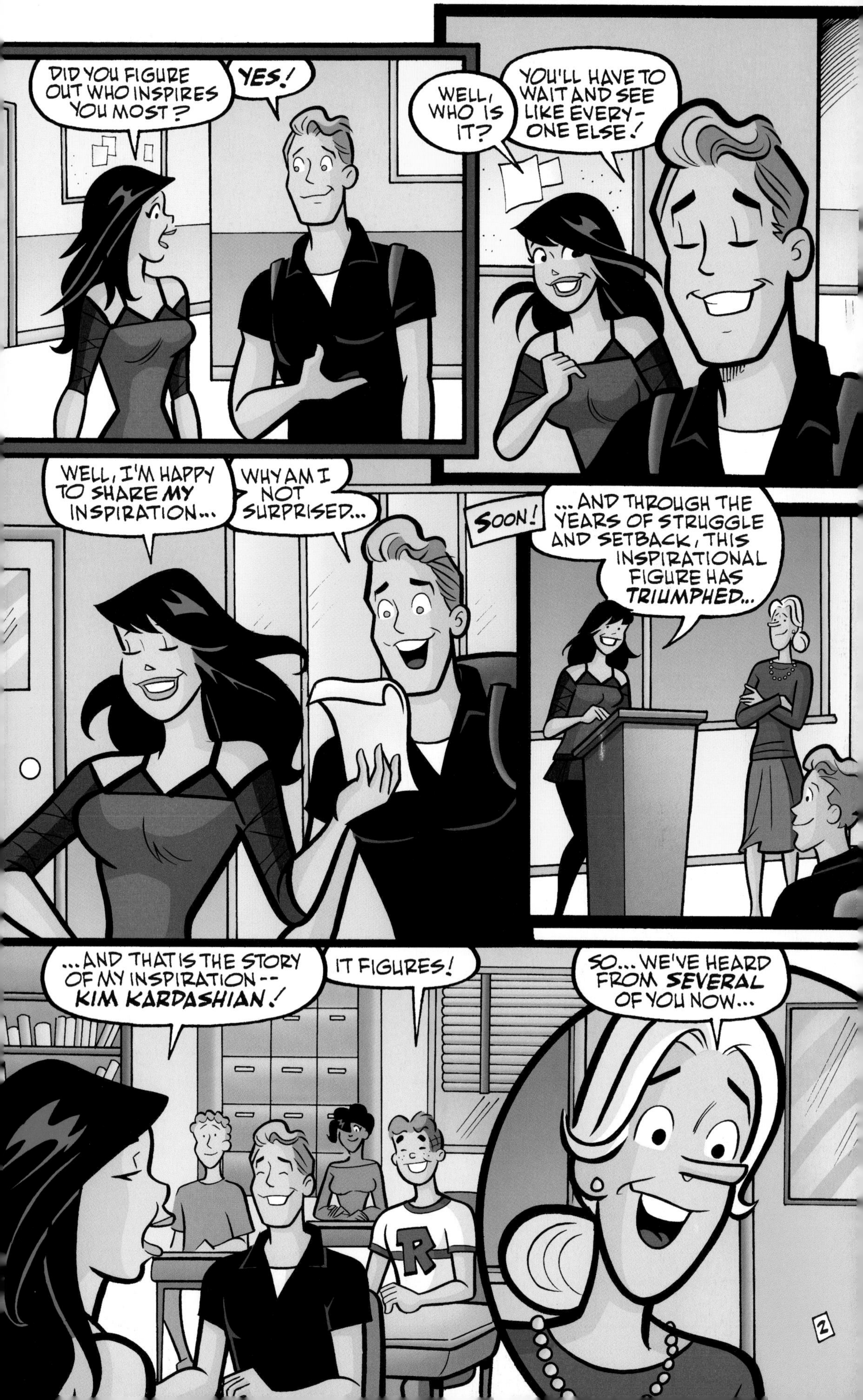
DID YOU FIGURE OUT WHO INSPIRES YOU MOST?
YES!
WELL, WHO IS IT?
YOU'LL HAVE TO WAIT AND SEE LIKE EVERY-ONE ELSE!
WELL, I'M HAPPY TO SHARE MY INSPIRATION...
WHY AM I NOT SURPRISED...
SOON!
...AND THROUGH THE YEARS OF STRUGGLE AND SETBACK, THIS INSPIRATIONAL FIGURE HAS TRIUMPHED...
...AND THAT IS THE STORY OF MY INSPIRATION-- KIM KARDASHIAN!
IT FIGURES!
SO... WE'VE HEARD FROM SEVERAL OF YOU NOW...
R
2

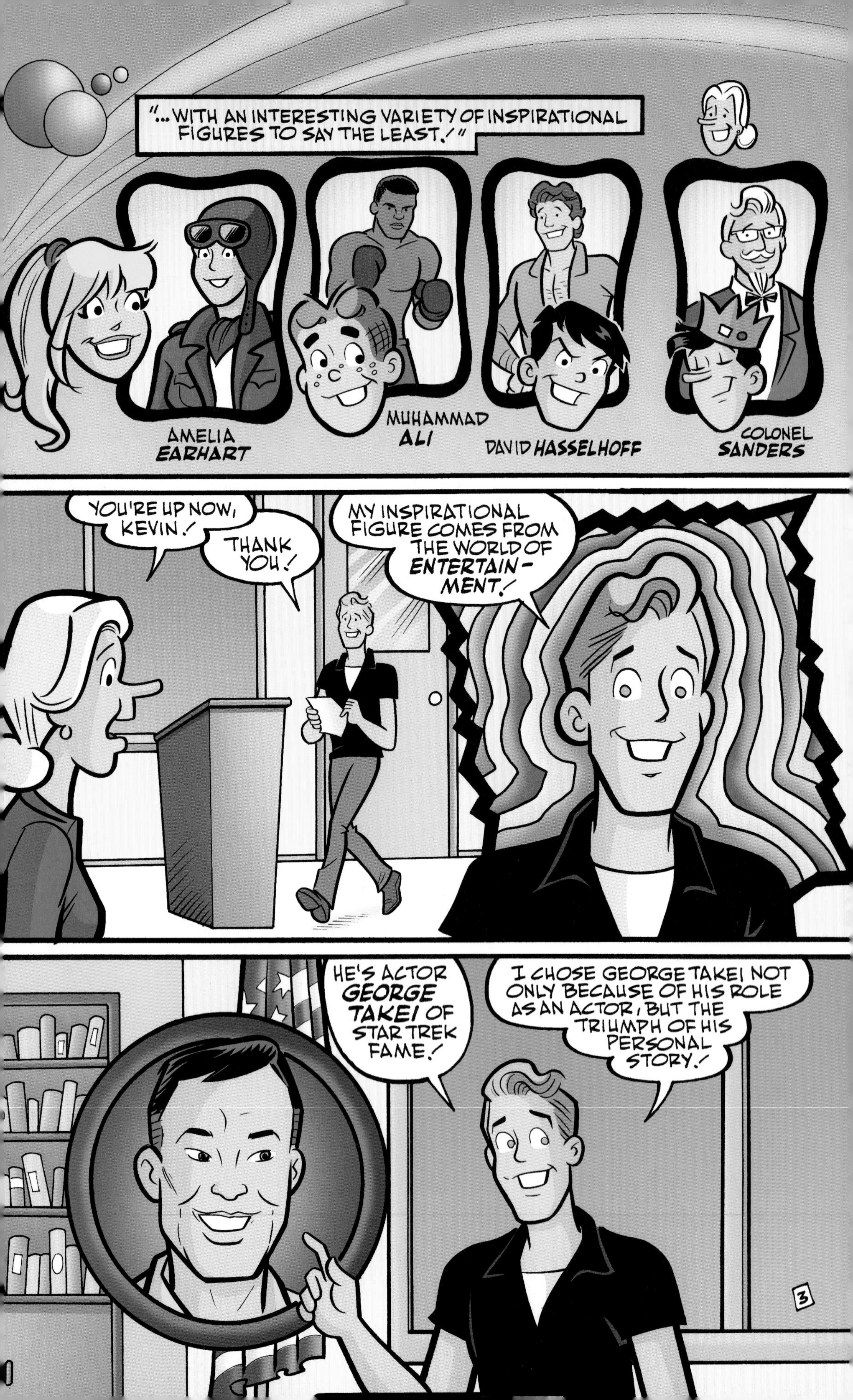
"...WITH AN INTERESTING VARIETY OF INSPIRATIONAL FIGURES TO SAY THE LEAST!"
AMELIA EARHART
MUHAMMAD ALI
DAVID HASSELHOFF
COLONEL SANDERS
YOU'RE UP NOW, KEVIN!
THANK YOU!
MY INSPIRATIONAL FIGURE COMES FROM THE WORLD OF ENTERTAIN-MENT!
HE'S ACTOR GEORGE TAKEI OF STAR TREK FAME!
I CHOSE GEORGE TAKEI NOT ONLY BECAUSE OF HIS ROLE AS AN ACTOR, BUT THE TRIUMPH OF HIS PERSONAL STORY!
3

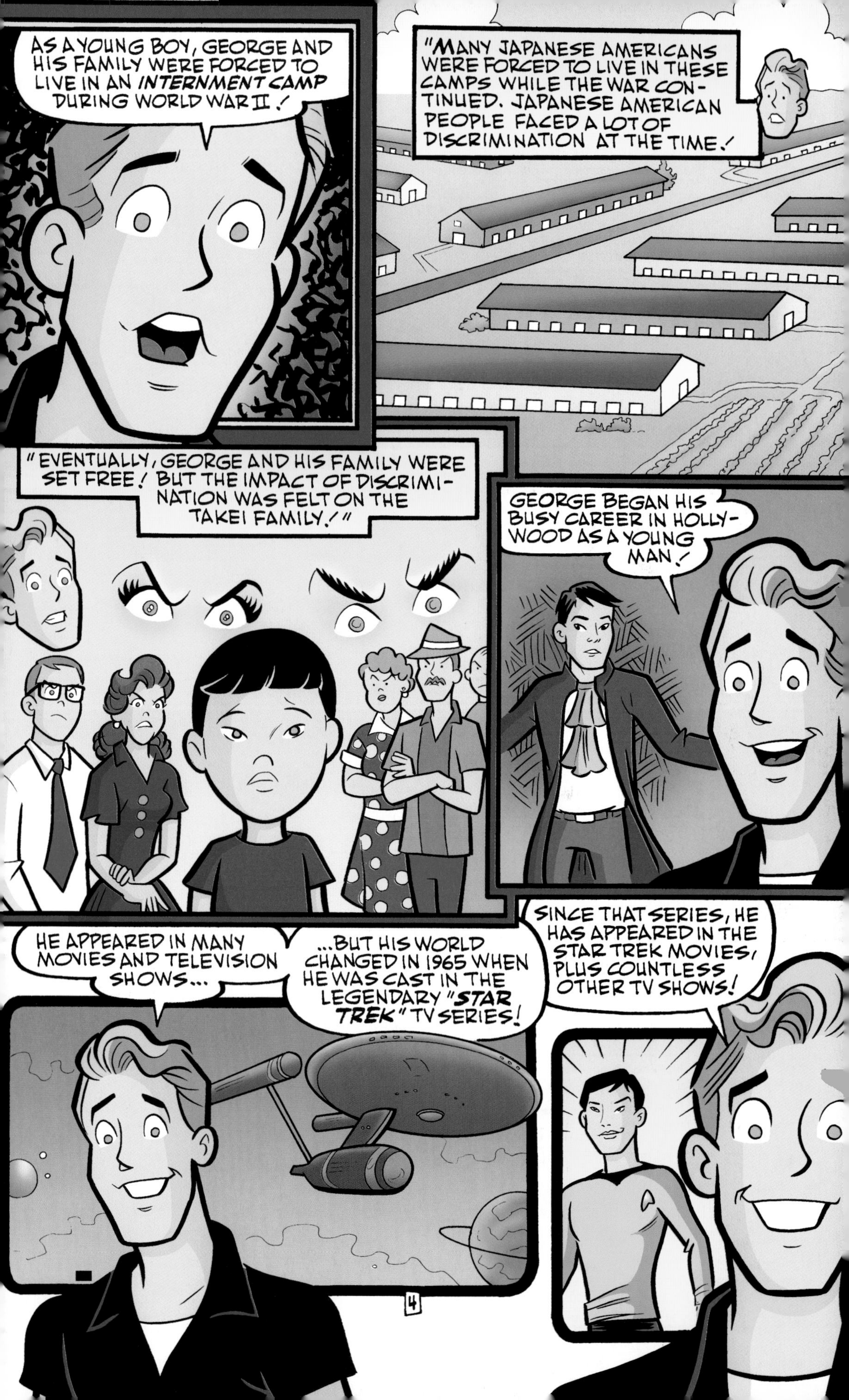
AS A YOUNG BOY, GEORGE AND HIS FAMILY WERE FORCED TO LIVE IN AN *INTERNMENT CAMP* DURING WORLD WAR II!
"MANY JAPANESE AMERICANS WERE FORCED TO LIVE IN THESE CAMPS WHILE THE WAR CONTINUED. JAPANESE AMERICAN PEOPLE FACED A LOT OF DISCRIMINATION AT THE TIME!
"EVENTUALLY, GEORGE AND HIS FAMILY WERE SET FREE! BUT THE IMPACT OF DISCRIMINATION WAS FELT ON THE TAKEI FAMILY!"
GEORGE BEGAN HIS BUSY CAREER IN HOLLYWOOD AS A YOUNG MAN!
HE APPEARED IN MANY MOVIES AND TELEVISION SHOWS...
...BUT HIS WORLD CHANGED IN 1965 WHEN HE WAS CAST IN THE LEGENDARY "*STAR TREK*" TV SERIES!
SINCE THAT SERIES, HE HAS APPEARED IN THE STAR TREK MOVIES, PLUS COUNTLESS OTHER TV SHOWS!

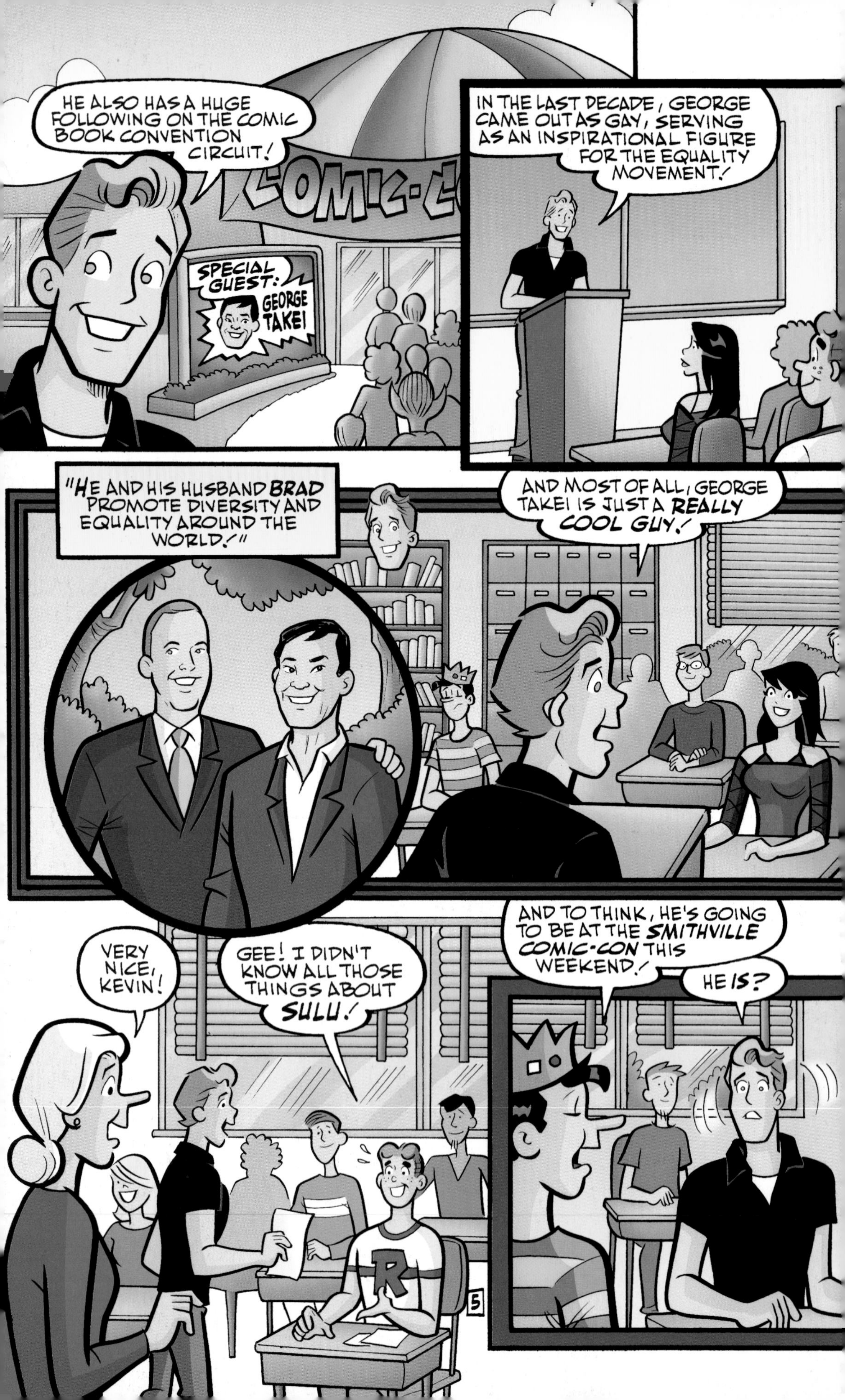

HE ALSO HAS A HUGE FOLLOWING ON THE COMIC BOOK CONVENTION CIRCUIT!
COMIC-CO
SPECIAL GUEST: GEORGE TAKEI
IN THE LAST DECADE, GEORGE CAME OUT AS GAY, SERVING AS AN INSPIRATIONAL FIGURE FOR THE EQUALITY MOVEMENT!
"HE AND HIS HUSBAND BRAD PROMOTE DIVERSITY AND EQUALITY AROUND THE WORLD!"
AND MOST OF ALL, GEORGE TAKEI IS JUST A REALLY COOL GUY!
VERY NICE, KEVIN!
GEE! I DIDN'T KNOW ALL THOSE THINGS ABOUT SULU!
AND TO THINK, HE'S GOING TO BE AT THE SMITHVILLE COMIC-CON THIS WEEKEND!
HE IS?
5

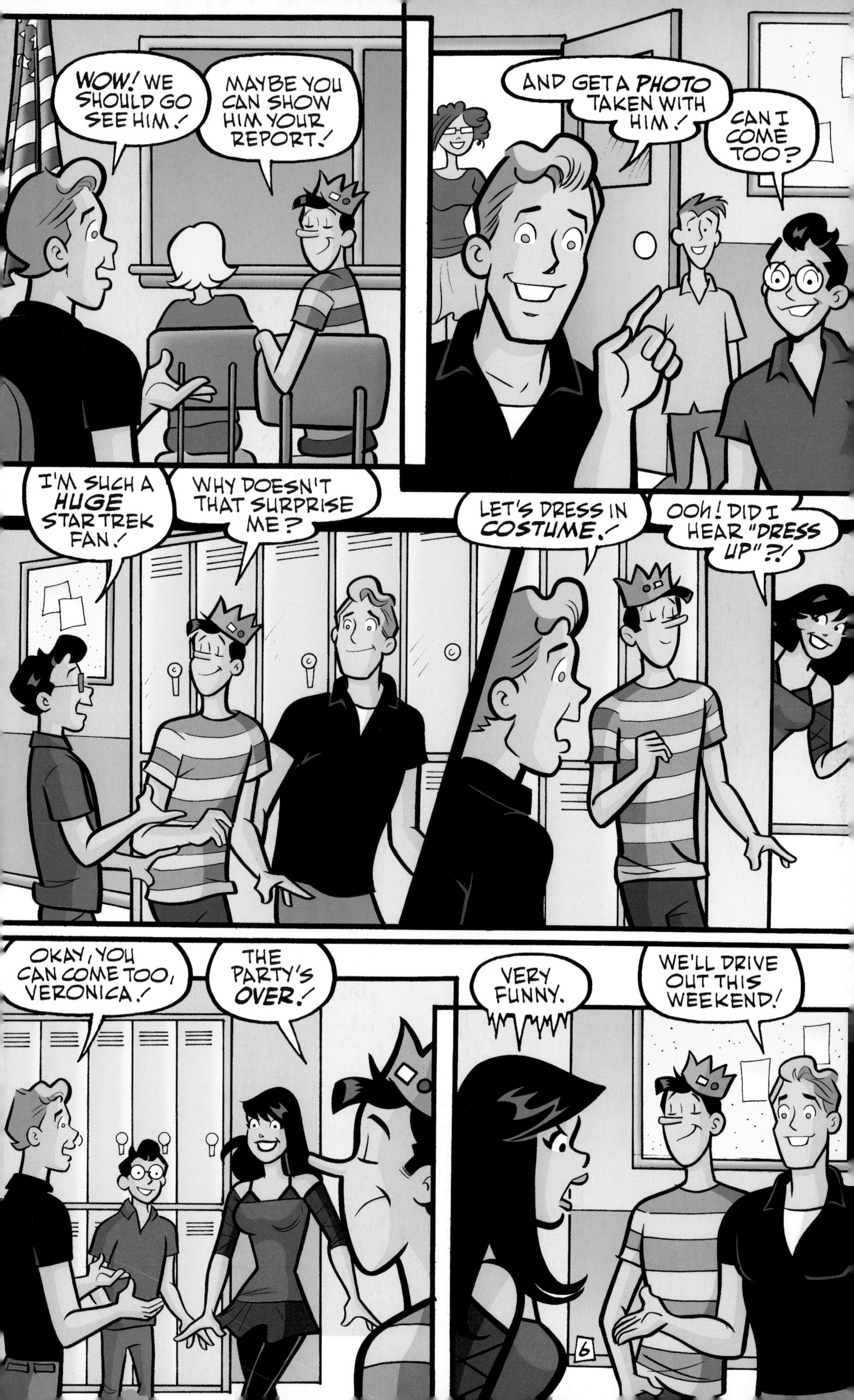
WOW! WE SHOULD GO SEE HIM!
MAYBE YOU CAN SHOW HIM YOUR REPORT!
AND GET A PHOTO TAKEN WITH HIM!
CAN I COME TOO?
I'M SUCH A HUGE STAR TREK FAN!
WHY DOESN'T THAT SURPRISE ME?
LET'S DRESS IN COSTUME!
OOH! DID I HEAR "DRESS UP"?!
OKAY, YOU CAN COME TOO, VERONICA!
THE PARTY'S OVER!
VERY FUNNY.
WE'LL DRIVE OUT THIS WEEKEND!
6

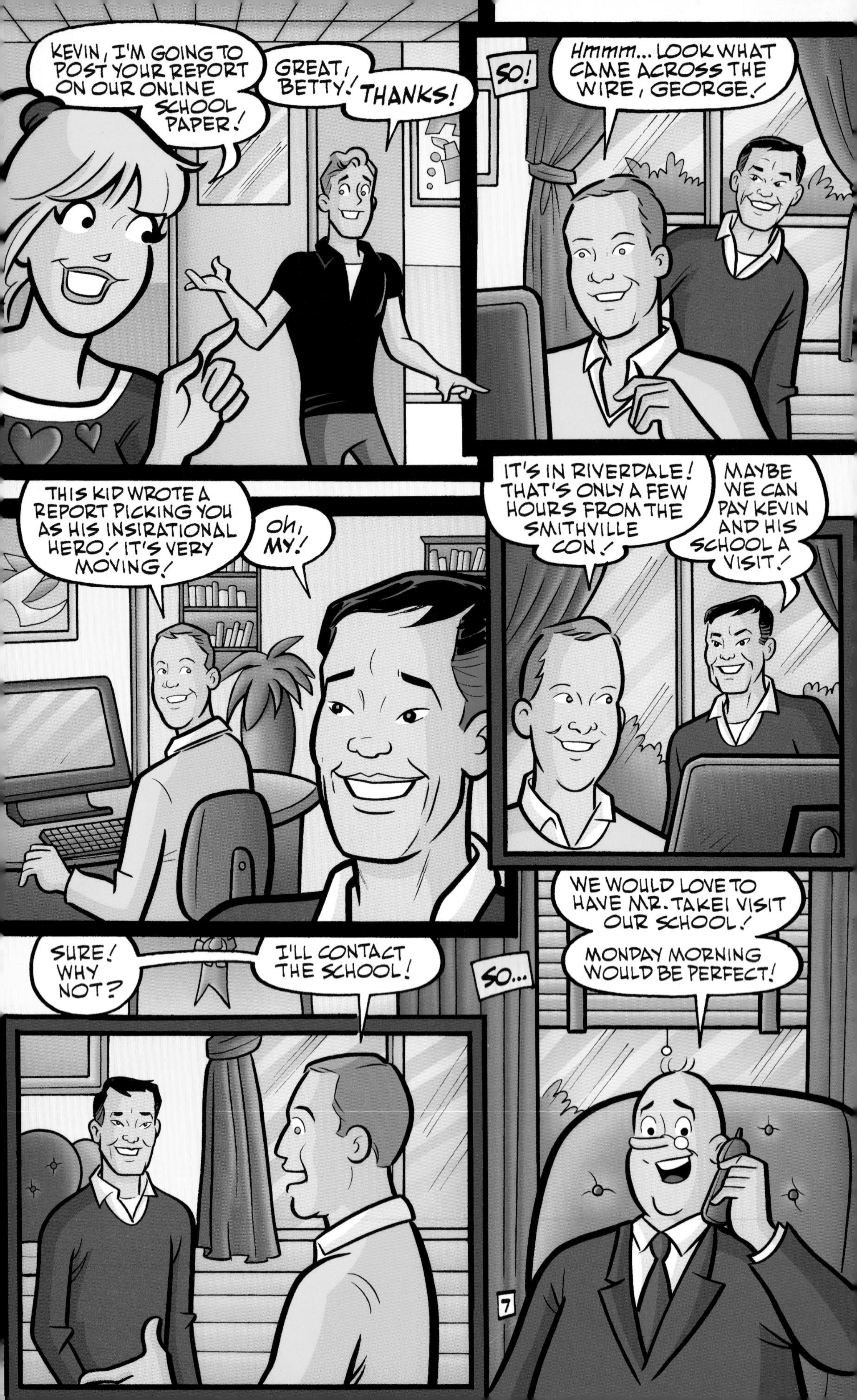

KEVIN, I'M GOING TO POST YOUR REPORT ON OUR ONLINE SCHOOL PAPER!
GREAT, BETTY!
THANKS!
SO!
Hmmm... LOOK WHAT CAME ACROSS THE WIRE, GEORGE!
THIS KID WROTE A REPORT PICKING YOU AS HIS INSIRATIONAL HERO! IT'S VERY MOVING!
Oh, MY!
IT'S IN RIVERDALE! THAT'S ONLY A FEW HOURS FROM THE SMITHVILLE CON!
MAYBE WE CAN PAY KEVIN AND HIS SCHOOL A VISIT!
SURE! WHY NOT?
I'LL CONTACT THE SCHOOL!
SO...
WE WOULD LOVE TO HAVE MR. TAKEI VISIT OUR SCHOOL!
MONDAY MORNING WOULD BE PERFECT!

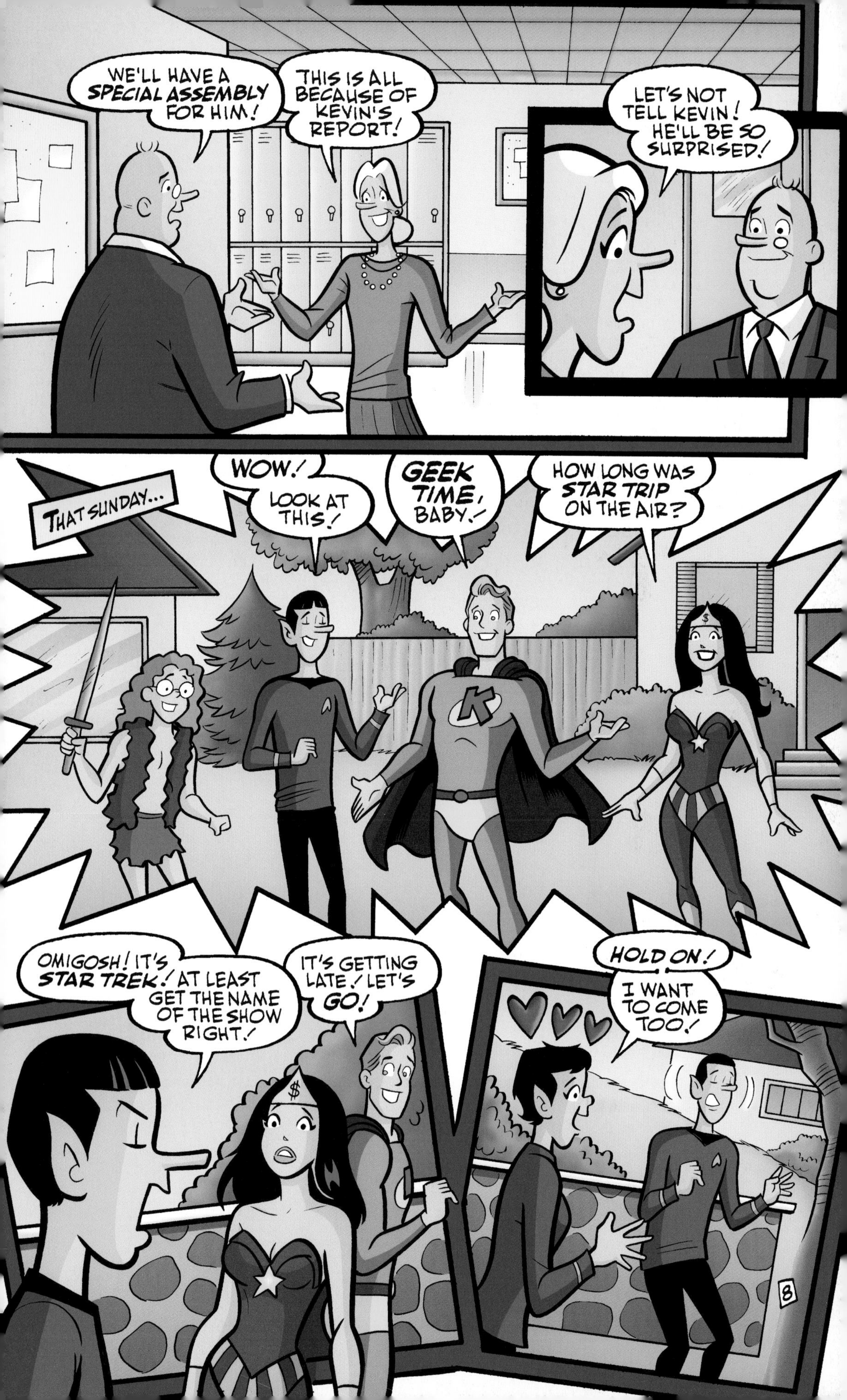
WE'LL HAVE A SPECIAL ASSEMBLY FOR HIM!
THIS IS ALL BECAUSE OF KEVIN'S REPORT!
LET'S NOT TELL KEVIN! HE'LL BE SO SURPRISED!
THAT SUNDAY...
WOW!
LOOK AT THIS!
GEEK TIME, BABY!
HOW LONG WAS STAR TRIP ON THE AIR?
OMIGOSH! IT'S STAR TREK!
AT LEAST GET THE NAME OF THE SHOW RIGHT!
IT'S GETTING LATE! LET'S GO!
HOLD ON!
I WANT TO COME TOO!
8

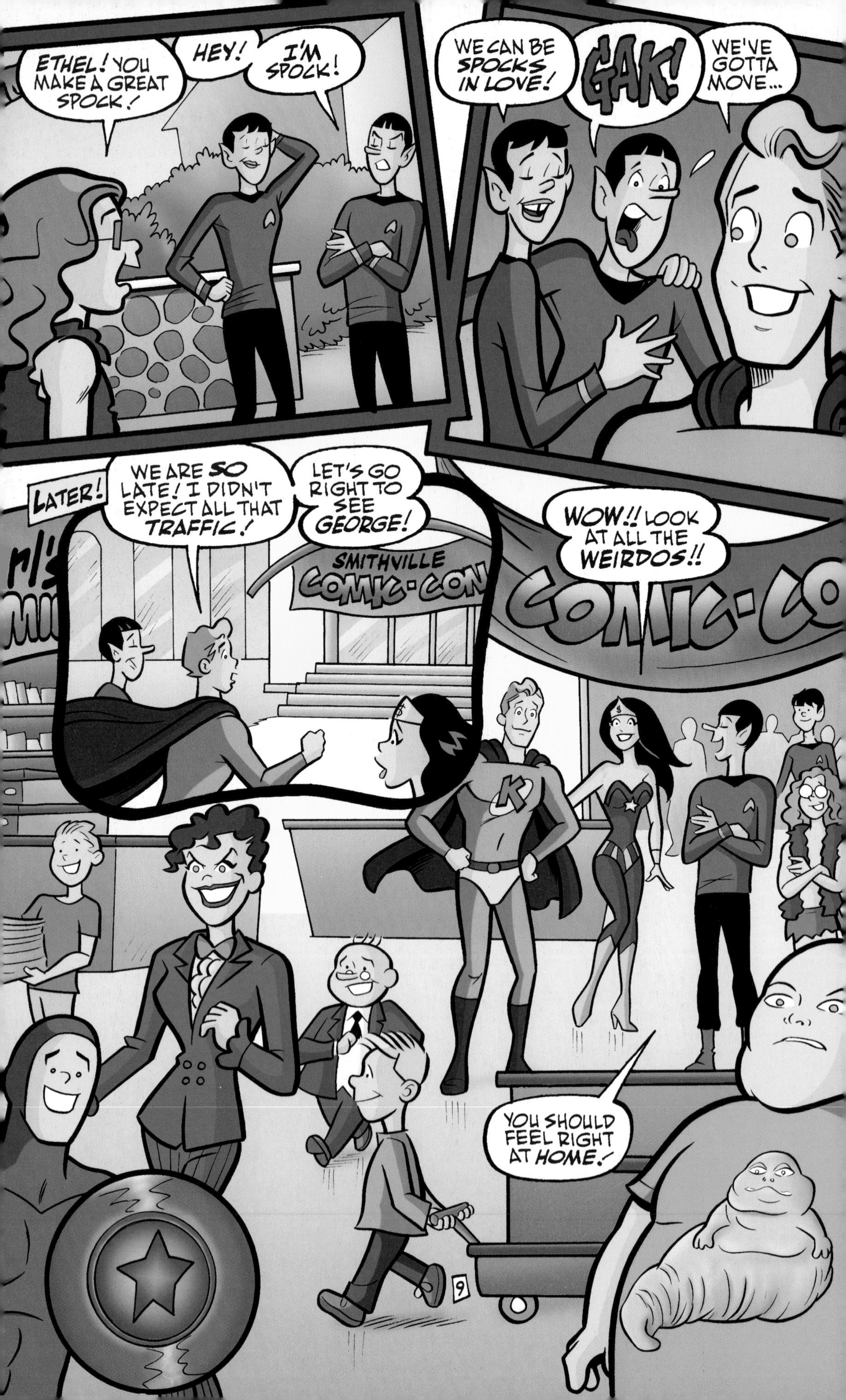
ETHEL! YOU MAKE A GREAT SPOCK!
HEY!
I'M SPOCK!
WE CAN BE SPOCKS IN LOVE!
GAK!
WE'VE GOTTA MOVE...
LATER!
WE ARE SO LATE! I DIDN'T EXPECT ALL THAT TRAFFIC!
LET'S GO RIGHT TO SEE GEORGE!
SMITHVILLE COMIC-CON
WOW!! LOOK AT ALL THE WEIRDOS!!
COMIC-CO
YOU SHOULD FEEL RIGHT AT HOME!
9

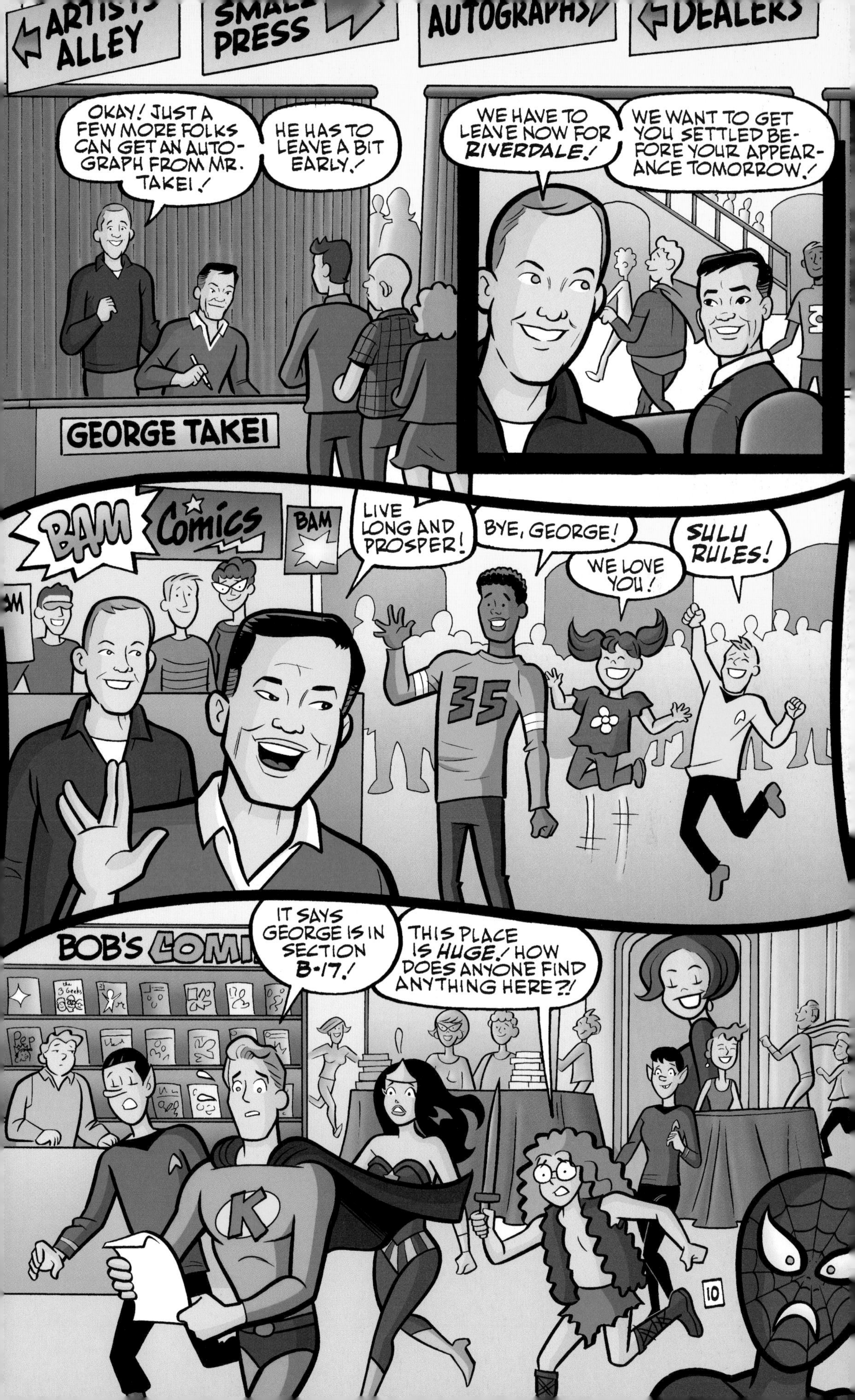
ARTISTS ALLEY
SMALL PRESS
AUTOGRAPHS
DEALERS
OKAY! JUST A FEW MORE FOLKS CAN GET AN AUTOGRAPH FROM MR. TAKEI!
HE HAS TO LEAVE A BIT EARLY!
GEORGE TAKEI
WE HAVE TO LEAVE NOW FOR RIVERDALE!
WE WANT TO GET YOU SETTLED BEFORE YOUR APPEARANCE TOMORROW!
BAM Comics
BAM
LIVE LONG AND PROSPER!
BYE, GEORGE!
WE LOVE YOU!
SULU RULES!
35
BOB'S COMI
IT SAYS GEORGE IS IN SECTION B-17!
THIS PLACE IS HUGE! HOW DOES ANYONE FIND ANYTHING HERE?!
10

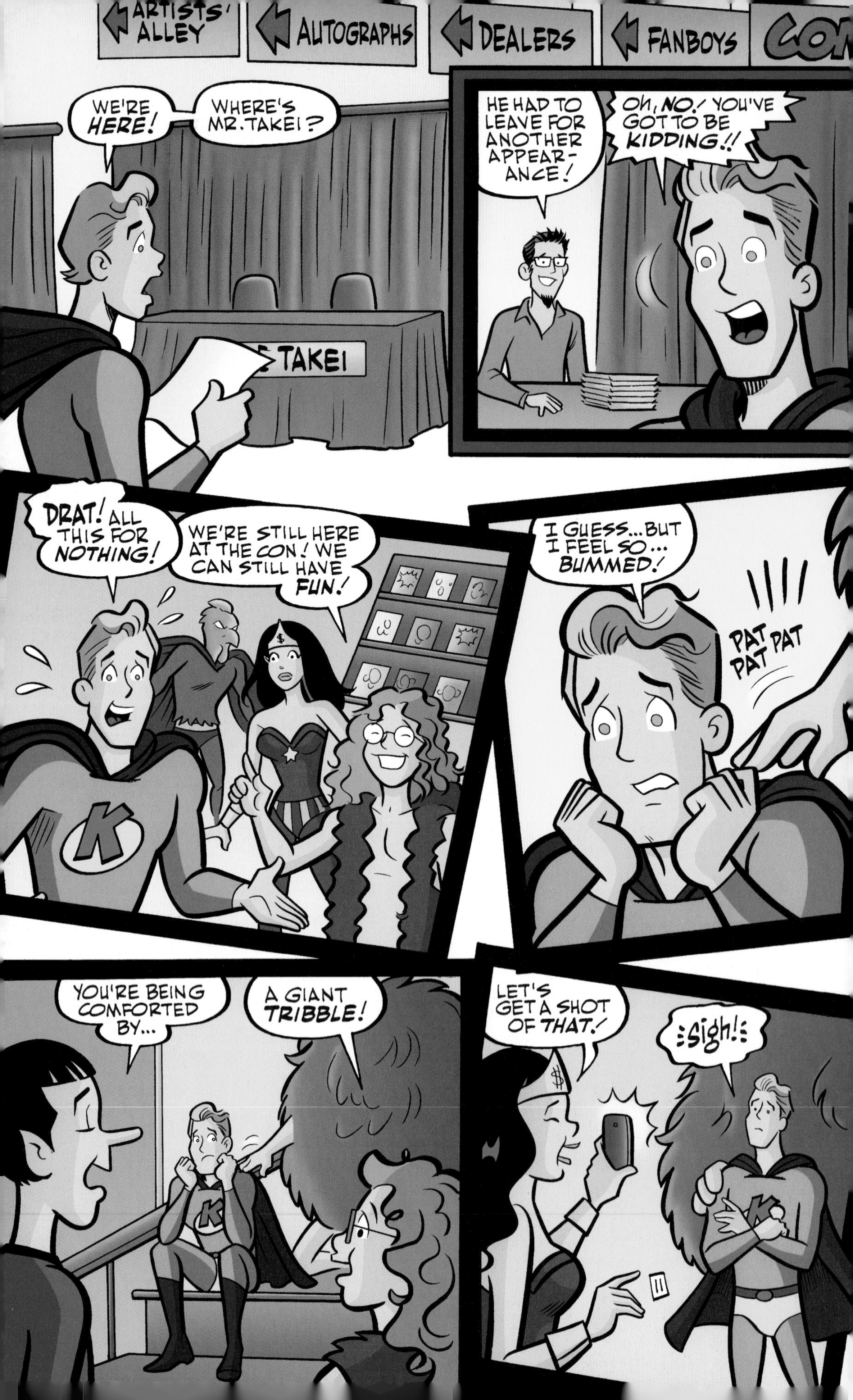

ARTISTS' ALLEY
AUTOGRAPHS
DEALERS
FANBOYS
WE'RE HERE!
WHERE'S MR. TAKEI?
TAKEI
HE HAD TO LEAVE FOR ANOTHER APPEAR-ANCE!
Oh, NO! YOU'VE GOT TO BE KIDDING!!
DRAT! ALL THIS FOR NOTHING!
WE'RE STILL HERE AT THE CON! WE CAN STILL HAVE FUN!
I GUESS...BUT I FEEL SO... BUMMED!
PAT PAT PAT PAT
YOU'RE BEING COMFORTED BY...
A GIANT TRIBBLE!
LET'S GET A SHOT OF THAT!
sigh!

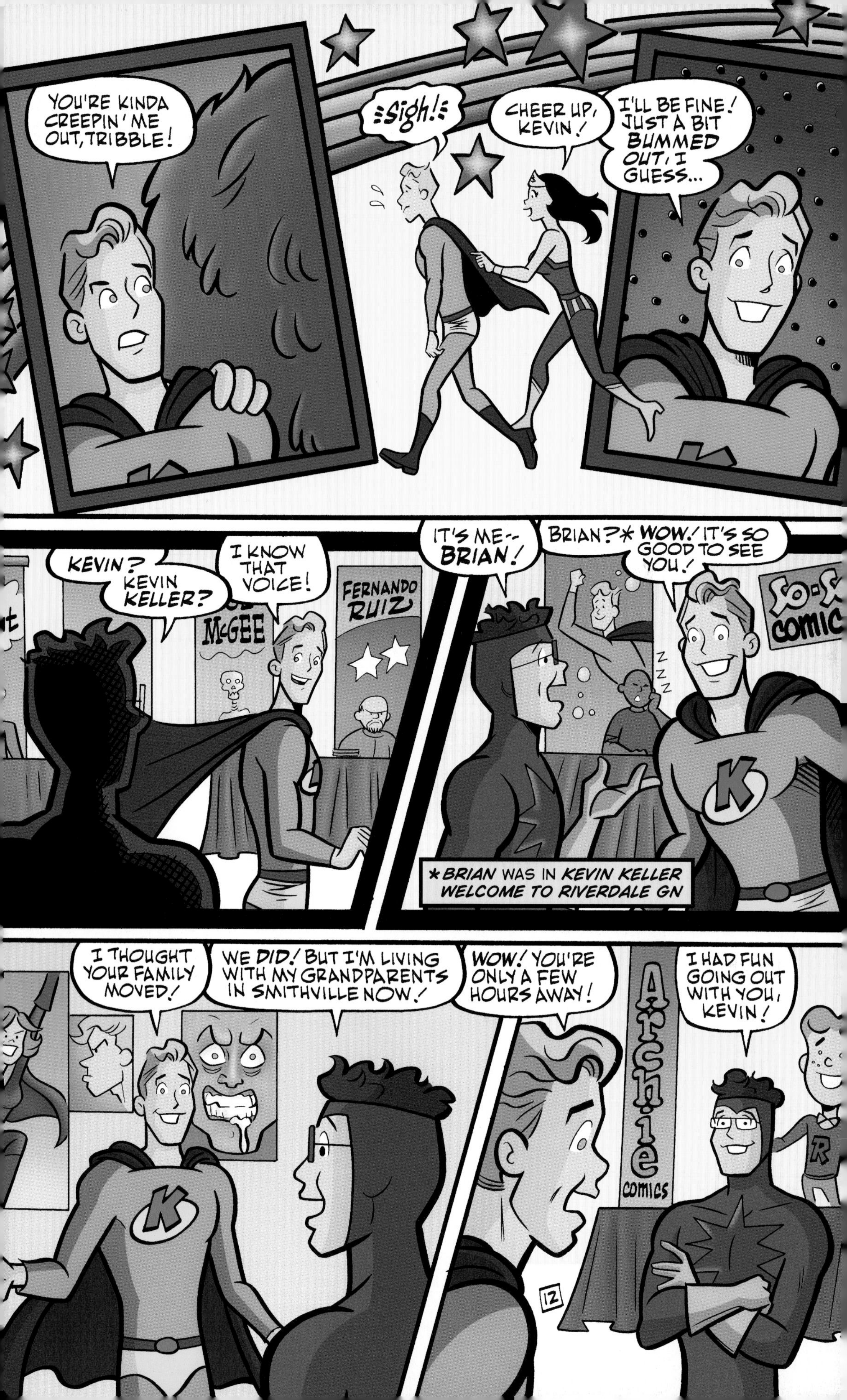
YOU'RE KINDA CREEPIN' ME OUT, TRIBBLE!
SIGH!
CHEER UP, KEVIN!
I'LL BE FINE! JUST A BIT BUMMED OUT, I GUESS...
KEVIN? KEVIN KELLER?
I KNOW THAT VOICE!
FERNANDO RUIZ
IT'S ME-- BRIAN!
BRIAN?* WOW! IT'S SO GOOD TO SEE YOU!
*BRIAN WAS IN KEVIN KELLER WELCOME TO RIVERDALE GN
I THOUGHT YOUR FAMILY MOVED!
WE DID! BUT I'M LIVING WITH MY GRANDPARENTS IN SMITHVILLE NOW!
WOW! YOU'RE ONLY A FEW HOURS AWAY!
Archie COMICS
I HAD FUN GOING OUT WITH YOU, KEVIN!
12

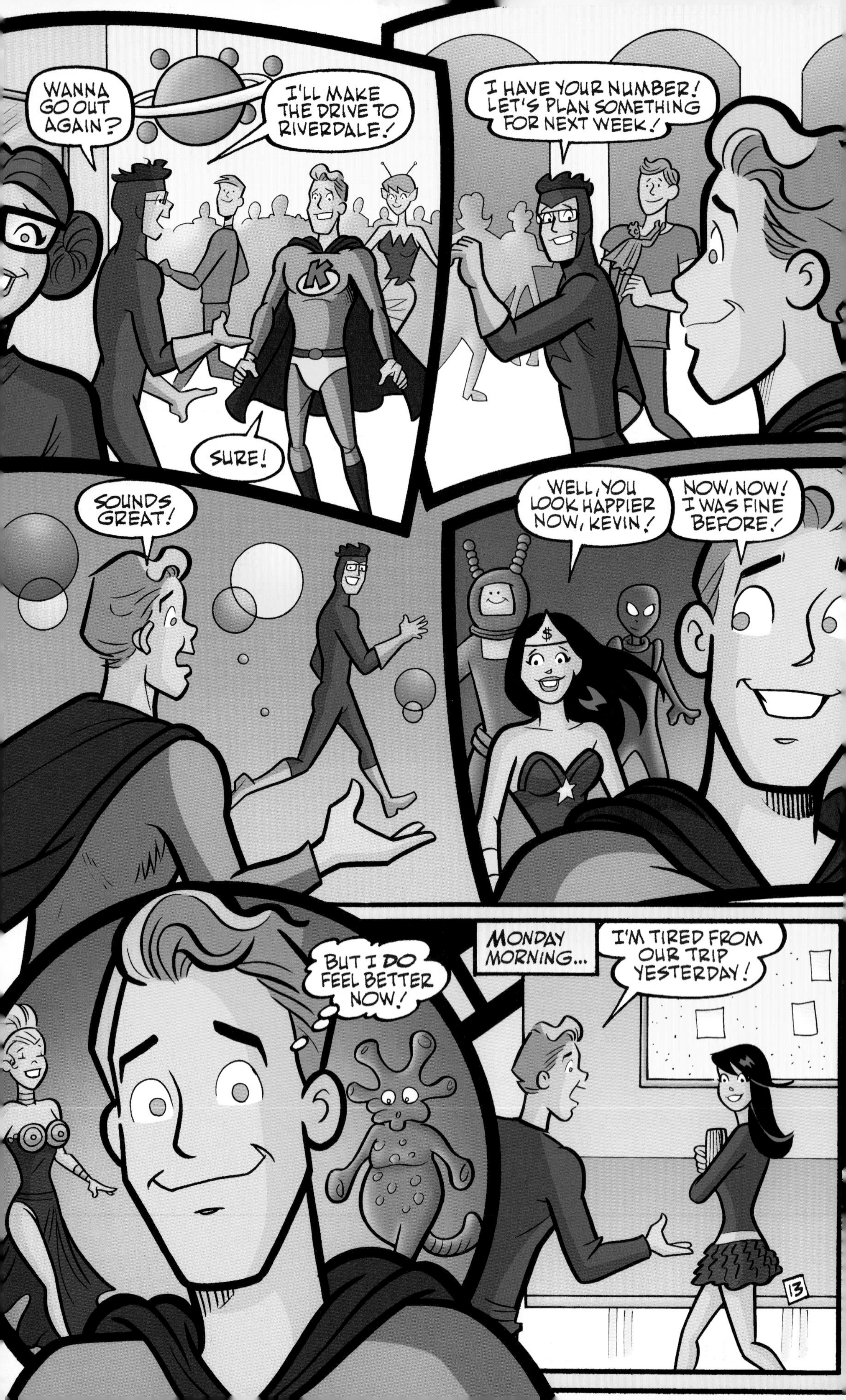

WANNA GO OUT AGAIN?
I'LL MAKE THE DRIVE TO RIVERDALE!
SURE!
I HAVE YOUR NUMBER! LET'S PLAN SOMETHING FOR NEXT WEEK!
SOUNDS GREAT!
WELL, YOU LOOK HAPPIER NOW, KEVIN!
NOW, NOW! I WAS FINE BEFORE!
BUT I DO FEEL BETTER NOW!
MONDAY MORNING...
I'M TIRED FROM OUR TRIP YESTERDAY!
13

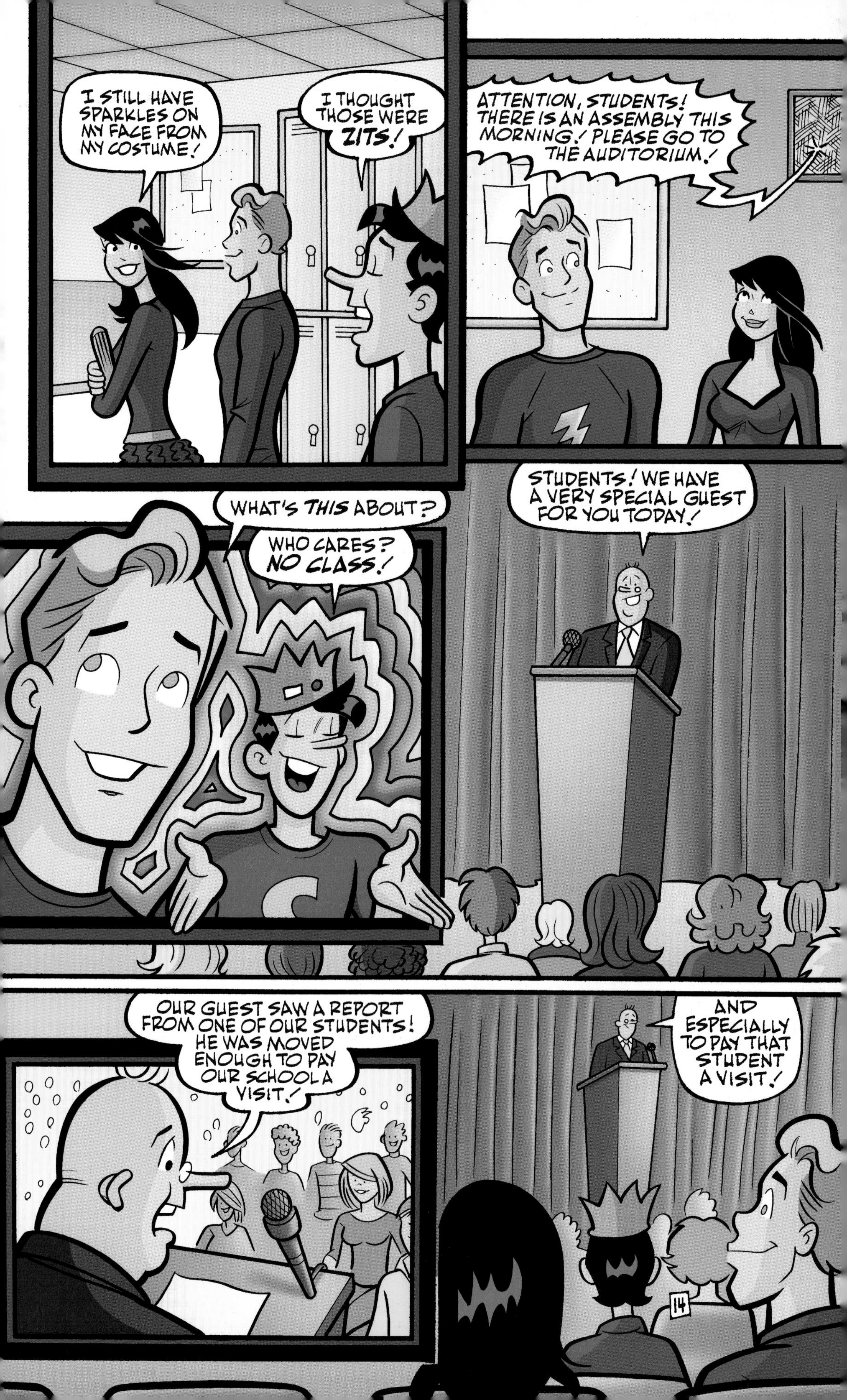
I STILL HAVE SPARKLES ON MY FACE FROM MY COSTUME!
I THOUGHT THOSE WERE ZITS!
ATTENTION, STUDENTS! THERE IS AN ASSEMBLY THIS MORNING! PLEASE GO TO THE AUDITORIUM!
WHAT'S THIS ABOUT?
WHO CARES? NO CLASS!
STUDENTS! WE HAVE A VERY SPECIAL GUEST FOR YOU TODAY!
OUR GUEST SAW A REPORT FROM ONE OF OUR STUDENTS! HE WAS MOVED ENOUGH TO PAY OUR SCHOOL A VISIT!
AND ESPECIALLY TO PAY THAT STUDENT A VISIT!
14

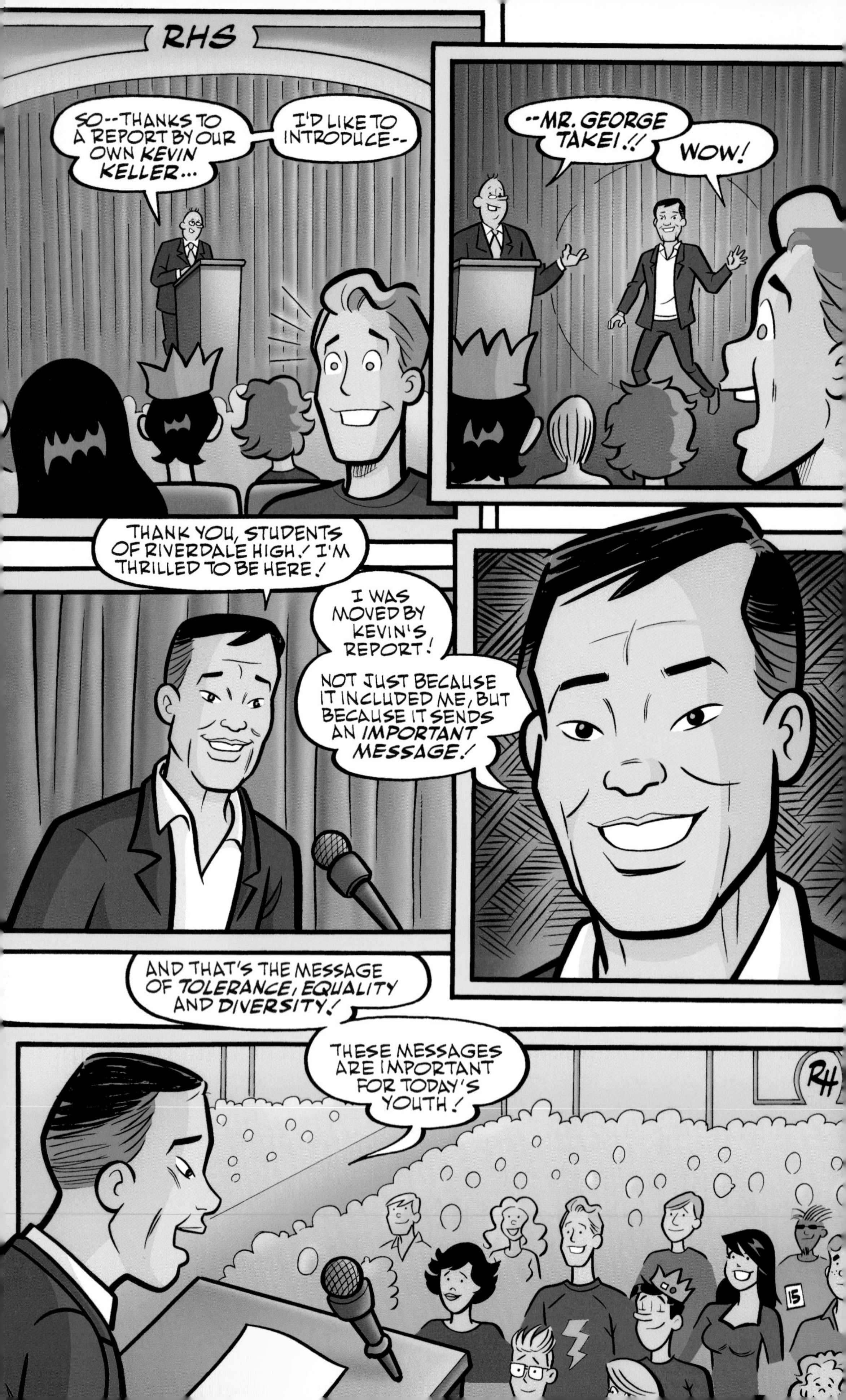
RHS
SO--THANKS TO A REPORT BY OUR OWN KEVIN KELLER...
I'D LIKE TO INTRODUCE--
--MR. GEORGE TAKEI!!
WOW!
THANK YOU, STUDENTS OF RIVERDALE HIGH! I'M THRILLED TO BE HERE!
I WAS MOVED BY KEVIN'S REPORT!
NOT JUST BECAUSE IT INCLUDED ME, BUT BECAUSE IT SENDS AN IMPORTANT MESSAGE!
AND THAT'S THE MESSAGE OF TOLERANCE, EQUALITY AND DIVERSITY!
THESE MESSAGES ARE IMPORTANT FOR TODAY'S YOUTH!
RH
15

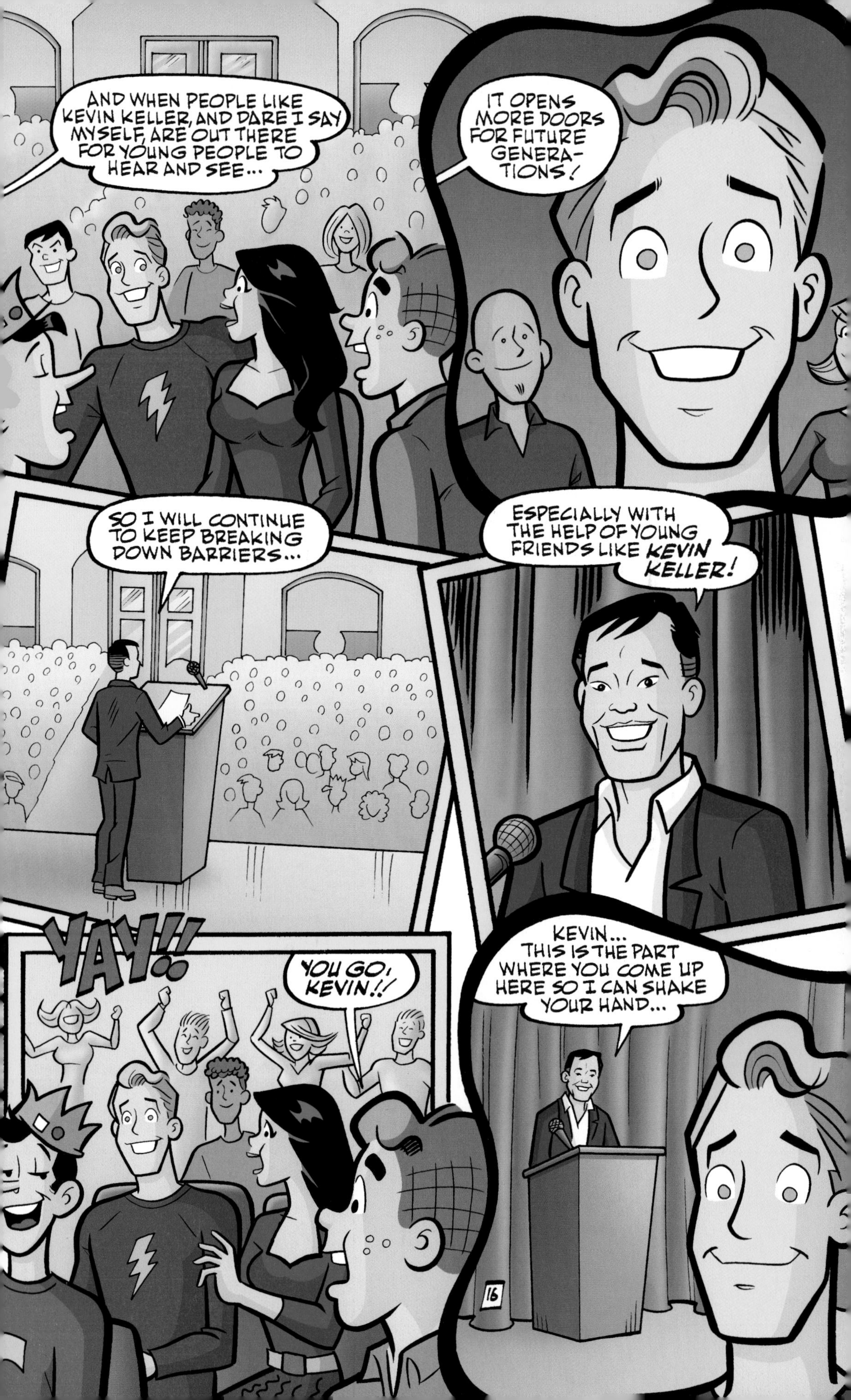
AND WHEN PEOPLE LIKE KEVIN KELLER, AND DARE I SAY MYSELF, ARE OUT THERE FOR YOUNG PEOPLE TO HEAR AND SEE...
IT OPENS MORE DOORS FOR FUTURE GENERA-TIONS!
SO I WILL CONTINUE TO KEEP BREAKING DOWN BARRIERS...
ESPECIALLY WITH THE HELP OF YOUNG FRIENDS LIKE KEVIN KELLER!
YAY!!
YOU GO, KEVIN!!
KEVIN... THIS IS THE PART WHERE YOU COME UP HERE SO I CAN SHAKE YOUR HAND...
16

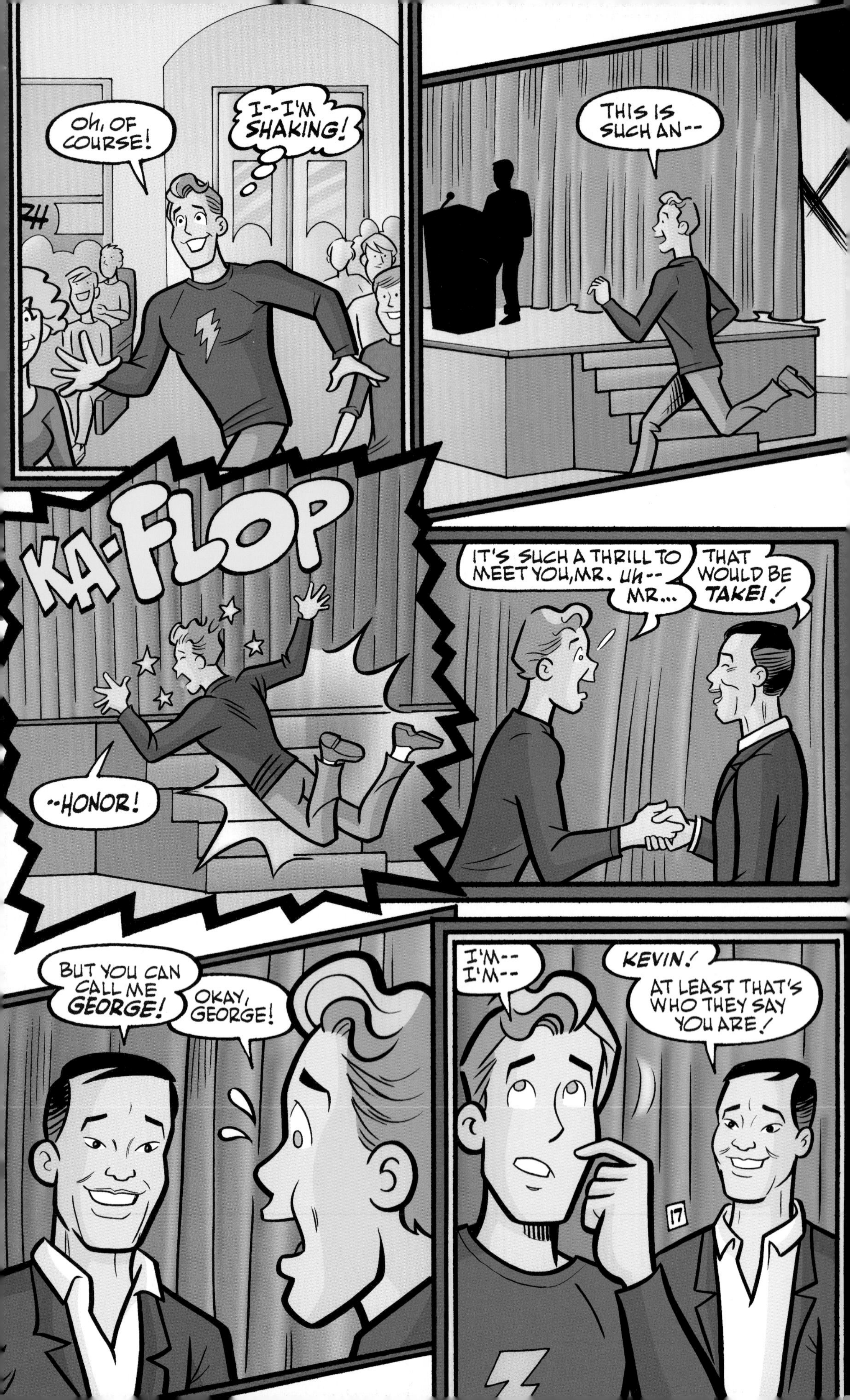
Oh, OF COURSE!
I--I'M SHAKING!
THIS IS SUCH AN--
KA-FLOP
--HONOR!
IT'S SUCH A THRILL TO MEET YOU, MR. uh-- MR...
THAT WOULD BE TAKEI!
BUT YOU CAN CALL ME GEORGE!
OKAY, GEORGE!
I'M-- I'M--
KEVIN!
AT LEAST THAT'S WHO THEY SAY YOU ARE!
17

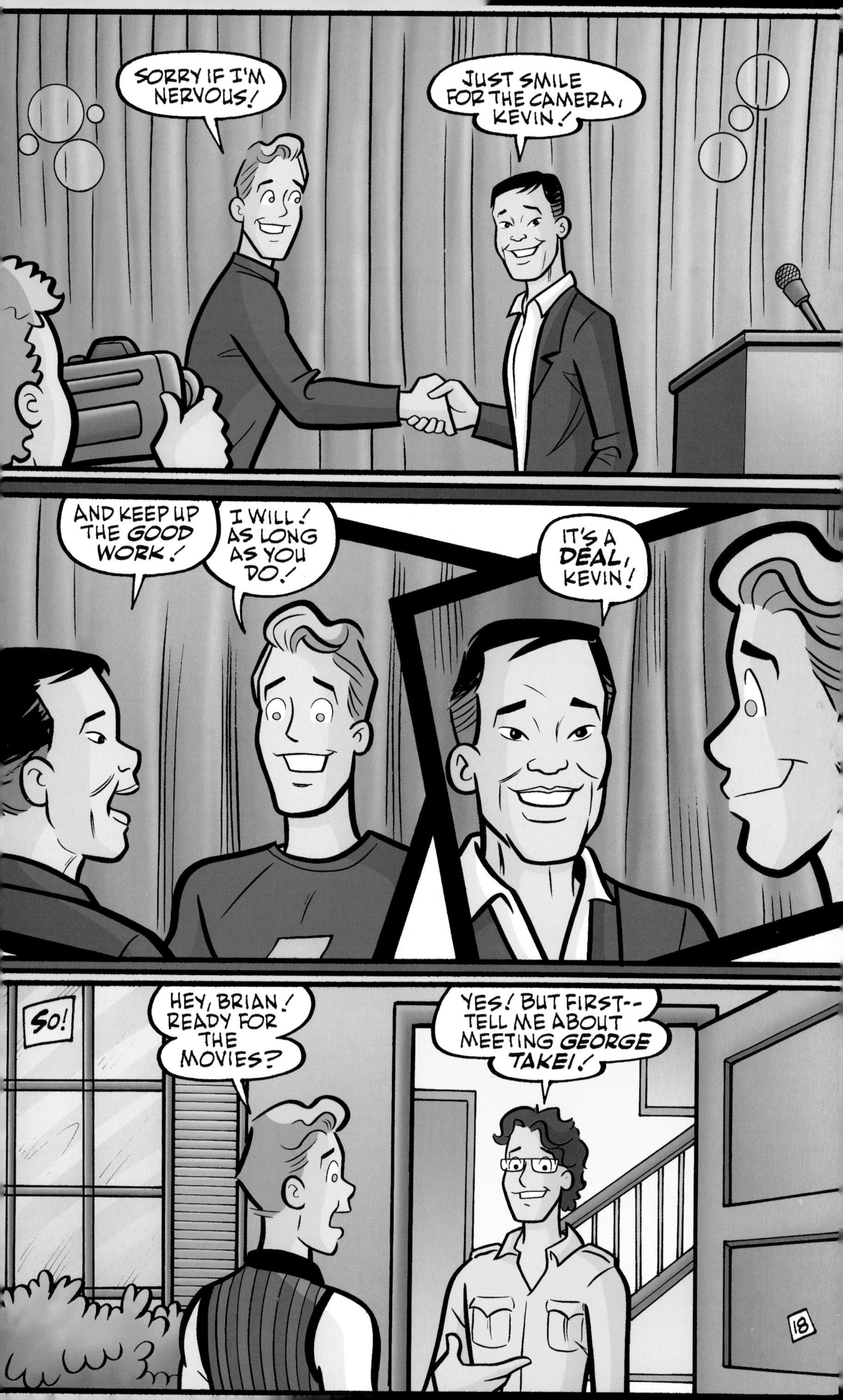
SORRY IF I'M NERVOUS!
JUST SMILE FOR THE CAMERA, KEVIN!
AND KEEP UP THE GOOD WORK!
I WILL! AS LONG AS YOU DO!
IT'S A DEAL, KEVIN!
SO!
HEY, BRIAN! READY FOR THE MOVIES?
YES! BUT FIRST-- TELL ME ABOUT MEETING GEORGE TAKEI!
18

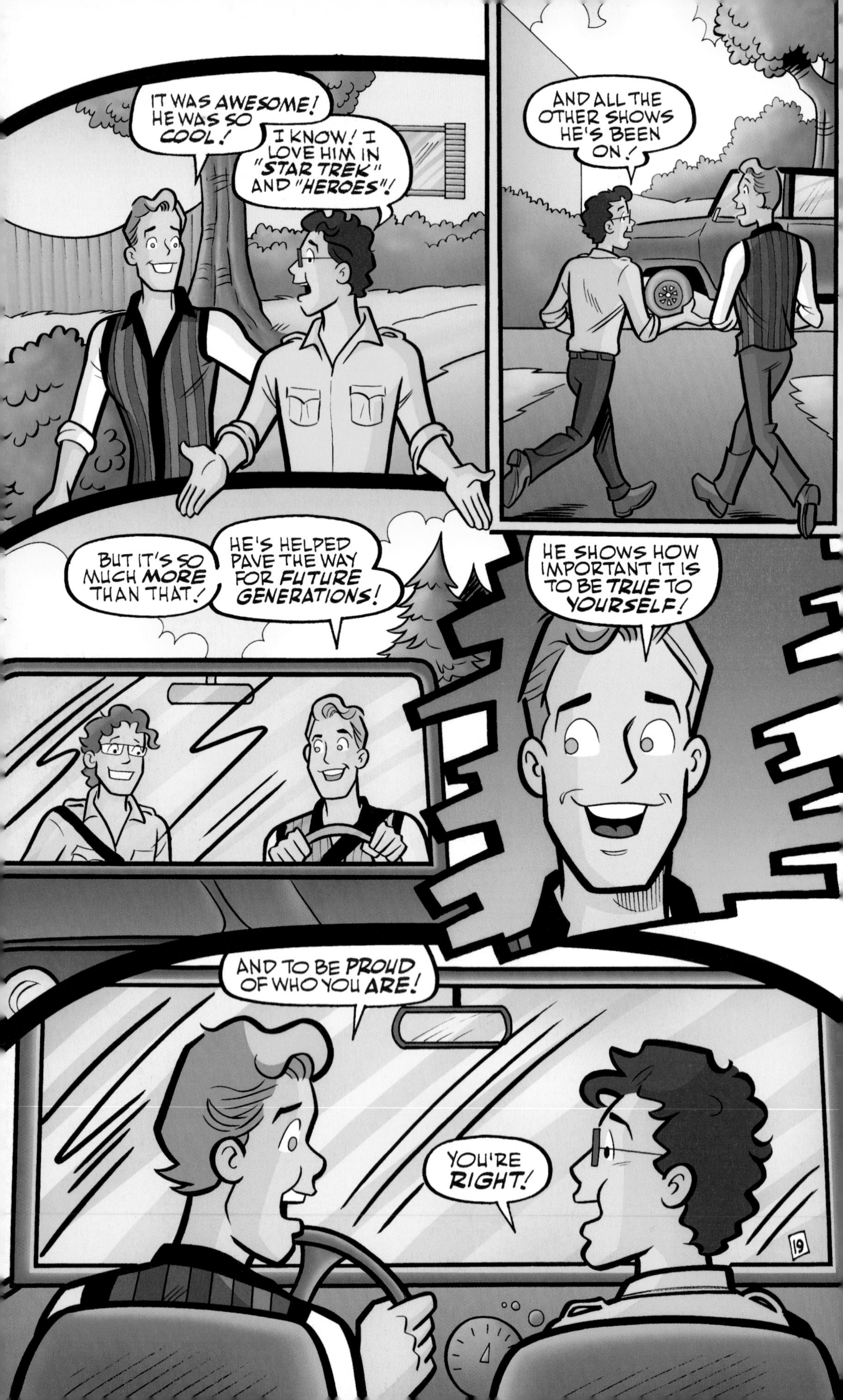
IT WAS AWESOME! HE WAS SO COOL!
I KNOW! I LOVE HIM IN "STAR TREK" AND "HEROES"!
AND ALL THE OTHER SHOWS HE'S BEEN ON!
BUT IT'S SO MUCH MORE THAN THAT!
HE'S HELPED PAVE THE WAY FOR FUTURE GENERATIONS!
HE SHOWS HOW IMPORTANT IT IS TO BE TRUE TO YOURSELF!
AND TO BE PROUD OF WHO YOU ARE!
YOU'RE RIGHT!
19

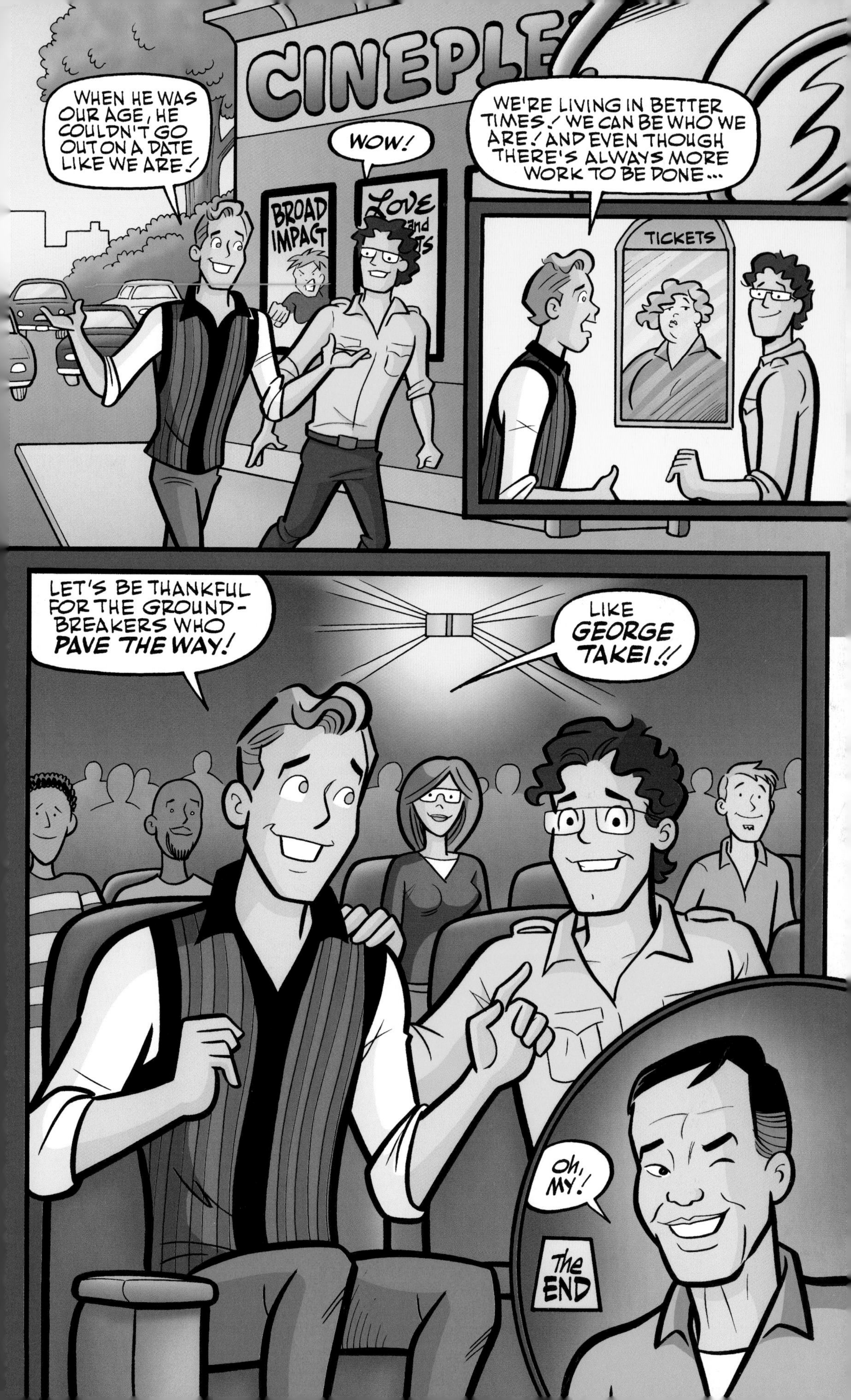
CINEPLE
WHEN HE WAS OUR AGE, HE COULDN'T GO OUT ON A DATE LIKE WE ARE!
WOW!
BROAD IMPACT
WE'RE LIVING IN BETTER TIMES! WE CAN BE WHO WE ARE! AND EVEN THOUGH THERE'S ALWAYS MORE WORK TO BE DONE...
TICKETS
LET'S BE THANKFUL FOR THE GROUND-BREAKERS WHO PAVE THE WAY!
LIKE GEORGE TAKEI!!
Oh, MY!
The END

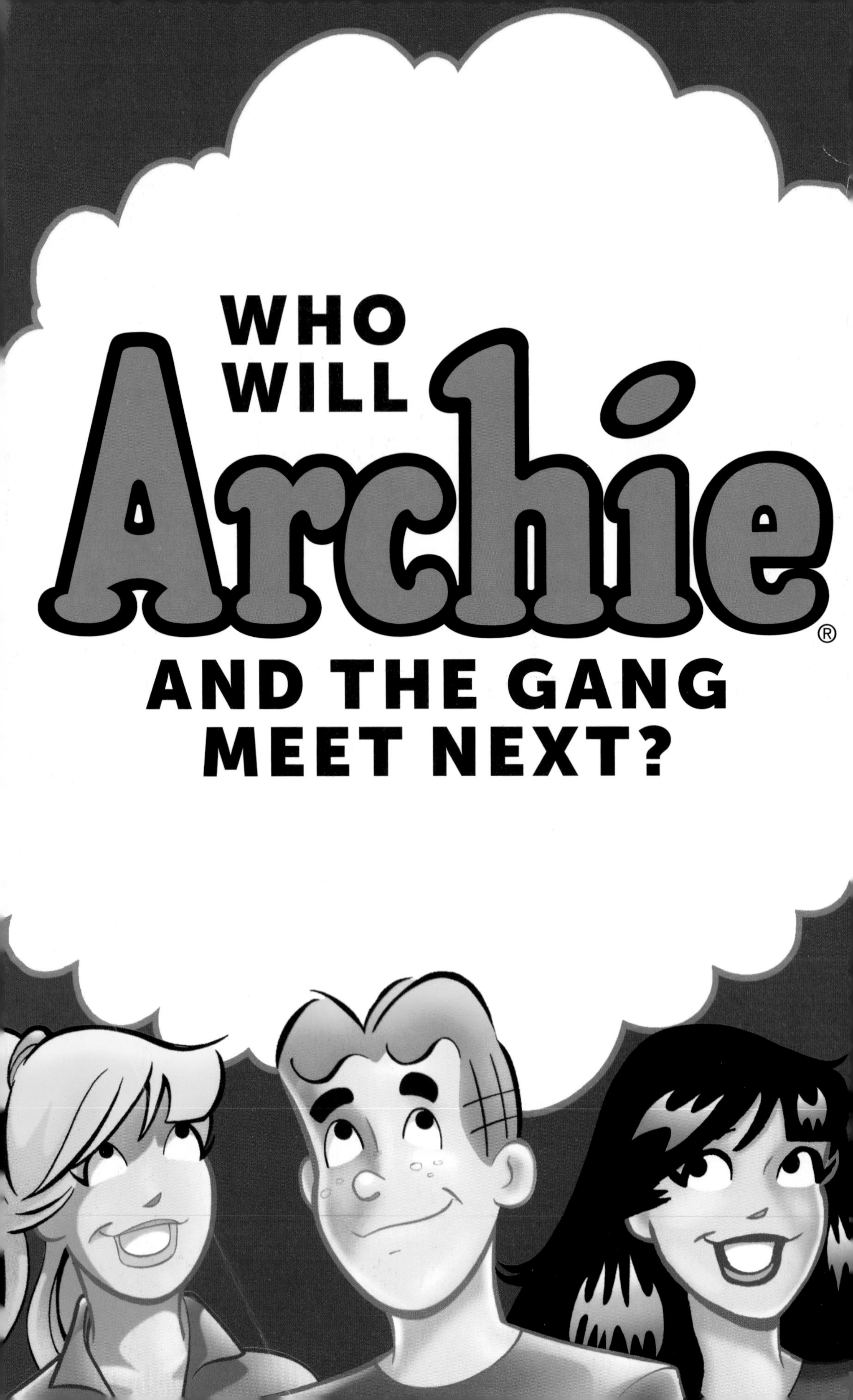
WHO WILL
Archie®
AND THE GANG
MEET NEXT?